A BIT OF LIGHT

YOUR DEAR FRIEND

HAROLD

Murderous Birmingham

Murderous Birmingham

The executed of the Twentieth Century

John J. Eddleston

The Breedon Books
Publishing Company
Derby

First published in Great Britain by
The Breedon Books Publishing Company Limited
Breedon House, 44 Friar Gate, Derby, DEl 1DA.
1997

Dedication

During the writing of this book, Joe Lobo, someone I was honoured to know passed away.

I would like to dedicate this volume to his memory.
Farewell old friend.

ISBN I 85983 085 4

Printed and bound by Butler & Tanner Ltd., Selwood Printing Works, Caxton Road, Frome, Somerset.
Colour separations by RPS Ltd, Leicester.
Jackets printed by Lawrence-Allen Colour Printers, Weston-super-Mare, Avon.

CONTENTS

ACKNOWLEDGEMENTS

I would like to offer my thanks to the staff of the Public Records Office at Kew. I have always found the people there to be most helpful and I would especially like to mention Edward Tilley and Josephine Matthews of the image library and Brian Carter the photographer who duplicated many of the pictures in this and other books in the series.

My greatest debt must however be to Yvonne Berger who helped with the research, proofreading and all other parts of the creative process. Without her most valuable assistance, my task would have been much more difficult.

Finally I would also like to thank my publishers, Breedon Books and particularly Anton Rippon, who has encouraged me throughout the preparation of this and indeed all the other volumes in the series.

INTRODUCTION

This century has seen the execution of 33 men and one woman at Winson Green prison in Birmingham. In addition, others who had a strong connection with England's second city were executed elsewhere and by the time we include those who perished on the gallows at Warwick, Stafford and Worcester, our totals have risen to 49 men and that lone woman, Dorothea Waddington, who was hanged in 1936.

It would be impossible to cover every one of these stories, in depth, in a book of this size, so I have concentrated on those who killed in Birmingham itself, or who committed their crimes in the surrounding towns and villages, but had a connection with Birmingham. Nevertheless, there are some absorbing tales to tell.

The reader will discover family feuds, such as that in the first chapter of this book, where John Joyce, the first man to die at the end of a rope in Winson Green this century, killed one of the members of a family he held a grudge against. The last Birmingham execution, that of Oswald Augustus Grey, in 1962, is also told in these pages. Between these two there are the child killers such as William Quayle, the wife murderers such as Elijah Pountney, and those who killed perfect strangers, such as James Joseph Power. There is the terrible story of Henry Gaskin who was rightly compared to Jack the Ripper, and John Davis who suggested that cutting someone's throat was a good way to cure a headache!

The reader should remember that in every single chapter, a man was found guilty of murder and was consequently given the exact date and time of his own death. He waited in the condemned cell, counting the days, hours and minutes until the door opened and the executioner came in to claim his life. Judge for yourself if all were guilty, and so deserving of that fate.

CHAPTER ONE

BAD BLOOD

ON Friday, June 7th, 1901, a case of assault was heard in the Birmingham police court. Two men, George Kelly, described as a labourer, and Herman Franey, a gun barrel fitter, were accused of assaulting Michael Nugent in Weaman Street on May 24th that year.

At first glance it appeared to be a simple enough case. Nugent claimed that Kelly had hit him with a heavy iron bar and then, before he even had time to recover from this blow, Franey had knocked him down and kicked him while he was on the ground. However, two witnesses were called, both of whom swore that it had been Michael Nugent who brought the iron bar to the scene in the first place and Kelly had managed to wrestle this from him. The magistrate considered that everyone in this case was equally to blame and the charge was dismissed. Later that day, another case was heard in the same court. Now it was John Joyce, a man known to all as Toby, who was charged with stabbing Michael Nugent, but this time it was shown that John Nugent, the father of the so-called injured party, had brought the bayonet with him. The stipendiary magistrate, Mr

T.M. Colmore, had heard enough and said that there was obviously some kind of family feud going on here, and so he dismissed this case as well.

Emma Moore lived at 8 House, 9 Court, Price Street, Birmingham, and at 7.00pm on Monday, June 10th, she saw 36-year-old John Joyce, one of the men who had appeared in court three days earlier, in the yard of number 5, a house belonging to Mrs Williams. Emma Moore watched as Joyce knocked at number 5 and saw the door opened by Elizabeth Matthews, a woman who was separated from her husband and lodged with Mrs Williams. As soon as the door opened, Joyce said politely, "Oh, I beg your pardon, I've come to the wrong house."

Emma Moore saw Elizabeth Matthews close the door and Joyce walked off down the court and stood for a time on the corner of Price Street and Lancaster Street. Perhaps Mrs Moore was an unusually watchful person, but when Joyce had first knocked on Mrs Williams' door, she saw that he held a knife in his hand, which he quickly concealed when Mrs Matthews came to the door. Suspicious as to what Joyce might be up to, Emma Moore kept a vigilant watch.

It was around 9.45pm when Joyce walked back into the court and went directly to a house occupied by the Nugent family. Joyce hammered on the door and Emma Moore, aware of the long standing arguments between Joyce and the Nugents, decided to go across and obtain a better view of events.

The door was opened by 61-year-old John Nugent, the father of Michael, the man Joyce had been accused of stabbing. As Joyce stormed into the house, Emma Moore stood in the doorway, determined to miss nothing at all.

John Nugent had taken a seat on the sofa in the front room and he did not move from this spot as Joyce first insulted him and then picked up a lighted oil lamp from the table and threw it at him. The lamp was made of metal, and so although it fell at

Nugent's feet, it did not burst into flame and no damage was done. Nugent, still calm, said, "Toby, go out. I don't want any row here tonight."

The throwing of the lamp had caused Emma Moore to scream and this in turn brought Elizabeth Nugent, John's wife, running into the room from the house next door. By now, John Nugent had gone to stand near the fireplace and Joyce was framed in the doorway, not far from where Emma Moore still kept watch.

Elizabeth demanded to know what Joyce wanted and he replied, using the foulest language imaginable, that he wanted Michael, their son. Elizabeth told Joyce that Michael had gone to the theatre and had not yet come home to which Joyce replied, "I will put a knife in one of you." Seeing that there would be further trouble if Joyce did not leave, Elizabeth grabbed Joyce and sought to hold on to him, at the same time telling her husband to go for the police. John Nugent left the house to do as he had been asked but almost immediately, Joyce shook himself free of Elizabeth's grip and dashed after him.

It did not take Joyce long to catch up with Nugent and when he did, he drew a knife from his sleeve, cried, "Take that you old cow," and stabbed him. Leaving the bloody body of John Nugent on the pavement, Joyce then walked down Price Street and into Lancaster Street. Without hesitating, Elizabeth Nugent went after him and caught hold of him again. Twice he lifted the knife as if to stab her before shouting, "If you were not an old woman I would put your lights in." Meanwhile, the ever-watchful Emma Moore was still following and still observing all that transpired. Joyce once more ran off and Emma followed him as far as Canal Street before she gave up the chase and returned to offer whatever help she could to John Nugent.

Constable George Stafford was on duty at the corner of Lancaster Street and Aston Street when he heard that there had been a stabbing incident in Price Street. Stafford headed for the spot, to be met by a group of people who were carrying Nugent, as gently as possible, towards the hospital. Constable Stafford saw that the injured man was bleeding badly from a chest wound. Within minutes, Thomas Edward Nugent, yet another of John's sons, arrived and helped carry his father to the General Hospital. Alas, by the time they arrived, John Nugent had already breathed his last.

The police now began to look for John Joyce but he was not at his lodgings in Summer Lane. It was not long, however, before he was in custody. Inspector Joseph Clarke, one of the senior officers involved in the search, turned into Lancaster Street and almost bumped into Joyce who was walking the other way. He was immediately taken into custody, escorted to the police station, and there charged with the murder of John Nugent.

On June 11th, 1901, Joyce appeared before the same stipendiary magistrate who had dismissed the earlier assault cases, Mr T.M. Colmore. Mr Philip Baker appeared on behalf of Joyce and made no objection to a remand until the following day.

The inquest opened on June 12th, before Mr Isaac Bradley, Joyce now being represented by Mr T.B. Eastley. It was here that Thomas Nugent told a most tragic story. He had been walking down Lancaster Street when he saw a crowd of people coming towards him, carrying a man. Thomas asked what the matter was and someone shouted, "Your father is stabbed." To his horror, Thomas saw that the man the people were carrying was John Nugent and he crouched down and cried, "Speak to me father," John moaned, "Is that you Tommy?" and Thomas said that it was and asked his father who had done this to him. John replied, "Toby Joyce has done it to me. Goodbye, I'm done." Those were the last words John Nugent ever uttered.

Having heard all the details of the feud between Joyce and the Nugent family, and the testimony of various witnesses who had seen some of the attack, the inquest jury found that John Nugent had been murdered and that the culprit was John Joyce. No sooner had the court concluded its business than Mr Bradley called two young schoolgirls, Jennie Holmes and Annie Taylor, into court. Elizabeth Nugent had reported that after she had tried to seize Joyce, these two girls had pushed her over, allowing him to escape. Mr Bradley demanded an explanation and the girls told him that they had seen Joyce in Lancaster Street and he had asked them to escort him home as he was drunk. They denied pushing Mrs Nugent but Mr Bradley said he doubted their truthfulness and if Joyce had managed to escape justice, they would now have found themselves on a serious charge. The two girls left the court, no doubt suitably chastened.

Earlier that same morning, June 12th, the police court had reconvened but had immediately adjourned until after the in-quest was concluded. Joyce appeared before the magistrates for the third and last time on June 19th, when he was formally sent for trial. Those proceedings took place at Birmingham on July 31st, 1901, before Mr Justice Phillimore. Joyce was defended by Mr S.G. Dorsett and Mr Norris Foster while the case for the prosecution was led by Mr Etherington Smith who was assisted by Mr J.W.P. Mosley.

Thomas Nugent told the court that there had been bad blood between his family and Joyce for more than two years. On May 28th, Michael had given evidence in court against two of Joyce's friends who were accused of assaulting him. Those men had been remanded in custody but at 11.45am that same day, as Thomas and his brother were walking home, they were accosted by Joyce who asked Michael if he were determined to give evidence against his friends. Michael had confirmed that he was and Joyce was furious. That evening, at 10.45pm, the Nugent brothers, who had been in the Apple Tree pub, were on their way home after last orders when Joyce rushed out of a side street and stabbed Michael in the back. The wound was not serious and somehow,

Joyce was also injured and required hospital treatment. Joyce was arrested and remanded to June 7th, when both of the cases were dismissed.

Turning to June 10th, Emma Moore outlined exactly what she had seen while Joyce was in Price Street. She stated that after John Nugent had left the house, Joyce had pushed Mrs Nugent out of the way. Joyce had caught up with the old man close to Sarah Duffy's house and it was there that the stabbing took place. Emma said that in her opinion, Joyce had been drinking.

Sarah Duffy lived at 2 House, 9 Court, Price Street and she, too, had seen Joyce go into Mrs Williams' house, only to come back out minutes later, apologising for his mistake. Sarah witnessed the actual attack upon Nugent later that night. She reported that as Nugent came out of his house, he shouted, "Police, police," but Joyce said, "Get away you old bastard, don't follow me." Joyce was pushing Nugent until he drew out a knife and plunged it into Nugent's side. John Nugent cried out, "Oh, Sarah, he's stabbed me in the heart," before staggering for a few steps and then falling by the kerbside at the bottom of an entry. The day before all this had taken place, Sunday June 9th, Sarah had seen Joyce who spoke about his troubles with the Nugents and added, "You know the Nugents? God blind me, I'll do them in."

James Clifford was in Lancaster Street on the night of June 10th and he saw Joyce walking down the street, followed by a growing crowd of people, one of whom shouted that he had a knife. As Joyce approached Clifford, he drew out the knife from his right trouser pocket and handed it to Clifford who went to his place of work where he stayed all night, with the knife still in his possession. When he found out that Nugent had been stabbed by Joyce and had died in hospital, Clifford took the weapon to the police station in Newton Street. He explained that he had only taken the knife in the first place to stop Joyce using it on anyone.

Dr Alex Wathen Nuthall was the resident surgical officer at the Birmingham General Hospital. He testified that by the time John Nugent arrived at the hospital, he was already dead. His clothes were soaked in blood and there was a single small wound in the lower part of his chest, just below the breast bone. Dr Nuthall also did the post-mortem and said that the blade used had entered the cavity of the abdomen, wounding the upper surface of the liver before passing through the diaphragm and into the aorta. The wound was four inches deep and had needed a good deal of force to inflict. Dr Nuthall was also able to say that John Nugent had been suffering from cancer of the right tonsil, with secondary cancers in his liver, spleen and abdominal glands, although these were not an imminent threat to his life.

Inspector Clarke said that after he had arrested Joyce and told him that he would be charged with murder, he had replied, "I know nothing about it." Joyce's clothing was examined and there were bloodstains on his coat, waistcoat and trousers. Joyce had said that this must have come from the earlier fight with the Nugents, in May. The blood did seem to be quite old but a fresh stain was found in his right trouser pocket, where James Clifford said he had seen the knife kept.

Giving evidence on his own behalf, Joyce explained that the feud had only been between him and Michael Nugent. Joyce explained that he had been in the Army for some time and had been demobbed a couple of years earlier. Meeting Michael Nugent in a public house, they enjoyed a drink together before Nugent invited him back to his house. There, for no apparent reason, Michael had struck him with a three-cornered file. Joyce had tried to defend himself whereupon John Nugent, the man he was now accused of killing, had lashed out with a poker.

Turning to the day of Nugent's death, Joyce denied that he had taken a knife to the scene, claiming instead that Nugent had produced the knife and he had merely wrestled it from him.

Some of this testimony had in fact already been backed up by other witnesses. Thomas Nugent had confessed that his brother Michael was sometimes 'strange in his behaviour' and medical evidence had shown that the wound inflicted on John Nugent was horizontal and not, as the witnesses to the event had claimed, a downward, slashing blow

However, having heard all the sordid details of the constant arguments between Joyce and the Nugent family and having listened to the witnesses, the jury had no doubt that this had been a premeditated crime of revenge. Joyce was found guilty and sentenced to death, but even now there was drama. Asked to give the verdict, the foreman of the jury said that they had found Joyce not guilty with a recommendation to mercy before hurriedly correcting himself and saying that, of course, he meant to say guilty.

To the very end, Joyce had remained full of enmity towards the Nugent family and was still talking of revenge, believing that he might get a reprieve due to the fact that he had once suffered from sunstroke while serving in the Army in India, which he maintained had rendered him unaccountable for his actions. When it was announced that the Home Secretary had found no grounds on which to recommend that reprieve, Joyce's fate was decided.

By 7.30am on Tuesday, August 20th, 1901, a crowd of about 100 had gathered outside Winson Green prison. By the appointed hour of 8.00am, this had grown to more than 3,000, all of whom stood in silence as John Joyce was hanged by James Billington who was assisted by his son, William. As the black flag was hoisted to show that the sentence had been carried out, someone in the crowd shouted, "There it is!" Then everyone began to disperse. The feud was finally at an end.

CHAPTER TWO

IMMORAL EARNINGS

MARTHA Eliza Simpson was an attractive 21-year-old woman who used her charms to earn her living as a prostitute. Known to her friends as 'Pattie', Martha, despite her profession, also had a special man in her life. It was at Christmas time 1903 that she had first encountered a 25-year-old general dealer who called himself Charlie Hammond although his real name was Charles Samuel Dyer. At first, Dyer moved in with Martha at her lodgings in Hurst Street, but in mid-January, 1904, he took lodgings at a small cottage, number 2, Back 21 Inge Street, and Martha joined him there.

One of Martha's closest friends was Margaret Moran, who lived at 15 Birmingham Place, on Bristol Street. Indeed, Martha had lodged with Margaret's mother in Hurst Street and the two women had remained close ever since. Martha often called at Margaret's house where there were two lodgers, John Moran, who was no relation to Margaret, and Arthur Lockley.

At some time after 1.15pm on Wednesday, February 3rd, 1904, Martha Simpson called on Margaret Moran at Birmingham Place. After chatting for a few minutes, the two women walked to Martha's cottage where they arrived at 2.00pm and saw Charles Dyer. The three had some dinner together, after which Dyer went out for a drink or two. Martha and Margaret stayed at Inge Street until around 7.30pm, when Dyer returned and handed some personal items of clothing to Martha, asking her to pawn them for him. Martha and Margaret went to the pawn-shop, pledged the items and headed back towards Inge Street. On their way, they met Dyer, who was accompanied by Arthur Lockley, one of Margaret Moran's lodgers. Lockley had arrived at Dyer's house earlier that evening and the two were going to a public house when they met Martha in the street. She handed Dyer the shilling which she had received from the pawnshop. Dyer took the money and both men continued on to Cutler's public house on the corner of Hill Street and Station Street. Here, Dyer and Lockley enjoyed a quiet drink together.

At 8.45pm Margaret and Martha called Dyer out of the pub and Martha asked him if he would give her some money for a drink. Dyer handed over three pennies and then returned to his pint. The two women walked on to another pub, in Old Meeting Street, near Dudley Street. It was there that Martha met up with another man who treated both women to a drink. Not wishing to cramp Martha's style, Margaret Moran left the pub at 11.00pm and returned home. Half an hour later, however, Martha Simpson appeared at Birmingham Place with the young man in tow. He and Martha went upstairs, where no doubt business was transacted. In all, the young man stayed for perhaps 15 minutes before leaving and as he strolled out of the house, Dyer and Arthur Lockley arrived. Although Dyer appeared to be the worse for drink, he was friendly enough towards the people in the house and when he and Martha left, close on midnight, there still seemed to be a pleasant enough atmosphere.

However, Dyer had not been gone more than ten minutes when he reappeared, white-faced, and threw himself into a chair in Margaret Moran's house before crying out, "Oh, Maggie! I've done it. Save her if you can." Even by the gloom of the candle-light which flickered in the room, Margaret could see that there was blood streaming down Dyer's fingers. Something terrible must have happened back at Inge Street and without seeking further clarification, Margaret, together with both her lodgers, ran to the house Martha Simpson shared with Dyer. There they found Martha sitting in an armchair, a massive gaping wound in her throat and blood pouring down her clothes. She was already beyond all help.

There had been a witness to Dyer's flight back to Birmingham Place. Police Sergeant Godfrey Hodgkins was on duty at the corner of Essex Street and Bristol Street and as he spoke to one of his officers, Constable Thomas Parnham, he saw Dyer running up Essex Street. As the sergeant watched, Dyer turned into Bristol Street before vanishing down the alley which led to Birmingham Place. Even as Sergeant Hodgkins started to follow, down the narrow alley, Margaret Moran, Arthur Lockley and John Moran came running past him down Essex Street. Hodg-kins continued down the alley until he came to a house where the door had been left open. There he found Charles Dyer, still sitting in the chair, and after taking brief details of what had taken place at Inge Street, Hodgkins took Dyer into custody.

Constable Parnham was immediately despatched to Inge Street to see what assistance he could offer there, while the sergeant escorted Dyer to the police station. On the way, Dyer remarked, "I struck her on the head with a poker, and then drew the razor across her throat. I gave 3s 6d for it." Upon arrival at the Moor Street station, Dyer was cautioned. Information then arrived that Martha Simpson had been found dead and Dyer was charged with her murder. To that he replied, "Correct, I plead guilty."

Martha had died at about 12.10am on February 4th and later that day, Dyer made his first appearance at the police court before the stipendiary magistrate, Mr T.M. Colmore. Brief details of Dyer's history were given which showed that he had served eight years in the Army, enlisting under the surname Smith, this being confirmed by his discharge papers which were found on him when he was arrested. The first five years of his military service had been in the Royal Artillery and three of those years had been spent in Malta. Dyer had then transferred to the 1st Warwickshire Regiment where he had spent three years, two of them in India. On December 9th, 1903, he had returned to Birmingham and soon afterwards had met with Martha Simpson. They had started living together on Boxing Day. When this evidence had been given, the magistrate remanded Dyer to the following day.

In early reports on the case, Martha Simpson's nickname 'Pattie' had been quoted and she had been referred to as Patricia Simpson. By February 5th though, when the inquest opened before Mr Isaac Bradley, Martha's correct name was being used. Further details of Dyer's Army career were given and it was now stated that his papers were dated December 11th, 1903 and were marked, 'Having been sentenced to be discharged with ignominy.' All the witnesses then gave evidence and the coroner's jury had no trouble in returning a verdict of wilful murder against Dyer. Later that day, the police court hearing resumed and Dyer was remanded again, this time until February 10th. On that date, Dyer was formally sent for trial on the capital charge.

Dyer's appearance at the assizes took place at Birmingham on March 17th, 1904, before Mr Justice Wills. The case for the prosecution was led by Mr J.J. Parfitt who was assisted by Mr J.W.P. Mosley, while Dyer was defended by Mr S.G. Dorsett and Mr Norris Foster.

Evidence was given that the dead woman was a native of Wolverhampton. George Albert Simpson, who lived at 9 Church Street, Heath Town, Wolverhampton, said that he was Martha's half-brother. Simpson had not seen Martha for four months but he had written to her on January 25th. She had replied to that letter, stating that she was now married to a man named Hammond who had until recently been a soldier. Simpson had never met Hammond, but he was, of course, none other than Charles Samuel Dyer.

A problem arose for both the prosecution and defence teams when certain witnesses gave contradictory testimony. Just before midnight on February 3rd, Margaret Moran and her two lodgers had been in the house in Birmingham Place with Martha and Dyer. All three witnesses denied that there had been any altercation between Dyer and the woman he was now accused of murdering. Margaret said that she had seen no incident whatsoever and that there had been no argument over the man Martha had brought back to the house with her. John Moran also confirmed that there was no argument although he added that he had seen Martha stumble and fall at one stage and simply assumed that she had, taken too much drink. Finally, Arthur Lockley said that although he heard no harsh words spoken, he also saw Martha fall and claimed that this was because Dyer pushed her but this had been accidental because Dyer, too, had had rather a lot of drink and had lost his balance. This testimony was, however, contradicted by two other witnesses: two ladies who Margaret Moran, John Moran and Lockley swore had not even been in the house that night.

Mary Ann Bayliss, Margaret Moran's sister, she said that at about 11.30pm on February 3rd, she, a man friend and a woman named Alice Tatlow had gone to the house at Birmingham Place. Only Bayliss and Tatlow gave evidence at the trial and they both reported that when they arrived at Birmingham Place, everyone there seemed to have been drinking. Bayliss stated that at one stage, Martha stood up to give her a drink of whisky but Dyer hit her and knocked her back down into the chair. Martha climbed to her feet but Dyer hit her again and knocked her under the table before pulling a razor from his pocket and hissing, "I will put this across you tonight." When the two women left the house, Martha was still under the table and called out to Margaret Moran, "Maggie, Maggie, don't let me go home tonight, he'll murder me."

Alice Tatlow backed up much of this evidence and added that when Dyer had first hit Martha, he had shouted, "Catch that." The argument between them had apparently been something to do with money for Tatlow claimed that Dyer had also said, "I don't give you five shillings a day for nothing; it's to keep you in, not to go out." Both witnesses also claimed that they had not given evidence at the police court or inquest because John Moran and Arthur Lockley had issued threats against them.

The defence called no witnesses but relied instead on a plea that Dyer had been sorely provoked. Dyer had apparently been so drunk at the time that he had made a statement to the police which proved that he did not recall the correct version of events. Dyer had claimed that he had first used a poker to strike Martha but when this weapon had been examined, the only head hairs adhering to it were dark, like Dyer's. Martha had fair hair and it was clear that for some reason, it had been Martha who picked up the poker and lashed out at Dyer. He had then defended himself with his razor. This provocation, together with the fact that he had been so drunk that he had not known what he was doing, meant that the verdict should be one of guilty of manslaughter, not murder.

Some of this suggested scenario was backed up by the medical testimony of Dr Oglethorpe Barrett, who had examined Martha in Inge Street and later performed a post-mortem on her. Although there were minor bruises on Martha's arms and legs, there was none on her head. Dyer had certainly not struck her with the poker.

One of the final witnesses was Rosannah Cotterill, who lived at 21 Inge Street and was Martha's neighbour. While it was true that she had heard no disturbance on the night that Martha was attacked, her testimony indicated that Dyer had offered violence to Martha on an earlier occasion. A few weeks earlier, Martha had shown Cotterill a burn on her arm and had explained that Dyer had caused this after an argument, when he pushed her back on to the hot fire-grate.

The jury retired at 4.20pm and took an hour and a half to decide that Dyer had realised what he was doing and was, therefore, guilty as charged. Two separate petitions were organised in an attempt to obtain a reprieve for the condemned man. One was signed by his friends, while the other was open to the general public, but despite these efforts, the sentence was confirmed.

Dyer rose very early on the morning of Tuesday, April 5th, 1904, and ate a breakfast of poached eggs, toast and tea. By the appointed hour of 8.00am, a crowd of between 700 and 800 people had gathered outside the prison gates at Birmingham as Charles Samuel Dyer was hanged by William and John Billington. Later that morning, Dyer's body was buried within the prison precincts in a plain black coffin.

CHAPTER THREE

A SOLDIER'S TALE

ON June 30th, 1904, a woman who gave her name as Mrs Holden, called on Ellen Mahoney at 2 Back 109 Coventry Street, and asked if she and her husband could rent a room from her. Mahoney gave the couple a furnished room on the first floor at a rent of 3s 6d per week.

In fact, 'Mrs Holden' was not, after all, a married woman. Her real name was Susan Humphries and she had taken her lovers' name. He was 43-year-old Samuel Holden, a former soldier with a distinguished record. Holden had served in the Boer War where he was wounded and had been awarded the South African Medal, with no fewer than four clasps representing actions in which he had been involved. A furnished room in such a poor area of Birmingham was quite a come-down for Holden, now a market porter, who had fallen on very hard times indeed.

It was perhaps largely because of the reduced circumstances they found themselves in that Holden and Susan Humphries sought solace in alcohol. Both were often seen to be much the worse for drink and this led to constant arguments between them. They had been living in Coventry Street for only a matter of days before the neighbours became used to hearing shouting and sometimes even worse from the new occupants of the rooms at number 109.

It was around 4.10pm on Saturday, July 2nd when Martha Davis, who lived directly beneath Holden and Susan, received a visitor. Already, the sounds of yet another argument had come from upstairs and now Susan Humphries appeared at Martha's door, sporting a small wound on her chin, which was bleeding a little. Susan greeted her neighbour with, "He's on again. He's stabbed me in the chin."

Martha Davis took a closer look at the wound and saw that Susan had indeed been stabbed. Even though the wound was not serious, it was clear that Holden was not in the best of moods and Martha advised, "Let him sleep. Let his temper cool down." Susan, though, would have none of this advice and after having her wound attended to by Martha, said she was determined to go back upstairs.

Eliza Jane Walton lived at 7 Back 109 Coventry Street, and that address shared a common yard with the house where Holden lived with Susan Humphries. It was some 20 minutes after Susan had left Martha's rooms that Eliza Walton heard a terrible scream. Eliza was in her kitchen at the time and, pulling back the curtain, she looked up at Holden's window. She had a reasonable view into at least part of the room and since Holden's window was open on this pleasant summer's day she could see clearly what was going on.

Holden was sitting on a sofa by the window, eating something. Susan was standing off to one side and Eliza now saw Holden strike out at her with something he held in his hand. There were four or five blows, all aimed at Susan's head, and after these had hit home, Eliza saw Susan throw up her hands and fall forward. Eliza Walton wasted no time in running across to Holden's house.

Martha Davis had also heard those screams and she had also made to go upstairs to see what was going on. She and Eliza were just about to go up to Holden's rooms when they met him coming down. Turning to Martha, Holden said, "Fetch a doctor. I've done her in." And with that, he walked out into the yard.

Eliza Walton and Martha Davis continued up to Holden's room and there they found Susan Humphries lying on the floor, face downwards, her head towards a table and her feet towards the window. She was still alive but deeply unconscious and her head lay in an ever-widening pool of blood. Martha Davis ran to fetch a doctor.

In fact, one of the first people Martha saw was Constable Frederick Lines. After being told what had happened, he returned with her to the house and made a quick examination of Susan. She was still breathing and there were stab wounds around her neck which were still issuing blood. After rendering basic first-aid and sending for a doctor, Constable Lines helped carry Susan to the ambulance, but even as she was placed gently in the vehicle which would take her to hospital, she seemed to breathe her last. Lines returned to the room where the tragedy had taken place and on the floor, close to the window, found a knife with blood on the blade, and nearby, a broken sauce bottle.

By now, Holden had walked off into the streets around the house where he lived and police officers were warned to be on the lookout for him. It was not until 6.50pm, though, that Detective Sergeant James Whitehouse and Detective Sergeant William Evans saw him, in Digbeth, a thoroughfare which ran parallel to Coventry Street. Whitehouse seized Holden's arm to restrain him but Holden offered no resistance. He merely turned to face the officers and asked, "How is she?" Sergeant White-house replied, "She's dead and I charge you with causing her death."

Holden remained silent for a few seconds and then continued,

"I thought it would come to it, but she has done herself in and it is not murder, Mr Whitehouse, and you might let me go and see my father in Meridian Street before I go with you." Not surprisingly, this request was refused and Holden was taken to Moor Street police station where it was noted that he had blood on the back of his left hand and between his fingers. There were obvious signs that the prisoner had been drinking but he was nevertheless told that he would be charged with murder later, to which he replied, "I only gave her a punch under the chin." Down in the cells he remarked, to Sergeant Evans, "I ought not to get a day for this. It's all through the drink."

It was 8.15pm when Detective Superintendent Joseph Daniel interviewed Holden and formally charged him with murder. Holden replied, "I deny the charge. I admit giving her a punch under the chin. I deny stabbing her whatever. It seems a funny thing, sir, that I can be in a public house for three parts of an hour afterwards. That is all I have to say.

The next day being a Sunday, it was not until July 4th that Holden was put up at the police court where he appeared before the stipendiary magistrate, Mr T.M. Colmore, when after evidence of arrest was given, he was remanded until the following day.

It was on July 5th that the inquest opened before Mr Isaac Bradley. The public prosecutor here was Mr Hill, while Holden was represented by Mr Herbert Willison. One of the early witnesses was Mary Gilliver who lived at 233 Mossley Street, but had once lived in Coventry Street. She told the court that she had known Susan Humphries for more than five years and at one stage, she and Holden had lodged at her house. There had been constant arguments between the couple and Holden had occasionally hit Susan, but they had always made up their differences quite quickly. However, under cross examination, Mary had to admit that she had once heard Holden say to Susan, "I'll do a Dyer on you," referring to the Inge Street murderer.

Martha Davis, in addition to relating the conversation she had with Susan Humphries about her being stabbed in the chin, also referred to an earlier conversation that same day. Susan had come down in the morning and said she was going to get some eggs for Sam's breakfast. It was clear that at that time, she and Holden were on good terms and Martha saw him go off to work at the market some time later. It was when he returned in the afternoon that an argument broke out and Holden inflicted the wound on Susan's chin.

Both Eliza Watson and Martha Davis had reported a scream, but in fact it was not Susan Humphries who had made this sound. It was made by Alice Rowen, who lived at 8 Back 109 Coventry Street. Her front door was directly opposite to the rooms which Holden occupied and on July 2nd, Alice was sitting on her doorstep when she heard a woman shouting as if involved in an argument. Looking across she saw Holden next to Susan, by his open window. Holden had a sauce bottle in his hand and as Alice watched, he hit out at Susan with this bottle before finally dropping it. Alice had seen Eliza Walton go across to the house and followed her. She, too, saw Susan lying on the floor of her room.

In fact, Alice's testimony was quite curious. In her initial statement to the police, she had said that after hitting out with the bottle, Holden had dropped this and picked up something else, which she soon saw was a knife. Now she made no mention of this weapon and maintained that she had only seen him use the sauce bottle. She also suggested that some of the other neighbours had issued threats against her, telling her what would happen to her if she gave evidence against Holden.

All the witnesses being heard, a verdict of murder against Holden was returned. The police court hearing, later that day, was adjourned until July 13th, and it was only then that Holden was committed for trial.

Holden appeared at Birmingham assizes on July 29th, before the Lord Chief Justice, Lord Alverstone. The prosecution was led by Mr Disney, assisted by Mr Reginald Coventry while Holden was defended by Mr S.G. Dorsett and Mr Norris Foster.

Alice Rowan had once more changed her story and now claimed she had seen Holden with a sauce bottle in one hand and a knife in the other. Constable Lines, in addition to describing what he had found in the bedroom, produced a green scarf which Susan had been wearing when she was attacked. Holding this up, he showed the court three distinct holes where a knife had passed through. There was dried blood encrusted around each of the slits.

Medical evidence was given by Dr James Young who had attended the scene at just after 5.00pm on July 2nd. By then, Susan had been placed in a chair but she was still unconscious. Dr Young could see three wounds in the back of the neck, towards the middle line and a fourth in the front of the right shoulder. The wounds were dressed but as Susan was being placed into the horse-drawn ambulance, she died. The next day, he performed the post-mortem along with Dr James Thomas Jackman Morrison. They saw that all the wounds were around five-eighths of an inch long and ranged in depth from one and a quarter inch to just over two and a half inches. The wound which was directly responsible for Susan's death had cut the auxiliary artery and considerable violence had been used. The artery in question had been preserved in spirits and was exhibited in court. Dr Morrison ended by saying that it was just in the bounds of possibility that the wounds could have been self-inflicted, but it was extremely unlikely.

For the defence, Mr Dorsett placed Holden in the witness box. Holden stated that he had joined the Army on January 14th, 1890, and had soon been sent to India where he spent three months before being shipped to Ceylon (Sri Lanka) for five years. After returning to England he joined the Army reserve and was sent to South Africa on November 20th, 1899. Among the actions he was involved in were Orange Grove, Johannesburg and Diamond Hill where he was wounded in the buttocks.

Turning to his relationship with the dead woman, Holden agreed that they argued a lot but this had all been her fault. He would give her money but, instead of spending it on food for the house, she would fritter it away on drink. Holden detailed exactly what he claimed had taken place on the afternoon of July 2nd. According to him, "When I came home in the afternoon she got me some eggs to eat, and I said 'Could not you get some meat on a Saturday?' She said 'No,' and I made a clout at her, and missed her, and she ran at me with a chair. She dropped the chair and I gave her a clout under the chin. Then she ran downstairs. I sat down to eat some sardines, which I had opened with a knife. She came back again and shut the door, got hold of the chair, and rushed at me again." Holden claimed that after this, he had no memory of what took place until he saw her lying on the floor in a pool of blood.

Addressing the jury, Mr Dorsett said that since the deceased had attacked his client with a chair, he had been sorely provoked and as a result, the crime should be reduced to one of manslaughter. The jury took just half an hour to decide that Holden was guilty. He listened to the sentence of death impassionately but as he was being led down to the cells, clasped his hands together and waved to someone in the public gallery.

There was no reprieve. On the morning of Tuesday, August 16th, 1904, Holden rose at 6.00am and ate a breakfast of sardines and ale. By 8.00am a crowd of more than 300 had gathered outside Winson Green prison as Samuel Holden was hanged by William Billington, who was assisted by John Ellis. Holden had marched to the scaffold smoking a large, expensive cigar. The cigar was removed by Billington as he placed the hood over

Holden's head and just before the trap was released, Holden said, "Farewell; I will see some of you again." The handle was pulled and Holden died instantly at the end of a 6ft 7ins drop. At the same time, John Thomas Kay was hanged at Leeds for the murder of Jane Hirst in Rotherham.

CHAPTER FOUR

A NEW CURE FOR HEADACHES

IN 1900, Jane Harrison was a happily married woman, running the White Hart Inn with her husband, Edwin. Unfortunately, soon after this date, Edwin Harrison fell ill and was admitted to the Hatton Mental Asylum and Jane was forced to give up the inn and had to move, with her children, to lodgings in Great Lister Street, Birmingham.

One of the regular customers at the White Hart was John Davis, who knew both Jane and Edwin Harrison very well. It appeared, though, that there might be something more than just friendship between Davis and Jane, for shortly after she had moved to Great Lister Street, she received a visit from Davis' wife and an argument ensued over the relationship which she claimed was going on between her husband and Jane.

Over the next few years, Jane Harrison and her sons moved first to John Street and then, finally, to 17 Tower Place in Aston. Tower Place was a narrow thoroughfare with the houses leading off what was little more than an entry, coming down from Tower Road. Davis, meanwhile, had moved to Garstang, Lancashire, but this did not signal the end of his friendship with Jane for they corresponded regularly and he visited Birmingham from time to time, so that he could see her.

It was clear that Jane's family did not approve of the relationship between John Davis and their mother. For instance, when a letter was received at Easter 1906, postmarked Liverpool and bearing Davis' handwriting on the envelope, Jane's eldest son, also named Edwin, opened it and threw it on the back of the fire after reading the words of love it contained. Edwin did not even tell his mother that the letter had ever existed.

At around 7.00pm on October 27th, 1906, Jane accidentally bumped into another old friend of hers, Charles Hunter. They had a drink together before Jane invited him back to her home at Tower Place. By then it was 8.00pm and Jane, realising that she had nothing to drink in the house, said she would fetch something from the shop at the corner of Tower Place and Tower Road.

After waiting for what seemed to be a considerable time, Charles Hunter went out to look for Jane and found her at the top of Tower Place, apparently quarrelling with someone. This person turned out to be John Davis who had decided to pay a visit on Jane but had seen her in the company of Hunter and was now accusing her of being unfaithful to him. Hunter, not one to see an old friend being abused in this way, told Davis to stop harassing her. Davis, feeling that Hunter might be about to reinforce this request with some physical action, ran off down the street. It was only the fact that Jane grabbed Hunter's arm and stopped him from following Davis that prevented Hunter from sorting him out properly.

This episode, though, certainly preyed upon Davis' mind for some time later, on November 15th, he was speaking to Annie Bailey about it and made it plain that he believed that the man he had seen with Jane had now replaced him in her affections. He told much the same story when he saw Annie again the next day.

On Saturday, November 17th, 1906, Edwin Harrison went off to work at his usual time of 6.15am. He returned to Tower Place for his breakfast at 8.15am and went back to work at 8.50am. At that time, Jane complained to him about a bad headache. She told him it simply would not go away no matter what she did.

It was exactly 10.00am when Ada McLaughlin, a neighbour of Jane Harrison's who lived at 16 Tower Place, saw a man she recognised as John Davis, go into Jane's house. Almost from the moment Davis went inside, Ada heard loud voices, as if there was some kind of argument going on at number 17, but she was unable to distinguish exactly what was said. There could be no mistaking the sound which rent the air at 10.20am, though, for a bloodcurdling scream rang out and it, too, appeared to have come from 17 Tower Place.

Rushing to her door, Ada McLaughlin watched horrified as Jane Harrison walked out of her own house, her head hanging on one side with a gaping wound in her throat. Jane managed to gasp, "What shall I do? What shall I do?" before Davis calmly walked out of the house and strode purposely off down the passageway towards Tower Road. Still numb with shock, Ada managed to dash after Davis and called out, "Stop him, he's cut a woman's throat." To Ada's relief, other neighbours now rushed to her aid.

Walter Redwood lived at 177 Tower Road and he was at the back of his house when Jane Harrison's terrible scream shattered the silence. Walter ran around to the passageway and saw Davis walking towards him. After Ada McLaughlin had shouted for someone to stop Davis, Redwood had blocked his way and held him until help could arrive. At the time, Redwood had asked Davis, "Was it your wife?" to which Davis had replied, "No, it's a whore I've been living with."

Alice Riley's house was on the corner of the entry leading to Tower Place and she, too, ran into the passage when she heard the scream. She saw Redwood stop Davis and speak to him and, seeing that he had been detained, ran along to Jane Harrison's house where she found Jane standing just inside the door, still bleeding heavily from her neck wound. Jane had tried to staunch the bleeding with a rag but this was now soaking with blood and she threw it down on to the floor. Alice gently led the injured woman to a chair, sat her down and after taking off her own apron, tried to use this to stop the bleeding. Once the ambulance had arrived, Alice Riley went with Jane to the hospital and remained with her until she passed away. Whilst there, Alice noticed that Jane's hands were covered in black lead.

Constable Thomas Parker arrived at Tower Road at 10.30am and immediately took charge of Davis from Walter Redwood. Davis was then escorted back to number 17 where Constable Parker found Alice Riley still tending to the injured woman. Turning to see who had entered the house, Alice Riley shouted that Davis was the man responsible for this terrible deed, where-upon Davis admitted his guilt and pointed to the inside pocket of his coat. It was there that Constable Parker found the blood-stained razor Davis had used. Davis was taken to the police station where he was properly searched and Parker found a small notebook on one page of which Davis had written, 'J. Davis. Late of 135 Ashted Row, Vauxhall, Birmingham. No 17 Tower Place, Tower Road, Aston Cross. Will know me.

Once Jane Harrison had died, Davis was charged with her murder and, consequently, appeared before the magistrates at Aston on November 19th. After evidence of arrest had been given, Davis was remanded until November 23rd and on that date, the evidence having been heard, he was sent for trial.

John Davis appeared before Mr Justice Ridley at Birmingham on December 10th, 1906. The case for the Crown was put by Mr J.J. Parfitt who was assisted by Mr Cave, while Davis was defended by Mr Richard A. Willes.

Ada McLaughlin told the story of what she had seen in Tower Place on the morning of November 17th. She also said that Davis seemed to be completely indifferent to what he had done, for when he was stopped by Walter Redwood, Davis had said, "You can fetch the police," in a very matter of fact tone.

Mary Ann Taberner ran the off licence at 181 Tower Road which was situated at the top corner of Tower Place and she, too, had heard the scream on November 17th and run out in time to see Walter Redwood stop Davis. Mary Ann also took hold of the man and heard Davis say, "I don't want to go. It's all through jealousy. Fetch a policeman." Mary Ann told the court of an incident which had taken place some three weeks before the attack. On that date, Davis had come into her shop and asked her if she knew a woman named Harrison, adding that he was a friend of hers and had come up from Liverpool to see her. Mrs Taberner told Davis where to find Jane but instead of going there himself, Davis had handed a note to a child outside the shop. Some minutes later, Mary Ann saw the child return, hand the note back to Davis and say that Mrs Harrison was not at home. At 10.00pm that same night, Jane Harrison had come into the off licence and even as Mary Ann was telling her about her visitor, Davis appeared outside and Jane went out to speak to him. Later still, at about 11.00pm, Davis was back in the shop when he handed yet another note to Mary Ann and asked her to pass it to Mrs Harrison next time she saw her. Mary Ann gave Jane the note the next day.

Another witness to the aftermath of the attack upon Jane Harrison had been Mabel Griffiths who lived at 5 Tower Place, a house almost directly opposite number 17. After hearing the scream, Mabel saw Jane in her yard, bleeding badly from her throat. Mabel saw Davis leave soon afterwards and was there when he was apprehended at the top of the passageway.

Jane Woollaston was Jane Harrison's step-daughter and lived

with her husband, Albert, at 15 John Street, Birmingham. She told the court of an incident which had taken place some four years before, when Jane Harrison and Edwin, her step-brother, lived in the same street. Edwin had come round to her house between midnight and 1.00am complaining that Davis was at their house and was showing no inclination to leave. Jane and her husband then went around to Jane's house where Albert Wool-laston invited Davis to leave. Rather reluctantly he did so and Albert followed him for some distance to make sure that he did not return. An argument followed during which Albert struck Davis twice. He then walked off, leaving Davis lying on the pavement, nursing his wounds.

Dr Allan Johnston Fairlie-Clarke was the house surgeon at the Birmingham General Hospital. He told the court that Jane Harrison had been admitted at 11.15am on November 17th but died just 15 minutes later. The cause of death was a single clean cut wound on the right side of Jane's neck, which had severed her jugular vein. The doctor was also able to say that Jane's hands had been covered in black lead and when he had examined the razor used to inflict the wound upon her, he had found no trace of black lead upon it.

George Baxter was a prison officer detailed to return Davis to Warwick jail after he had been committed for trial by the magistrates. On the way, Davis had asked, "How do you think I shall get on?" Quite properly, Baxter had then cautioned Davis by saying, "I caution you, for I don't know anything about the matter." Davis had apparently ignored these words for he continued, "I have got to have my say yet, now they have had theirs, and I shall be defended at the assizes.

"I know very well I did not do it. She inflicted the wounds herself. I was going to shave myself and she had put a saucepan of water on the fire for me to do so and I had got the razor in my hand for the purpose of shaving me. She was then on her knees black leading the grate, and all at once she jumped up and shouted, 'Oh Jack, what shall I do my head is so bad,' and at the same time she caught hold of my hand and drew the razor across her throat. I struggled with her but was unable to prevent her cutting it. I then said to her, 'Oh Jennie, what have you done? I'll go and fetch a policeman.' and I was coming out of the house and down the passage when I was stopped by the crowd of people."

In his summing up for the defence, Mr Willes commented on the absence of any motive for his client. Mrs Harrison's husband was in an asylum and this, allied to the fact that she had fallen on hard times and was short of money, might well have disposed her towards suicide. The jury, though, preferred the prosecution version of events, believing that it was highly unlikely that a woman engaged in a task as mundane as black leading a grate would suddenly decide to kill herself, allied to which there was, of course, no trace of black lead on the razor even though Jane's hands were covered in the substance. It took them just a few minutes to decide that Davis was responsible and after being sentenced to death, he thanked the judge in a loud and firm voice.

Davis managed to see in the New Year, but only just. On the morning of Tuesday, January 1st, 1907, John Davis, the man who suggested that throat cutting was a cure for a headache, was hanged at Warwick by John Ellis.

CHAPTER FIVE

WARNINGS

BY the spring of 1913 there were signs that the relationship between Frank Greening, a 34-year-old painter, and his lover, 27-year-old Elizabeth Ellen Hearne, was deteriorating. On March 26th that year, Elizabeth paid a visit to a friend, Beatrice Matthews, at 21 Ashley Street, Birmingham. Edith Mumford, another close friend of Elizabeth's was also there, as were Annie West — Edith's mother — and two other women. Also present was Frank Greening.

During the visit, Annie called her daughter outside for a moment and while they were talking, there was the sound of a loud crash from the room and a flash of light filled the house. Frank Greening emerged and a shaken Annie West asked him what had happened. Greening replied, "The lamp has been upset. I haven't thrown it."

Going back into the room, Annie was horrified to see Elizabeth Hearne with her clothes on fire. A small chair was also ablaze and a broken oil lamp lay on the floor. The other occupants of the room were busily pouring water on Elizabeth, who claimed that Greening had thrown the lamp at her. Fortunately, the fire was soon brought under control and although Elizabeth Hearne was unconscious for some time, this was due mainly to shock and she was not badly burned. She did not even go to hospital and that night, rather surprisingly perhaps, she met up with Greening, announced she had forgiven him and they went home together, apparently quite friendly with each other.

Even before this incident there had been much happening between Greening and Elizabeth Hearne. Edith Mumford, who lived at Back Bissell Street, had known Greening for some years but had been friendly with Elizabeth only since February 1913. There were suggestions that both ladies, and indeed others in the life of Frank Greening, earned their living by selling their favours, but this apparently did not deter Greening. When Elizabeth went down to London, possibly to ply her trade, he wrote to Edith, when he discovered that she too was about to take a trip to the capital, and asked her to meet Elizabeth in the Albion, a public house which he knew she frequented, close to Kings Cross, and ask her to come back to Birmingham. Edith did as she was asked and handed another letter to Elizabeth, from Greening. The upshot was that Elizabeth agreed to return to Birmingham, if he paid the fare.

The letter had been handed over to Elizabeth around February 12th, and the next day she went back to Birmingham with Edith, and met Edith's mother, Annie West, who let out furnished rooms. Elizabeth took a room at 52 Rea Street South. Greening moved in with her, although they were there for only eight days. Elizabeth then went to visit her nephew at Kidderminster, returned in early March and moved into another house, 30 Gooch Street, again with Greening. Two weeks later they were on the move again, this time to 24 Claybrook Street where Elizabeth rented the room using the name Davies. The rent at Claybrook Street was 7s a week. Sometimes Greening paid and other times it was Elizabeth who gave the money to Annie West.

Just over a week after the alleged throwing of the oil lamp at Elizabeth, there was another incident, again involving a lamp. It was Sunday, April 6th when Annie West visited Claybrook Street to collect some rent. Elizabeth, Greening and a woman named Rose Butler were there and, seeing that Elizabeth was crying, Annie asked her what the problem was. Elizabeth replied that Greening had 'buried the lamp' in her head and then she took off her cap to show Annie some wounds.

Upon hearing of this second attack, Annie West told Greening what she would like to do to him. Greening listened in silence but when Annie had finished, he turned to Elizabeth and said, "I will close your lips tonight so that you may tell no one else what I have done, nor go to public houses telling people what I have done, and when I have done it, they can say mad Frank has done it."

Annie West told Elizabeth to get washed and come with her for her dinner. Elizabeth replied that Annie's daughter, Edith Mumford, had already asked her but Greening interjected with an announcement that she was going with him to his mother's house. When Elizabeth said she was never going there again, Greening flew into a rage and took a running kick at her, but Annie West managed to pull Elizabeth out of the house.

Greening followed the two women into Claybrook Street and twice threatened to punch Elizabeth's face in. The women began walking to Annie's house, followed all the way by Greening who stopped them in Kent Street and asked Elizabeth for 4s she had promised him in order to buy some clothes for his mother. Elizabeth replied that she had given him 3s the day before, when he had said that he would put the extra shilling to it. Greening, though, kept following, arguing all the way until Elizabeth stopped outside a chemist's shop and said that if it was open she would buy 6d worth of poison and end this misery by taking it.

The group continued until they reached the junction of Macdonald Street and Barford Street where Elizabeth said she must have a drink or she would 'drop'. All three went into a nearby pub, the Queen's Head, where Elizabeth had 2d worth of whisky while Annie and Greening each had a stout. Greening did not touch his drink and when Annie told him to go back home, lock the house and bring her the key, in effect evicting him from their home, he simply walked out of the pub.

Edith Mumford was also in the pub and in due course, Annie left Elizabeth with her while she went back to her own house, having first invited Elizabeth to come over later for something to eat. Elizabeth replied that she would go back to Edith's house at 5 Back 115 Bissell Street.

Frederick West, Annie's husband, had also been in the Queen's Head and when Annie had given Greening the order to fetch the front door key, he had followed him out to ensure that he did as he had been told. Frederick returned to the pub with the key but he also had a postcard with a hastily scrawled message for Elizabeth. Although the writing on the card was very bad, Elizabeth could just about make out, 'You can do your best and see who will win. You have asked for it and you have got it.' It was signed 'Frank'.

It was 2.20pm when Edith and Elizabeth left the pub and went to Edith's house at Back Bissell Street. Another woman, Ida Ann Bolding, lived at the same address and all three women were in the house when Greening arrived there at around 3.00pm, asking for his key. Told that his landlady had it, Greening persisted in his demands and, seeing that he was getting nowhere with this approach, he again asked Elizabeth to come to his mother's house for her dinner. As she refused and added that she was staying exactly where she was, Edith got to her feet and said she was going into the kitchen to strain the potatoes.

Further conversation followed between Elizabeth and Greening but Edith could not hear any of the details until suddenly

Elizabeth shouted, "I don't care about the shooter." Greening then replied something like, "Woman, you must be mad," and as Edith turned, she saw him take a revolver out of his pocket, aim it at Elizabeth and fire three times. Edith Mumford shouted the single word, "Murder!" whereupon Greening fired one shot directly at her. The bullet, though, only grazed Edith's eyebrow and Greening ran out into the street as Ida Bolding bravely gave chase. Edith, meanwhile, moved Elizabeth to a chair as the wounded woman exclaimed, "Oh my stomach." Soon afterwards, Annie West, who lived only across the yard and had heard the four shots, came in to see what had taken place.

Constable William Morris, having been informed that there had been a shooting incident in Back Bissell Street, arrived at the scene at 2.55pm. Elizabeth Hearne was still in the chair, groaning loudly and bleeding from the abdomen and thigh. Constable Morris rendered basic first aid, after which he sent for the ambulance and accompanied the stricken woman to the hospital.

It was 3.45pm. by the time Elizabeth arrived at the General Hospital where she was administered to by Dr Herbert Henry Sampson, the resident surgical officer. Dr Sampson noted two puncture wounds in Elizabeth's right shoulder, two on the right thigh and one in the abdomen. Emergency treatment was applied in an attempt to stabilise Elizabeth's condition and relieve her pain.

The police were told that the man responsible for the shooting was Frank Greening and a search was now launched for him. Rose Butler had also been living with Greening and Elizabeth at Claybrook Street, along with another woman, Kate Cawley. She had not heard of the shooting incident when she returned to her lodgings at 3.45pm and found the house locked up. Determined to gain access, Rose got into the house through the cellar grating and then went up to her attic room to sleep. Some time later,

Rose's slumber was disturbed by police officers knocking on the door and shouting that they were looking for Frank Greening in connection with the shooting of Elizabeth Hearne.

In fact, it was not until 9.20pm that Rose saw Greening. At that time he was coming out of 24 Claybrook Street and walked to the door of number 12, which he tried to open. While all this was going on, one of the police officers involved in the search, Detective Constable Henry Jones, was just a few yards away and he advanced towards Greening, who immediately moved his hand to his hip pocket. Constable Jones shouted, "Stand still Frank. I might have got a weapon as well as you." Greening stopped in his tracks and replied, "I haven't got it now." Nevertheless, to be on the safe side, Jones told his prisoner to throw up his hands and after searching him and confirming that there was no gun, marched Greening to the police station where he was charged with inflicting grievous bodily harm.

Back at the hospital it was clear that Elizabeth's condition was worsening rapidly and it was thought that she would not survive long. For that reason, on April 7th, Greening was taken to the hospital, under police escort, to hear Elizabeth give her deposition to Charles Edward Barker, the chief assistant clerk to the court.

Elizabeth explained that she was a married woman but had not seen her husband for nine years and had lived with Greening for the past eight weeks. On April 6th, she had been having dinner at a friend's house when Greening came in and demanded his front door key. Seconds later he drew a gun and fired at her, after which she had no memory of anything else that took place.

Just a few hours after that deposition was taken, at around 4.00pm on Monday, April 7th, Elizabeth Hearne succumbed to her injuries and died. Greening was immediately charged with wilful murder and appeared at the police court on that charge the same day when matters were adjourned pending the result of the inquest.

The inquest opened before Mr Isaac Bradley on April 10th, Greening being represented by Mr Arthur Hall Wright. Evidence of identification was given by George Pitt of 5 Jerusalem Walk, Kidderminster, who testified that the dead woman was his sister and her maiden name was Elizabeth Ellen Pitt. She had married Arthur Hearne but left him some nine years before when she moved in with a man named Davies and began to use his surname. George said he had last seen his sister when she visited Kidderminster four or five weeks before her death. He had heard about the shooting on April 6th and went over to Birmingham to see her in the hospital, when Elizabeth had told the ward sister, in his presence, that Greening had shot her five times. George also admitted that his sister had had quite a sharp tongue and could stand up for herself in a quarrel but she was by no means a short-tempered woman.

Once all the other witnesses had been called, the jury did not even bother to leave the court before returning a verdict of wilful murder against Greening, who was sent for trial on the coroner's warrant. Just a week later, on April 17th, the police court reconvened and Greening was again committed to the assizes on a charge of murder.

Greening faced his trial at Birmingham before Mr Justice Atkin on July 14th, 1913. The Crown's case was led by Sir Ryland Adkins who was assisted by Mr Costello while Greening was defended by Mr Richard A. Willes.

In his opening speech for the prosecution, Sir Ryland Adkins stated that this was a story which was 'short and squalid — a story of misery and suffering, a tale of mean streets'. He then called his first witness, George Pitt, who again spoke of his sister's relationship with Greening.

Edith Mumford told the court of her trip to London and of

being given a letter by Greening, who told her to go to a public house near King's Cross and ask for 'Birmingham Lizzie'. Elizabeth had travelled back to Birmingham with Edith, Greening met them at the station and that night they all stayed with Annie West, Edith's mother. The following day, Greening and Elizabeth moved into one of Annie's houses at Rea Street and after this, moved to various other addresses, all owned by Annie, until they finally settled down at Claybrook Street. Having detailed these movements, Edith then outlined the incident with the oil lamp on March 26th and of the shooting itself, on April 6th.

Ida Bolding said she had been in the Queen's Head public house at 1.30pm on April 6th. Elizabeth and Edith were there and Ida joined them. Eventually all three went back to Back Bissell Street and after they had been there for perhaps ten minutes, Greening came in and demanded his door key, saying that both he and Rose Butler needed to get their clothes from the house. Ida, of course, remained in the room when Edith went to strain the water from the potatoes in the kitchen and she could hear clearly all that was said. Elizabeth had at one stage mentioned that Greening had a 'shooter' to which he had replied, "Woman, you must be mad. I have not got such a thing." And as he spoke, Greening turned to look out into the yard as if checking whether anyone was there or not. As soon as he saw that the coast was clear, Greening put his hand into his coat and pulled out a gun. Without saying another word, he fired three shots at Elizabeth and one at Edith when she ran into the room. Greening then calmly pulled down his hat, put up his coat collar and ran off up the yard as Ida shouted after him, "You dirty dog, you've shot her." Ida tried to follow but he was much too quick for her and by the time she had reached the street, there was no sign of him.

Rose Butler told the court that she was now living at 40 Inge

Street but at the time of this incident had been living with Greening and Elizabeth in Claybrook Street. She had mentioned to Greening, on March 31st, that she and Kate Cawley needed fresh lodgings and he had suggested they move in to his house. Rose reported that all the time she was at the house, Greening and Elizabeth were always arguing and on more than one occasion she had heard him threaten to shoot Elizabeth.

On April 2nd, Rose had come home to find Elizabeth sporting a fresh head wound and she said that Greening had hit her with an oil lamp. When Greening came in later he seemed totally unconcerned about this and merely said to Elizabeth, "You are not dead yet," adding that he would take her life before the week was up. That night Elizabeth had slept on the floor of the attic room which Rose shared with Kate.

The following morning, Greening announced that he was going to Coventry and Wolverhampton and asked Rose if she wanted to go with him. When she said no, he repeated his threat to kill Elizabeth before the week was out. On April 5th, the threat was issued for a third time, Greening adding that he had a revolver in his pocket. Rose did see something there but did not think for one minute that Greening was serious and joked, "Oh, that's only a piece of wood." Greening pulled his pocket tight to reveal the shape of a gun and replied, "That don't look like a piece of wood does it?"

On April 6th, Elizabeth was cleaning the grate and tidying up the house when Greening started yet another argument and said that he would 'close your lips before night'. Rose left the house soon afterwards, at 12.10pm, and when she returned, the house was all locked up. She knew nothing of the shooting until the police came looking for Greening.

Kate Cawley was the other woman who had been invited to move into 24 Claybrook Street by Greening. She agreed that Greening and Elizabeth never seemed to be friendly and confirmed some of the threats which Rose Butler had mentioned. Kate had left the house with Rose at 12.10pm and they returned together to find the house locked and no one in.

Many of the threats which Greening had made were also heard by Annie West, who also mentioned the throwing of the oil lamp on March 26th. Turning to the afternoon of the shooting, Alice said she had heard four shots and someone shout, "You dirty dog." She ran across to Edith's house and saw Elizabeth on a chair, saying that she had been shot. It was Annie who sent someone for a doctor while she herself went for the police.

Percy Smallwood lived in the house next door to Edith Mumford and he saw a man he did not know, standing in the yard outside, just before 3.00pm on April 6th. Soon afterwards, Smallwood heard four shots and going outside saw the same man, who was wearing a grey overcoat, going towards the entry which led to the street. On April 10th, Smallwood attended an identification parade at the police station and picked out Greening as the man he had seen.

Clara Garrattley was a friend of Greening and lived at 85 Lower Essex Street, and she said that he had visited her twice on April 6th. The first occasion was at 1.30pm when he told her that Elizabeth had 'gone on the beer' and that he would be happier if she came off it. Later that afternoon, Greening returned. He seemed to have been running, was out of breath and gasped, "Liz has met with an accident. In fact she is dead. I have shot her and this is what I have shot her with." He then pulled a revolver from his pocket, showed it to her briefly, and put it back. He was laughing at the time, so Clara thought he was joking. Her testimony was corroborated by Clara's husband, Alfred Garrattley.

Medical testimony was given by Dr Sampson who had also performed the post-mortem with Dr James Thomas Jackman Morrison. They reported an old scalp wound, some one and a quarter inches long, and not too deep, which might have been caused by a blow or a fall. Describing the bullet wounds, Dr Sampson said that the one in the abdomen had passed in and up on the right side, perforating the intestines five times. It had been this bullet which caused peritonitis which, in turn, led to Elizabeth's death. Other bullets were found in the armpit, having passed through the upper arm, against the shoulder blade and the two wounds in the thigh were caused by a single bullet which passed right through.

The final prosecution witness was Constable Henry Jones. He stated that when told he was being arrested for the shooting of Elizabeth Hearne, Greening had replied, "I was there about three o'clock but I done no shooting." Taken to the police station at Claybrook Street, Greening added, "I was at Edith Mumford's house this afternoon, but I know nothing about it." After Elizabeth's deposition had been taken, the charge was altered to one of attempted murder and after she had died, this was changed yet again, to one of murder. To this Greening had said, "I had better be defended on that."

Giving evidence on his own behalf, Greening agreed that he and Elizabeth had argued frequently but these had all been minor affairs and were soon forgotten. He said that he had objected to Elizabeth visiting the house in Ashley Street, because he, believed it to be a house of ill-repute. He had certainly never threatened to take her life and on the day in question, had a loaded gun on him only because he had borrowed it and was about to return it. After yet another argument about him being locked out of the house, Greening said he had taken out the gun and fired 'on impulse'. Asked why he had fired three times if that was the case, the prisoner replied that he had simply lost his temper.

In his closing speech for the defence, Mr Willes urged the jury to return a verdict of manslaughter but after a short deliberation, they announced that Greening was guilty of murder and he was sentenced to death. An appeal was entered and heard on July 29th before Justices Bray, Avory and Lush. Here Mr Willes stated that at the trial, the prosecution had referred to two separate attacks upon Elizabeth with oil lamps as this suggested that he had been violent towards her before, even though in neither case had it been proved that these were deliberate or even that Greening was responsible. There was also a suggestion that Greening had been provoked but in giving their decision, the appeal court judges ruled that when he spoke to Elizabeth before the shooting, Greening had appeared calm and collected, which was hardly the behaviour of a man who considered himself provoked. As a result, the appeal was dismissed.

At 7.00am on Wednesday August 13th, 1913, a crowd began to gather outside Winson Green prison and by 8.00am there were between 400 and 500 there. Meanwhile, inside the condemned cell, Greening was defiant to the end. He spent a restless last night, rose early and sent for a prison official who he then abused verbally. Greening was rude to the prison chaplain and ranted all the way to the scaffold where he continued swearing until the white cap was placed over his head. Right at the last moment he admitted that the sentence was just, before he was hanged by Thomas Pierrepoint and George Brown. At the same time, James Ryder was hanged at Manchester for the murder of his wife.

CHAPTER SIX

SICK OF LIFE

FLORENCE Beatrice Butler was a 29-year-old married woman, although she had been separated from her husband, Thomas George Butler, for more than five years. Since the break up of her marriage, Florence and her nine-year-old daughter, Nellie, had lived with Florence's mother, Frances Julia Griffiths, at 2 Bath Terrace, Chequers Walk, Birmingham. There was one other person living at 2 Bath Terrace, a lodger, and, by coincidence, although he was no relation to the family, his surname was also Butler.

William Allen Butler had first come to lodge at Bath Terrace in July 1915 and by February the following year, it had become clear that he was attracted to Florence, his landlady's daughter, and they started walking out together. The relationship developed quickly, for in March 1916, Florence found herself pregnant by Butler. Frances knew of her daughter's condition and made no move to interfere. Neither did Frances interfere when an almost constant series of arguments broke out between Florence and her new lover.

Verbal arguments were one thing, physical violence was another. On the night of Friday, May 19th, 1916, Florence and

Butler went out together but Florence came home alone, in tears, to tell her mother that Butler had been knocking her about. The following morning, Florence showed Frances some bruises on her legs which she said had been caused by Butler kicking her. Enough was enough – when Frances got home from work that night, she faced Butler with what had been going on, told him she wanted no more trouble in her house and gave him one week's notice to quit. All this took place at around 3.30pm and Butler offered no argument, preferring instead to go up to his room and lie down.

At some time between 6.00pm and 6.30pm, Butler came back downstairs and seemed to be friendly enough towards Florence until she said she was going out. By then it was 6.50pm and Butler demanded to know where she was going. Florence replied, "That's my business," and left. Ten minutes later, Butler, too, went out. Florence returned alone at 9.30pm and Frances prepared her supper for her. It was not until just after 10.00pm that Butler came in and at that time, Florence was still sitting at the table, eating.

Whilst Florence was finishing her meal, Elizabeth Rice and her children, who lived next door at 1 Bath Terrace, were present in the house, visiting Frances. However, as soon as Frances Griffiths announced that she was going upstairs to make the beds, Elizabeth returned to her own home, leaving Florence and Butler together. At the time, little Nellie was asleep in one of the armchairs in the same room.

It was just a few minutes later when a scream rang out. Something had woken Nellie and frightened her so much that she had called out. Frances Griffiths ran downstairs and saw her daughter standing at the foot of the stairs, holding on to the back of a door. Even before Frances could ask what had happened, Florence said, "Mother, he's on again." Frances turned towards her lodger who was standing near the sofa, and asked him what he had done. Butler replied, "What I said I would do long ago."

Florence went next door to Elizabeth Rice's home. Butler followed her and Frances went after him, fearful that he might attack her daughter again. In order to discourage just such an event, Florence threatened to fetch a policeman but Butler said, "No, I'm going to give myself up," and walked off into the night.

Frances Griffiths went into Elizabeth Rice's house to find her daughter on the floor by a sofa. Seeing a spot of blood on Florence's blouse, Frances unfastened a couple of buttons, to find more blood issuing from a wound in Florence's side. It was then that Butler came in to the room, brandished a knife and announced, "This is what I done it with," before once more going out into the street. Frances, seeing that Florence needed help, ran to fetch the police.

Constable Samuel Dexter was on duty in Broad Street when Butler, a man he did not know, walked up to him and said, "I want to give myself up. I have stabbed a woman." Butler did not give his name and when asked the identity of the woman, replied that it was someone he had been keeping company with. Dexter asked for the address, which Butler provided, along with the comment that Florence was with some neighbours. When Constable Dexter asked whether Florence was badly injured, Butler replied, "She's bleeding badly." Taking Butler into custody, Dexter told him that he would be escorted back to Bath Terrace but Butler objected and shouted, "No, I'm going straight to Ladywood to give myself up." Surprisingly, Dexter let his man go free and went alone to the scene of the crime.

Butler was true to his word and at 11.05pm he strolled into the Ladywood police station, walked up to the desk where Sergeant Frederick Shereston was on duty, and admitted that he had stabbed his 'wife' with a knife. Sergeant Shereston demanded to know when this had taken place, whereupon Butler said, "Just now. I have come straight here," but then added that he had first spoken to a policeman in Broad Street.

Still taking down the details, Sergeant Shereston asked Butler if he had any family. Butler retorted, "No, but this one is in the family way and that's the cause of the trouble." He then produced a bloodstained knife, placed it on the counter and added, "That's what I did it with." Butler was detained and later, when it was ascertained that Florence had died, he was charged with her murder. In reply, Butler said, "Oh dear!"

Butler was put up at the police court on May 22nd, two days after Florence had died. The stipendiary magistrate was Lord Ilkeston and he heard that the inquest had been fixed for May 24th. Having heard evidence of Butler's arrest, the magistrate remanded him to May 25th.

The inquest, before the deputy coroner, Mr Arthur H. Herbert, proceeded rapidly and the jury, having listened to the testimony of the various witnesses, returned a verdict of murder against Butler that same day. The following day, the police court having come to the same conclusion, Butler was sent for trial at the next Warwickshire assizes.

Those assizes opened in July and Butler faced his trial on the 12th of that month, before Mr Justice Avory. The defence rested in the hands of Dr W. Dawson Sadler, while the case for the Crown was led by Mr H.M. Giveen who was assisted by Mr Reginald Coventry.

Frances Griffiths reported that when Butler had come into the house on the night of May 20th, he did not appear to be drunk. He did not speak, except for once when she asked Mrs Rice for a match and Butler told her to feel for one in his jacket pocket. Frances went on to detail what she had seen and heard after the attack had taken place, before she went out to fetch a policeman.

Elizabeth Rice said that she had heard many arguments

between Florence and Butler. On the day Florence had died, she had come into Elizabeth's house at dinner time and shown the bruises on her legs, explaining that Butler had kicked her during their last disagreement. Florence went on to say that she was so fed up with the situation that she wanted to move in with Elizabeth.

That night, just after Frances had gone up to the bedrooms, Elizabeth had returned to her own house. Just a few minutes later she heard Nellie scream and soon after that, Florence ran into her house and collapsed on the floor. All this was seen by Mrs Maria Keeton, who lodged with Elizabeth, and these two tried to minister to Florence who seemed unable to speak. Elizabeth was bathing blood from Florence's eye when Butler came in. She turned to him and cried, "Good God, what have you done?" Butler did not reply, but showed Elizabeth the knife he had used to inflict the wound. Seeing this, Elizabeth said that she was going to go for the police but Butler said he was going to give himself up. His last words, when asked to hand over the knife, had been, "No fear."

Mrs Keeton said that almost every time she saw Butler and Florence together, they were arguing. On the night of May 20th, Florence had run into the house and shouted, "Oh me! Do protect me." She then tried to get up the stairs, probably to hide from Butler if he should follow her but finally Florence collapsed and when Butler came in, Maria shouted at him, "You have killed her." To this Butler replied, in a matter of fact way, "That's what I intended to do."

The only witness to the actual attack had been nine-year-old Nellie. She told the court that as soon as Frances had gone upstairs, Elizabeth Rice left the house and almost immediately Butler had risen from his chair, walked over to Florence who was still eating her supper, taken a pen knife from his pocket, opened out the blade and without a word, raised his arm above his head and plunged the blade into Florence. She squealed in pain and fell off the chair and seeing that she had been hurt, Nellie screamed instinctively. As soon as Frances had followed Florence out of the house, Nellie, showing remarkable common sense, ran to the corner of William Street where she found a policeman and told him what had happened.

In fact there were a couple of policemen close by the house at the time of the stabbing. Constable Harry Taylor was at the corner of Granville Street and Holliday Street at 10.55pm when he heard that there had been an incident in Bath Terrace. Going to the house, he found Florence lying on the floor. She tried to speak but seemed unable to do so. Constable Taylor helped another officer to bandage the stricken woman and tried to get Dr Bekew to attend, but he was out. No one else from the hospital was available at the time. When Florence was eventually placed in the ambulance, she was already dead.

Constable George Brown was the officer who assisted Constable Taylor. He had been in Chequers Walk when he heard of the stabbing. He went to Elizabeth Rice's house and asked her what had happened. She replied, "Billy Butler has stabbed her with a penknife." Brown had been sent to fetch the ambulance, but it arrived too late and after Florence had been pronounced dead, Brown took her body to the mortuary.

Detective Sergeant Frederick Stickland was at the Queen's Hospital when he heard that a woman had been stabbed. He went to the scene as soon as he could and was told that Dr Tooks had already attended and pronounced Florence dead. It was Stickland who, after he had returned to the police station, informed Butler that Florence had died and he would be charged with her murder. Butler had said, "That's all right," but went on to ask if Stickland had been present when Florence died. Stickland told Butler that he had not. Later, when he examined the knife that Butler had handed in at the station, Sergeant

Stickland noticed that it was not only stained with blood but also that it had recently been sharpened.

Dr Walter Pemberton Tooks was the doctor who finally attended to Florence at Mrs Rice's home at midnight on May 20th. By then she was already dead and on May 22nd, Dr Tooks performed a post-mortem which showed a single incised wound under the left breast. The blade used had penetrated the heart.

The left lung was also slightly cut but the direct cause of death was haemorrhage due to the wound. Dr Tooks also observed a number of recent bruises on Florence's legs and confirmed that she was three months pregnant.

When he had walked into the police station to give himself up, Butler had freely admitted his guilt and said that it was all because Florence was pregnant and he had been jealous of another male friend of hers, an elderly man named Ireland. Butler knew she had seen this man on the night she had died. Indeed, he had given her a crab which she was eating for her supper in front of him, as if flaunting what she had done.

When Butler was searched, a letter had been found on him. Addressed to his mother it read, 'Dear Mother, we like one another but it is better to part sooner or later as I am sick of my life.' Now, though, in court, Butler claimed that he had no memory whatsoever of the crime. He had no idea what had happened until he found himself at a neighbour's house with a knife in his hand. As a result, the defence asked for a verdict of manslaughter, claiming that there was no evidence that Butler intended to take Florence's life with malice aforethought. The jury, though, took just under an hour to decide that Butler was guilty as charged.

The execution was originally fixed for August 8th, but that was postponed when notice was given that Butler wished to appeal. The appeal was heard on July 31st, before the Lord Chief Justice, Lord Isaacs, and Justices Scrutton and Low. The main grounds of that appeal were that the trial judge had misquoted part of Butler's statement. When arrested, Butler had actually said, "This is what I have done it with, what I said I would do long ago." Mr Justice Avory had quoted this as 'what I intended to do long ago', and this suggested a premeditation which did not actually exist. Added to this, not enough had been said about the fact that Butler was in great pain at the time of the attack since his arm was bandaged as the result of an accident at work when molten metal had fallen on to him.

Giving the court's judgement, Lord Isaacs said that there was no doubt that Butler was jealous of the woman he had killed and it was plainly apparent that he intended to commit the crime and had carried out those intentions. It was said that Florence had admitted a relationship with Mr Ireland and the court held that such an admission was sufficient provocation to reduce a murder charge to manslaughter, but only if the woman had been Butler's wife. This rule did not apply to any woman who was not a wife and so the appeal must fail.

Butler's defence did not give up and an application was made to the Attorney General for permission to appeal to the House of Lords. When, on August 14th, that permission was refused, Butler's last hope was a petition, signed by 7,000 people, begging for a reprieve. Soon it was announced that the Home Secretary had found no reason to interfere with the sentence and Butler's fate was sealed.

At 8.00am on Wednesday, August 16th, 1916, a crowd of 200 people gathered outside Birmingham prison as William Allen Butler was hanged by John Ellis, who was assisted by Edward Taylor.

CHAPTER SEVEN

A TOUCH OF ADULTERY

IN 1914, World War One broke out across Europe, plunging the country into four years of bloody conflict. Although it is debatable which country suffered most in that terrible war, Belgium must rank as one of the worst affected, with many battles taking place upon its soil.

As it became clear that a long trench campaign would take place, some of that country's citizens chose to leave their native land and set up home in England in an attempt to rebuild their shattered lives. One such couple was Clemence Verelst and her husband, Pierre Axel. They came to England some nine months after the war had started and were given permission to work in the munitions industry in Birmingham. The couple worked hard, and saved every penny they could until they had enough to open a tea shop in London. Clemence and Pierre moved down to the capital, opened their new business, and settled down to a peaceful and prosperous life together.

Unfortunately, this peace was shattered within six weeks of the tea shop opening, for one of the customers of this new venture was another Belgian, Louis Van de Kerkhove, a native of Antwerp. He and Clemence soon found themselves attracted to each other and it was not long before they had run away together, first setting up home in Staines, where Louis took work as a labourer, but later moving to Birmingham when Van de Kerkhove obtained work at the Austin factory at Longbridge. The couple took lodgings together at 18 Great Lister Street, where they stayed for some four and a half months.

There was trouble between Van de Kerkhove and Clemence soon after they had started living together, caused mainly by her drinking habits, and eventually he said he had endured enough and intended to leave. Clemence took a knife, stood before the door to bar Van de Kerkhove's way and threatened to stab him if he tried to get out of the room. Van de Kerkhove decided to call Clemence's bluff but she was good to her word and plunged the dagger into his arm. Van de Kerkhove did not press any charges but, to all intents and purposes, at least as far as he was concerned, the relationship was now well and truly over. He walked out of his job at Austin's factory and took fresh lodgings at 3 Tower Street, Dudley. Clemence, meanwhile, returned to London but did not seek a reconciliation with her husband.

The separation was not very long lasting, for just ten days later, Clemence was back in Birmingham where she took a job at the National Projectile factory. Soon she had traced Van de Kerkhove and asked him to live with her again. At first he refused, but constant pressure from Clemence meant that he soon gave way and agreed, even promising her 50s a week from his wages to help out with the household expenses. It was a decision he soon regretted, for a fortnight later, Clemence sold most of his furniture and walked out on him with the proceeds. Once again she returned to London, but each week letters arrived from her, still professing undying love, even though Clemence, an illiterate, would have had to have these letters written for her.

For the next few months there were fresh attempts to rekindle the relationship on the part of Clemence Verelst. Van de Kerkhove visited London at Easter in 1917 and again she begged him to live with her once more. When he refused, she said she would follow him back to Dudley, which she did just a couple of weeks afterwards. There followed another brief reconciliation but towards the middle of December 1917, Van de Kerkhove made what he determined must be the final break. Clemence would not give up, though, and continued to visit his lodgings and his place of work in an attempt to win him back. Meanwhile, she, too, had taken new lodgings in Birmingham, living in rooms at 248 Windsor Street.

It was at that address that Van de Kerkhove called on the morning of Sunday, January 13th, 1918. The door was opened by Catherine Johansson, another Belgian who had come to England at the outbreak of hostilities in 1914. She told Van de Kerkhove, a man she knew, that Clemence was not at home but had taken a new job in Brun's coffee house in Dale End. Van de Kerkhove politely bid her goodbye and said he would speak to Clemence at her place of work.

Van de Kerkhove did indeed visit Clemence at the coffee house and there it was plain that he would cause a scene if she did not leave with him. Hilda Tudor, who also worked in the coffee house, saw Van de Kerkhove arrive. Clemence asked for an hour off and left with him at 6.00pm. At 7.00pm Hilda herself left work and went for a drink in the White Horse public house. She saw Clemence there, arguing with a man whose face Hilda could not see. They appeared to be speaking in a foreign language. Clemence saw Hilda and asked her to keep a seat for her, but she did not return to the pub that night.

It was just after 9.00pm that Van de Kerkhove and Clemence booked into the Shaftesbury Hotel on Station Street, where they were given room number ten. Van de Kerkhove filled out both registration cards, since, of course, Clemence could not write, and they then retired to their room. For a time, all was quiet.

Florence Powers was one of the chambermaids at the Shaftesbury and it was she who showed Van de Kerkhove and Clemence to their room. For the next half hour or so, Florence's work took her past room ten a number of times and she heard no sounds coming from within. Just before 10.00pm, another maid, Sarah Rosenthal, finished her duties for the night and retired to her own room, one she shared with yet another maid, Pauline Hyman. These two chatted for a short time and then, at almost precisely 10.00pm, they heard the unmistakable sounds of a major quarrel, coming from room ten. What began as raised voices and banging soon developed into loud screams and, fearful of what might be going on, Sarah and Pauline ran downstairs and reported what they had heard to Mary Casey, the wife of the hotel proprietor, Samuel Casey.

Mary Casey perhaps did not take the maid's story too seriously at first but nevertheless, she sent up James Kilkenny, the hotel's assistant boots, to see what was going on. He tried the handle of room ten and found that the door was locked. From within he could hear the sounds of a woman groaning and so Kilkenny knocked on the door and demanded entry. Within seconds, the door was slowly opened by Van de Kerkhove, who was wearing only his shirt. Without explaining what he meant, he muttered, "I've done it now," and threw down a bloodstained knife. As if further clarification of what precisely he had done were necessary, the door then creaked open a little more and Clemence Verelst crawled out on her hands and knees. She wore only her underwear and she was covered in blood. She managed to gasp out, "God help me, I'm dying," before collapsing on the landing. Van de Kerkhove, meanwhile, had gone back inside the darkened room.

There had been another witness present when Clemence crawled out of her room. Lawrence Jack Hughes, a friend of some guests at the hotel, had been downstairs when Sarah and

Pauline had reported a disturbance. He had heard the maids tell their story of the violence coming from room ten and had followed James Kilkenny up the stairs. Now, as Kilkenny ministered to the stricken woman, Hughes ran to summon further assistance. In the street outside the hotel, he found Constable Frederick Goodman, told him what had happened and took him back to the landing where Clemence still lay in an ever-widening pool of blood.

The room door was still slightly open but Constable Goodman now pushed it back against the wall. The gas was not lit inside the room and it was impossible to distinguish anything. Goodman called out, "Where are you?" and Van de Kerkhove immediately came to the door, still clad only in his shirt. Constable Goodman ordered him to dress, noticing that there was a good deal of blood on his hands. Within a few minutes, another officer, Constable Giles, appeared on the scene and when the ambulance arrived, the two officers lifted Clemence into it, also ensuring that Van de Kerkhove was inside before setting off for the hospital. On the way, the ambulance stopped to drop Constable Giles and his prisoner at Newton Street police station before carrying on to the General Hospital.

Once Constable Goodman had seen that Clemence was being attended to by the doctors, he travelled back to the police station himself and there charged Van de Kerkhove with causing grievous bodily harm. To this Van de Kerkhove replied, "That's right. She shouldn't have fooled me about the same as she has done her husband."

On the morning of January 14th, Van de Kerkhove appeared before the magistrates on the charge and here it was stated that the victim in this case appeared to be responding to treatment and was expected to survive. Those hopes turned out to be ill founded, for in the night, Clemence's condition worsened, her lungs collapsed and she died from her injuries on the morning of

Tuesday, January 15th. That same day, Constable Goodman and Detective Inspector James Macaulay visited Van de Kerkhove at Winson Green prison where he was being held and charged him with murder. Inspector Macaulay noted that Van de Kerkhove, when he heard the news that Clemence was dead, paled visibly and appeared close to fainting.

Things moved quickly from then on. On January 17th, the inquest opened before Mr Isaac Bradley, and on the same day it returned a verdict of murder against Van de Kerkhove. Soon afterwards, the police court came to the same conclusion and Van de Kerkhove was sent for trial.

The case of the Crown against Van de Kerkhove was heard at Birmingham on March 18th before Mr Justice Lawrence. Although Van de Kerkhove spoke reasonable English, he asked for and was granted the services of an interpreter and Mr Jacques Hubert Lonsberg attended the court for that purpose. During the single day that the trial lasted, Van de Kerkhove was defended by Mr Richard A. Willes, the prosecution being led by Mr T. Hollis Walker, who was assisted by Sir Ryland Adkins MP.

Catherine Johansson stated that she had been a close friend of Clemence Verelst and after Clemence had left her husband, she and Van de Kerkhove had come to Birmingham and visited her at Windsor Street. Clemence had told her that she had left her husband and soon afterwards, she and Van de Kerkhove had taken lodgings together in Great Lister Street. Three weeks before she died, Clemence had called on her again, this time alone, and told Catherine that she had left Van de Kerkhove, had no intention of going back to him and hoped to get back with her husband.

Catherine said that after hearing that Clemence was in the hospital, she had visited her and Clemence had told her some of what had taken place after Van de Kerkhove called at the coffee shop where she worked. It was clear that there was going to be a scene so Clemence obtained permission to leave early and she and Van de Kerkhove then went to a pub, the White Horse, where he consumed a large amount of whisky. From there they went to the hotel and once alone in the room, he accused her of sleeping with another man. She denied this but he would not listen and tried to strangle her and then, when this did not work, produced a knife. Clemence, in an attempt to escape, had hidden beneath the bed but he had knelt down and jabbed the knife at her a number of times.

Florence Powers, Pauline Hyman, Sarah Rosenthal, James Kilkenny and Mary Casey all told of what they had heard and seen on the night of January 13th. Lawrence Hughes also gave details of being downstairs in the hotel when Van de Kerkhove and his companion went to the office window and asked for a room for the night. After the attack had taken place and Hughes had gone to fetch the policeman, he had gone into the bedroom to light the gas so that the constable could keep an eye on Van de Kerkhove. Once the room was well lit again, Hughes saw a good deal of blood on the floor, most of it underneath the bed. Around the room were scattered various articles of women's clothing.

Dr William Arnold Clements was the resident surgical officer at the General Hospital and he testified that when Clemence was admitted, there were a number of stab wounds, mostly on the upper part of her back, but she also had a large wound in her abdomen. After Clemence had died, at 6.30am on January 15th, Dr Clements had performed a post-mortem, during which he counted 14 separate wounds, two of which he regarded as dangerous. Clemence's right lung had collapsed and her left lung was partially collapsed and this was the direct cause of death.

Edward Rowley Peirce was the resident pathologist at the hospital and he was on duty in casualty when Clemence was brought in. At one stage, as he was treating the injured woman, she explained to him that there had been a quarrel and at first, Van de Kerkhove had tried to strangle her with his bare hands.

When this failed he drew out a knife and attacked her. Clemence also told him that Van de Kerkhove had once before threatened her with a knife, although he had not touched her with it on that occasion. Edward Peirce pointed out to Clemence that she was rather stupid to have anything to do with a man who had threatened her with a knife. To this she had replied, "You don't understand; you do anything when you love them."

Van de Kerkhove stepped into the witness box and began by saying that he had been born in Belgium on September 15th, 1885. The woman he was now accused of killing had been 35 years old and a married woman, her husband still living in London. He went on to outline the rather tempestuous relationship he had shared with Clemence and of her constant attempts to get him to go back to her. Finally he had agreed to go to the hotel room with her but it had been his intention to tell her, once and for all, that it was all over between them. There was some sort of argument about this but he remembered nothing of the attack itself and his next memory was of someone knocking on the door. Only then did he notice that he had an open knife in his hand so when he opened the door, he threw this down on to the floor.

An attempt was made by the defence to show that Van de Kerkhove had been sorely provoked by Clemence and that he had taken so much drink that he did not know what he was doing at the time he stabbed Clemence It was plain that Clemence had gone willingly to the hotel and therefore had no fear of Van de Kerkhove at that time. When found, she was wearing only her underwear and it appeared that her clothing had been removed voluntarily, implying perhaps that she was the one trying to rekindle the relationship once again. Despite this evidence, the jury preferred to believe that Van de Kerkhove had attacked Clemence during a fit of jealousy and a guilty verdict was returned.

There was no appeal and on Tuesday, April 9th, 1918, Louis Van de Kerkhove was hanged at Birmingham by John Ellis and George Brown. He was only the fifth man to die on an English gallows in this year.

Note: Other writers have told the Van de Kerkhove story and in some, his name has been given as Louis Van Der Kerkhove and others have said he was Louis Van Der Kerk-Hove. In the original depositions, held at the public record office, both his statement and his identity card are preserved. On both of these he signed his own name as Louis Van de Kerkhove and this is why he has been referred to as such in this book.

CHAPTER EIGHT

THE HEDNESFORD RIPPER

IN 1913, Henry Thomas Gaskin, who was then just 21 years old, married Elizabeth Talbot of 72 Brindley Heath, Hednesford, Staffordshire. A child was soon born to the union but in March 1914, Gaskin received a prison sentence for theft. He was sent to Portland prison on the Isle of Wight, only being released in early 1916 when Gaskin answered the call to arms and joined up to fight in the bloody trenches of France. He did not return to England until September 1917, and then only on leave, but it was soon clear to Gaskin that while he had been away, his wife had not remained faithful to him, for in that long period of absence, she had given birth to two further children.

Gaskin's leave was only one week long and during that time they lived with Elizabeth's mother, Emily Ann Talbot, at Brindley Heath and by all accounts were happy enough with each other. The young soldier then returned to the front, not being finally demobbed until early 1919. In the meantime, on January 6th, 1919, Elizabeth Gaskin gave birth to her fourth child. Finally, Thomas Gaskin had decided that there was little point in trying to rekindle his relationship with his wife and when he turned to Hednesford, he did not go to Emily Talbot's home, but stayed instead with his own mother, Harriet Eliza Williams.

It was 1.50pm on Wednesday, February 19th, 1919 when Tom Saunders, a friend of Gaskin's called at Emily Talbot's house with a pencilled note for Elizabeth. The note read, 'Meet me round the pool at once important,' and although it was not signed, Tom explained that it had been given to him by Gaskin. Soon after receiving the note, Elizabeth Gaskin left her mother's house, never to return.

By February 20th, Emily Talbot had grown somewhat concerned and went to see Gaskin at his mother's house, 43 Longford Road, Bridgetown. Gaskin denied that he had seen Elizabeth the previous day, to which Emily replied, "You did see her. You sent her a note by Tom Saunders didn't you?" Faced with this, Gaskin admitted that he had arranged to meet Elizabeth because he wanted to discuss the possibility of a divorce, but after thinking it over he had decided that it might be best if he didn't. He had not kept the appointment and had no idea what had happened to his wife.

Emily Talbot was far from satisfied with this explanation and took her suspicions to the police. As a result of what she said, Inspector George Woolley went to the West Cannock Colliery at midnight on February 20th, to interview Gaskin, by now a miner, as he came off his shift. Gaskin again admitted sending the note to Elizabeth but said he had not gone to see her after all. In the meantime, though, Inspector Woolley had been making inquiries in the village and had found a number of witnesses who said they had seen Gaskin with Elizabeth on a road leading to the Valley Pit. Gaskin explained that these witnesses must be mistaken because he had been in a public house until 2.00pm, had been home at 3.00pm and that night, had gone to see a film at the cinema. For the time being, the matter was allowed to rest there and Gaskin was not detained.

Inspector Woolley, having spoken again to his witnesses, came to believe that Henry Gaskin was not telling him the whole truth and so, on the afternoon of February 21st, as Gaskin went to clock on at the mine, he found Woolley and Superintendent John Morrey waiting to take him to the police station. There Gaskin was cautioned and told he would be held in custody while the investigation continued. That evening, Inspector Woolley went to Gaskin's home and took possession of many of his clothes.

On the morning of February 22nd, the case took an interesting turn. Emily Talbot contacted the police and said that a letter had just been delivered, ostensibly explaining her daughter's disappearance. The letter was postmarked Birmingham and had been posted at 12.05pm on February 21st. The letter read, 'Mrs Talbot, Lizzie is quite alright. She is with me now. I met her at Hednesford on Thursday. She was crying, she told me her husband was making a fool of her so I told her to leave all and come with me.

'She will send you some money when we get to London. We are going there next week. She will write herself when we get there. She is very upset now. I can assure you she will be alright with me. Hoping you don't mind. From Lizzie's friend. W. Brooks.'

Emily Talbot had never heard of anyone named Brooks and had her suspicions that the letter had in fact been sent by Gaskin. The letter was passed on to the police but even before they had time to confront Gaskin with it, he had decided that he wanted to talk. Sergeant Charles Thomas Harrington was on duty in the cells at Hednesford police station when Gaskin told him that he wished to see the inspector. Harrington sent for Superintendent Morrey and when he saw Gaskin in his office, Gaskin simply announced that he wished to show him where the body was.

Gaskin was placed into a taxi cab, with a number of police

officers, and directed them to Victoria Street where he stopped the vehicle, pointed to the gasworks and said, "Over there." Proceeding on foot, Gaskin took the police to a large gas holder which was surrounded by a tank of water. He pointed down into the dark murky liquid but even before the water could be investigated, he was intimating that he would now take them to where he committed the deed. Getting back into the cab, Gaskin took the police to a corner of a wood near the offices of the Cannock & Rugeley Mining Company. There were no obvious signs of an attack having taken place at the spot Gaskin identified, but a light dusting of snow had covered the ground, so such indications would have been difficult to see anyway. Gaskin, though, had still not finished. Back at the police station he said he wished to make a full written statement. It made chilling reading.

The statement read, 'I, Henry Thomas Gaskin, being of a sober and sound state of mind, do make this statement of my own free will without any fear or favour.

'On Wednesday the 19th of Feb, 1919, I met my wife by arrangement on the Rugeley Road about 2.20pm and proceeded with her on the outscerts (sic) of the wood by the Cannock & Rugeley Collierie (sic) Offices. She said, "Why don't you come down home, there's nobody there, only mother and dad?" I said, "Come in the wood and we'll talk things over." In the wood I said, "What do you mean by having these bastard kids while I was away? I know you went to Yorkshire with Sgt Walker, then to Birmingham and then to London." She said "It is your fault, you should have come to me instead of going to the Army." I said "Who's (sic) is this last kid you've had?" She said "It's Monty's. He is at home now if you want to see him."

The statement went on to explain how Gaskin had refused to go to Elizabeth's home but she had then said that if he did, she would go to bed with him. This infuriated Gaskin who grabbed her around the neck and cried, "You dare to ask me to go to bed with you, after what you've done?" Elizabeth struggled free from his grip but Gaskin grabbed her again, insulted her and then said he would 'send her to Hell where she belonged'. Gaskin then dragged Elizabeth deeper into the woods and the narrative of how he had killed her then began.

It read, 'I dragged her some yards further into the wood, then stood over her for about a minute, when she attempted to get up. I pushed her down again and said, "I have not done with you yet," and hit her with my fist on her left ear saying, "That's for Sgt Walker," hitting her in the right ear saying, "That's for your Monty," struck her in the right eye, "That's for whoring in Birmingham," struck her in the left eye "That's for whoring in London."

'I then rolled my right sleeve up saying, "Now I'll tare (sic) your inside out and show it to you," and I forced my arm in her womb, up to my elbow, failing to draw anything out, I made about four snow balls and forced them in her inside saying, "These should cool you down a bit." In a fainting condition she began to kick, and make a noise with her throat.

'I said, "I'll stop that row for you," and breaking a thick twig off a tree I forced it down her throat saying, "Chew that if you like." I then took my knife and cut all her clothing off and while I was hiding her hat and shoes she got into a kneeling up position. When I got back to her she murmured, "Harry," and raised her arms up level with her shoulders. I knelt down in front of her and said, "Do you see me?" She shook her head, meaning no. I said, "Do you hear me?" and she nodded. I said, "Listen to me. I am going to kill you and cut you to pieces." I kicked her under the chin and she rolled over. I said, "Now we'll see what you're made of," and I cut her open from womb to nable (sic). I caught her by the heels and bent her up, saying "Do you see that?" She did not speak but put her hands over where I had cut her. I got up and put my heel on her neck until she had finished struggling, then I cut her up to the neck and pulled her bowels out saying, "Now the devil in hell can have you if he wants you, I don't."

'She was still breathing when I covered her up with her own clothes, saying, "If you get over that we'll say the devil don't want you." I left her where she lay the time being about 4.30pm. I reached home about 5.30pm went to the cinima (sic) Walsall Road with my brother. After being in there about half an hour I made an excuse to leave the building and proceeded to Hednesford by bus. Went to the wood where the body lay, dragged it to the edge of the wood, cut the head off and almost cut the left leg off. Then I dragged the body to a culvert near by, and took the head and clothes to the Hednesford gasometer.'

Gaskin went on to explain that after he had first been interviewed by the police, he had taken a roundabout route to where he had hidden the body, carried it to where he had dumped the head in the water around the gasometer and, after forcing a two-inch gas pipe down the torso to weight it down, and thrown it into the water with a cry of, "Now you can go to Monty if you like." The statement was finished at 2.30am, after which Gaskin was charged with murder.

Having been told exactly where they would find the body of Elizabeth Gaskin, police officers took grappling hooks and began to drag the waters around the gasometer. Sergeant Thomas John Heath found the headless body on the same day that Gaskin had been charged. Elizabeth had indeed been horribly mutilated in the manner her killer had described. The search continued but it was not until February 25th that Constable William Henry Baker found the battered head. The task of performing the post-mortem fell to Dr John K. Butter who would eventually catalogue a series of injuries which were never fully reported in the newspapers of the day but did, nevertheless, earn Gaskin the epithet of the 'Hednesford Ripper'.

The inquest on the dead woman concluded at Cannock on March 5th. So horrific were the words of Gaskin's confession that all females were asked to leave the court before the document was read out. Not surprisingly perhaps, a verdict of wilful murder was returned and after a number of appearances at the police court, Gaskin was sent for trial.

Gaskin's case came before Mr Justice Roche, at Stafford, on July 4th, 1919. The case for the prosecution was led by Mr C.E. Vachall who was assisted by Mr Granville Ram, while Mr Graham Milward represented Gaskin, putting forward the only possible defence, that his client was insane at the time the crime was committed.

In order to show that Gaskin was actually sane and therefore responsible for his actions, the prosecution had to prove that this was a deliberate and coldly planned act. The first thing was to detail Gaskin's movements on the day that his wife was killed.

Elsie May Garry lived at 22 Bradbury Lane, Hednesford, and she testified that she had seen Gaskin near her house at 10.40am February 19th. He appeared to be perfectly normal and passed the time of day with her as if he hadn't a care in the world. As Elsie chatted to Gaskin, her husband, John Thomas Garry, came out of the house and also engaged him in conversation. At 10.45am these two walked towards Hednesford railway station but called into a couple of public houses on the way. At around noon, Gaskin saw Tom Saunders in one of the pubs and asked to take a note to Mrs Talbot's house. Saunders later testified that he delivered the note to Elizabeth at around 1.40pm.

Continuing his narrative, John Garry said that at 1.00pm he and Gaskin were in the Uxbridge Hotel together. By 1.40pm they had moved on to the Plough and Harrow where they stayed until 2.00pm. At that time, Garry went back towards his own house while Gaskin headed off towards the old pool in the woods.

A number of witnesses reported seeing Gaskin with Elizabeth, either on the way to the woods where Gaskin said he had killed her, or in the woods themselves. Norah Digwell was only 16 and at some time around 2.30pm on February 19th, she was sitting on the doorstep of her house at 10 Rugeley Road, Hednesford. She saw Elizabeth Gaskin, a woman she knew well, with a man she subsequently identified as the prisoner walking under the bridge nearby. The couple seemed to be arguing.

Thomas Henry Borton worked at the Cannock & Rugeley Colliery offices and on February 19th, he was in the boardroom there when he saw Gaskin and Elizabeth walk along the edge of the plantation. At one stage, the couple parted, Gaskin going into the woods and Elizabeth skirting the edge. Borton lost sight of Elizabeth as she walked along the footpath over the hill.

Sarah Southall looked out of her front room window at Rugeley Road and she, too, saw Gaskin and his wife walking up the side of the plantation, putting the time at around 3.00pm or perhaps a little earlier. By 4.15pm, though, the attack on Elizabeth was apparently over, for Gaskin had been seen alone at that time by Joseph Owen Roadway, who lived at 48 Bradbury Lane. Gaskin was also seen, some 15 minutes after this, by Daisy Winfer of 41 Longford Road, the house next door to Gaskin's mother. She, of course, knew Gaskin very well and confirmed that he was alone at that time. Daisy also swore that when he was on leave in 1917, Gaskin had threatened to shoot his wife and even produced a gun which had turned out not to be loaded.

Gaskin had claimed that after killing Elizabeth he had gone to the cinema with his brother but made an excuse so that he could go to move the body. Herbert Wilfred Junemann had been adopted by Gaskin's mother as a child and he confirmed that he and Gaskin had gone to the pictures together, and the film had started at about 8.00pm. After an hour or so, Gaskin had muttered something which Herbert didn't quite catch and left him alone in the picture house.

In his interviews with the police, Gaskin said that at first he tried to move Elizabeth's body in a wheelbarrow, but left this when he realised it was making conspicuous tracks in the snow. James Bradbury, a miner, testified that at 11.50pm on February 19th, he had found a wheelbarrow abandoned in the middle of the road close by the plantation.

Medical evidence was given by Dr John Butter, who said that a piece of rusty iron piping, one inch in diameter, and just over six feet long, had been pushed through the chest part of Elizabeth's headless torso. It was in a slanting position and passed through the belly downwards to the left side of the body. The lower end of this pipe rested on the upper part of the hip bone and 3ft 4ins of pipe extended out from the opening in the neck.

There were many minor cuts on the body but among the more serious ones was one that opened the front part of the chest from the neck, down to the breast bone. The cut in the belly was ten inches wide at the lowest point and four and a half inches wide at the top. The left elbow was broken and Elizabeth's private parts had been cut away on the left side and were missing, as was the bladder. The head had been severed between the fourth and fifth vertebrae and when it was recovered, the total height of the body had been determined at 5ft 2ins. The cause of death was shock and loss of blood from the extensive wounds.

The prosecution had shown that Gaskin had arranged to meet his wife, had paid a stranger 2s 6d to write the 'Brooks' letter in order to hide his tracks, and had carefully disposed of the body. The defence team now called a number of witnesses to swear that Gaskin's behaviour was far from normal.

Ernest Woodall, a miner, had known Gaskin when he served in the Army and they were in the same Royal Engineers tunnelling company. One day, close to Ypres, they had been digging a tunnel towards the German trenches when it was blown up by the enemy. Gaskin was buried in the tunnel and it took some time to rescue him. Ever since his behaviour had been strange. Woodall had seen him sitting in the trench during heavy shell-fire, taking pot shots at bottles of water. This evidence had also been confirmed by Charles Dawson, another soldier in the same company who said that after the tunnel collapsed, Gaskin seemed to have no sense of danger and no fear of being killed.

The time came for Gaskin's mother, Harriett Eliza Williams, to give her testimony. She stated that Gaskin's troubles had started even before he was born, for she had been ill for 16 weeks when she was carrying him. As a child, Gaskin had never made friends with other children and had been anti-social in his behaviour, ending up at a reformatory school when he was 14. Since his return from the trenches, on January 4th, 1919, Gaskin's behaviour had been even stranger. He rarely drank but on the occasions he did, he became even more erratic.

Other instances of Gaskin's strange behaviour outlined in court were the occasion he had dressed as an Indian and driven through the town on a pony, and once when he had tied a scarf around his neck so tightly that he had collapsed and had to be revived. The jury retired at 4.28pm to consider their verdict and returned at 4.52pm to announce that Gaskin was sane and guilty of murder. After being sentenced to death Gaskin muttered, "I did not intend to kill her."

Gaskin's appeal was heard on July 21st before the Lord Chief Justice, Lord Isaacs, and two of his colleagues. The grounds were that Gaskin was demonstrably insane and that his wife's conduct had been such that he had been sorely provoked. Further examples of his strangeness were documented, including once when as a youth he had tarred his legs, put feathers on his head and ridden a bicycle through Hednesford. Giving his judgement, though, Lord Isaacs said it was plain that the crime was premeditated and that this was the behaviour of a sane man. Gaskin's appeal was lost.

Despite a petition of 6,000 signatures sent to the Home Secretary, there was no reprieve. At 8.00am on Friday, August 8th, 1919, Henry Thomas Gaskin was hanged at Birmingham by John Ellis and William Willis. A crowd estimated at somewhere between 150 and 200 had gathered to read the notices of execution.

CHAPTER NINE

CHINESE WHISPERS

I T was close on 4.30pm on Friday, June 27th, 1919, when a young lad, Henry Thomas Wilson, took a stroll through Warley Woods on the outskirts of Birmingham. Needing to relieve himself rather urgently, Henry walked off the pathway into a spinney where he would be hidden from public gaze. He was just about to answer his call of nature when some yards away, in a slight depression, he saw a dark object which stood out against the carpet of grass and leaves. At first, Henry thought it was a man sleeping but as he approached, he saw that the man was undoubtedly dead and that there was a wooden log across his face. Henry ran for the police as fast as his legs could carry him.

Inspector Francis Henry Drew was the first senior officer at the woods, arriving there at 5.15pm. Going into the spinney, Drew saw that the man was lying on his back, with his legs and feet fully extended, his head turned towards the right. A large piece of timber, which was later weighed and found to be just over 41lbs, was lying across his neck and face. The head had been badly battered, but it was still possible to distinguish that the man was oriental. Finally, since the jacket was tucked up underneath the body, it was obvious that he had been attacked some yards away and dragged to the spot where he now lay, probably to hide from the sight of people walking along the public footpath. Although death had taken place some days before, this still needed to be confirmed by a registered medical practitioner and at 7.15pm Dr Louis Charles Southall Broughton made an initial examination and stated that the man had probably been dead for four or more days.

This approximate time of death enabled the police to make a fairly rapid identification of the body. On the previous Wednesday. a Chinese gentleman named Li Ding Jig had visited the Central police office in Birmingham and asked to see the aliens registration officer, William Tudor. Jig had told Mr Tudor that he was concerned about one of his fellow lodgers at 109 Coleshill Street. The house was owned by the Di Mascio family who rented out rooms, almost exclusively to working men from China. One of Jig's closest friends was a man named Zee Ming Wu and he had last seen him on the evening of June 22nd. The next morning, Jig had heard Wu getting ready for work, although he did not actually see his friend, but that night, Wu had not returned home.

Another day passed and still there was no sign of Wu, so on June 25th, a worried Jig took his concerns to Mr Tudor. The next day, Thursday, Teresa Di Mascio, whose parents owned 109 Coleshill, also went to see Mr Tudor and added her own concerns to those of Jig. She said that Wu had first come to live at the house in April and he was one of six Chinese lodgers. All six had gone to work on the Monday morning but only five had returned home that night. When Wu had not returned by 8.00pm, Jig spoke to her and told her he was worried that something might have happened to his friend. She told Jig to give it a couple of days, but when Wu still hadn't returned or made contact with them by the Thursday, she, too, thought it was time to report him as missing.

Since a Chinaman had been reported missing and the body of a man who appeared to come from that country had now been found, Jig was taken to the mortuary and there made a positive identification. The missing person file was closed and a murder inquiry begun.

The inquest on Zee Ming Wu opened before the coroner Mr Arthur H. Herbert, at Oldbury, on July 2nd. One of the earliest witnesses was Lui Si Shin, a nephew of the dead man, who said that his uncle, a native of Chekiang near Shanghai, had been 41 years old at the time of his death. Although a married man, Wu's wife and three children had remained in China and Wu, who worked at the John Wright & Eagle Range factory used to send her money whenever he could. Tragically, since Wu's body had been found, a letter had arrived from China containing the good news that his daughter was about to be married.

Dr Broughton stated that he had performed a post-mortem on the body. Once the clothing had been removed it was seen that certain mutilations had been performed on the body. Wu had six lacerated wounds around his left ear and four around the right. He had been stabbed in the right temple and his lower jaw was broken in three places. Three ribs were fractured, as was the skull. The left side of the scrotum had been opened and the left testicle removed. A second wound on the scrotum started on the right side and extended up along the penis. Since there was little bleeding from these particular wounds, the heart must not have been beating at the time, which indicated that they were inflicted after death. Since the victim's trousers had not been cut, they must have been removed, the genital injuries inflicted and the trousers then pulled up again. Death was due to laceration of the brain and the weapon most likely to have been used to inflict the stab wound in the temple, was a screwdriver or possibly a thin chisel. Finally, Dr Broughton was able to suggest that Wu had probably been killed on Monday, June 23rd, the day he disappeared, and his body had remained undisturbed until found by Henry Wilson.

Having heard this catalogue of injuries, the jury deliberated for a very short time before returning the expected verdict of murder against some person or persons unknown. It was now up to the police to trace that killer.

In fact, it had already become clear that whoever had killed Wu had probably done so for one of the oldest motives of all – greed. Wu was known to be a frugal man and during his time in England had managed to save £240 which he had deposited in the Post Office Savings Bank. The deposit book was not found among Wu's belongings and proof that his assailant had stolen it came on the day after Wu's body had been discovered.

At some time between 2.00pm and 2.30pm on Saturday, June 24th, a Chinaman had walked into the Post Office in Blythe Road, West Kensington, London. The cashier who dealt with the man was Arthur Baron Powell, who was handed a passbook in the name of Zee Ming Wu. Opening the book, Powell saw that there had only been two transactions since the account had been opened; £200 had been deposited on May 24th, 1919, and a further £40 on June 7th. Inquiring politely what 'Mr Wu' wanted, Powell was told that he wanted to withdraw all the money. There was nothing unusual in the transaction and so Powell handed over a slip and asked 'Wu' to fill it in.

The first thing that aroused Arthur Powell's suspicions was the fact that 'Wu' asked for the book back, and then proceeded to carefully copy out the name on the heading. Even then he had made a basic mistake, for the book had been signed with a cross since Wu was illiterate, but this man had written the name Zee Ming Wu in full. This meant that the signatures were different so Powell asked the gentleman to step into a waiting room while he referred the matter to his superior.

Herbert Brigden, the superintendent of the office, spoke to

'Wu' and asked him why the signatures were so different. The man answered in Chinese and so, seeing that he was getting nowhere, Brigden said that he was putting the matter in the hands of his head office. Mr Wu, together with the passbook, would be handed over to another officer who would escort them to 10 West Kensington Gardens where the matter would be sorted out.

The passbook and withdrawal slip were handed to Peter Robert John Marr, who was told to escort 'Wu' to the head office. As they stepped outside, however, 'Wu' shouted, "Me no go." Marr tried to explain again that they were just going to another office where everything would be dealt with, but 'Wu' tried to snatch the book, refused to go back into the Blythe Road office and muttered something about wanting his dinner. Then, without another word, the Chinaman walked off into the crowded London streets, leaving his passbook and withdrawal slip behind.

When all this took place, of course, the real Zee Ming Wu was lying on a mortuary slab. The man with his passbook had almost certainly been Wu's killer and when the description was sent up to Birmingham, this along with other evidence which came to light, led to the arrest, on July 10th, of another Chinaman, Ah Chee. The evidence the police had against him was weak, however, and when he appeared in court on July 15th, the case was thrown out and Ah Chee was released. The police investigation was back to square one.

When the breakthrough came, it was not in Birmingham but once again, in London. Ernest Dyson lived at 15 Aldine Street, Shepherd's Bush, a house in which rooms were let out. The room above Dyson's was occupied by Kwo Doung Dsou and early on the morning of July 25th, Dyson heard some strange noises coming from that room. Looking out of his window, he saw another Chinaman passing the house and an hour or so later, when Dyson himself went out, he found a hammer near his front door. The hammer appeared to bear traces of blood.

In fact, Dsou had had a guest with him, staying for a few days, but after an argument, this visitor had attacked Dsou with a hammer. Fortunately, Dsou was not badly injured and the information he gave to the police led to the arrest of his guest on a charge of assault. That visitor was 33-year-old Djang Djing Sung, and it soon became clear that Sung, whose home address was in Birmingham, had also been an acquaintance of Zee Ming Wu.

On July 28th, Sung appeared at the West London police court, charged with the attempted murder of Kwo Doung Dsou, and with stealing property belonging to him. His home address of 73 Balsall Heath Road, Edgbaston was given. The arresting officer, Detective Sergeant Algernon Sprackling, told the court that Dsou had suffered seven scalp wounds, four other wounds and a shattered elbow and fractured rib. Dsou had named his assailant, but by then he had returned to Birmingham and it was there that he was arrested. Sergeant Sprackling had brought Sung back to London. On that journey, Sung had said that Dsou owed him '50 dollars' and had refused to pay even when he wrote to him asking for the money. As a result, Sung had decided to help himself and had broken into Dsou's flat at night, while the occupant was asleep. Dsou had woken, though, so Sung, according to his statement, 'went tap, tap on his head', claiming that he had used a small stick and not a hammer. The case was then adjourned until August 13th, and Sung was remanded in custody.

Before that date, the Birmingham and Metropolitan police had compared notes and as a result, on July 28th, Sergeant Sprackling saw Sung again and told him that he was now investigating the murder of Zee Ming Wu in Warley woods. Sung was told that he would be placed into an identification parade in order to see if he would be selected as the man who had tried to use Wu's bank passbook on June 24th.

Upon hearing this, Sung immediately admitted that he had taken Wu's passbook but denied that he was responsible for the man's death. Sung claimed that he had been given the passbook by Jig and it was Jig who had killed Wu and had then sent him down to London to try to obtain the money. Taken to the Lime-house police station, Sung was placed among a group of other orientals and picked out by Ernest Dyson and Peter Marr. He was also indicated by Philip Henry Besien, a doorman at the office, who had seen Sung talking to the counter staff.

On the way back to Paddington, Sung admitted to Sprackling that he had lied, but said that he now wanted to tell the truth. Back at the police station he was interviewed by Divisional Detective Inspector Percy Savage, to whom he made a full statement which was written down, read through and then signed by Sung.

According to this statement, Sung said that he had been to his work at Briscoe's factory which he left at 5.30pm on Monday, June 23rd. Outside, he met four other Chinamen, one being Wu and another being Jig. Wu, for some reason, asked Sung to steal a hammer from his work. Sung did so and handed it to Jig after which he, Jig and Wu caught a tram to Warley. Once they were in the woods, Jig shouted that there was a large rabbit and when Wu turned to look, he brought the hammer crashing down on Wu's head, saying afterwards that he had done it because Wu's family had cheated him in China.

Fearful that he might be next, Sung did as he was asked when Jig told him to get Wu's bankbook. As he was doing so, the other two men, Zee Bing Zar and Ling Gai Wu, who had caught a later tram, came upon the scene. They saw what had been done and went away saying they wanted nothing to do with it. The statement concluded with Sung saying that the murder had troubled him greatly and he had been unable to sleep. At one stage he had been so scared that he had even asked his landlord, Mr Grosvenor, to sleep with him.

On August 13th, Sung was back at the police court in London when matters were adjourned again, this time until August 21st. On the same day, he was interviewed again by Sergeant Sprackling but he repeated what he had said before. At the next hearing on August 21st, Sung was committed for trial on a charge of attempted murder but it was a case that would never be heard, for just over two weeks later, on September 6th, he was charged with the murder of Zee Ming Wu.

It was also on September 6th that Sung was taken back to the West London police court to face the murder charge for the first time. For the prosecution, Mr Travers Humphreys detailed the disappearance of Wu, the subsequent finding of his body, and of a man, since identified as Sung, attempting to use the dead man's passbook to withdraw cash from an office in London.

Mr Humphreys went on to show that on July 4th, Sung had travelled to London again and stayed with Dsou at Aldine Street. When Sung returned to Birmingham he wrote letters to Dsou and in some of these he made references to the murder of Zee Ming Wu. In one, dated July 7th, he had written, 'Zee Ming Wu is buried, but has had no revenge yet. I think Englishmen is careless of it.' In another, a postcard this time, and dated July 10th, he wrote, 'After all the real offender has been caught [referring to the arrest of Ah Chee] and that I am not the one. One would not murder Ming Wu for anything, and if the book was taken to London that must have been the object.

'Both yesterday and today the offender has been summoned to court, and he has been remanded. The manager of the Bank and several witnesses have said this man is not a bad one.

'Today I saw in the newspapers that there were four China-men concerned in the murder of Ming Wu, I do not know if it is true, and today's newspaper I shall send on to you tomorrow.'

After this, along with Sung's statements to the police had been read the magistrates remanded him to September 13th. On that date a further remand followed and it was not until September 20th that all the other witnesses were heard. It was also on that date that another letter from Sung was read out. This missive, dated September 17th on Brixton prison notepaper, was addressed to the magistrates themselves and read, 'Your worship, I am very sorry this occurred.

'I tell truth. Li Ding Jig is the man who kill Zee Ming Wu. I never touched him at all. I am married and have one child eight years old in China. I am also business man and never been in trouble before. This is the first time.

'Li Ding Jig got me to go for a walk in the park, I cannot understand English very much. Will you please be very lenient with me as I want to go back to my wife and business and my mother who is very good to me.' The letter carried a post script, 'Last Saturday I quite forgot to say that Li Ding Jig was the man who did the murder. I am very sorry. I could not understand what was said. I want to see him again.

Despite Sung's constant protests that it was Jig who killed Wu, he was ordered to be sent for trial at the next assizes. They opened at Worcester in October and on the 22nd of that month, Sung faced Mr Justice Rowlatt and an all-male jury on the capital charge. The case for the prosecution was led by Mr A. Powell who was assisted by Mr A.E.N. Jordan. Sung was defended by Mr Reginald Coventry. All the evidence was translated for Sung, by Mr Sen Tebes.

The man who Sung had claimed was the real killer, Li Ding Jig, was an important witness for the prosecution. Jig confirmed that Sung was a regular visitor to the lodging house at 109 Coleshill Street and he had last seen him there on June 22nd, the day before Wu vanished. Jig heard the two men talking about 30s which Sung owed Wu. Sung was trying to repay it but Wu refused to take it, saying he had no immediate need of the cash as he had £4 or £5 on him at the time. Sung's visits to Coleshill Street were also confirmed by Teresa Di Mascio.

George Aston was the timekeeper for W.H. Briscoe & Co of 51-53 Park Street, Birmingham. Sung had been employed there since August 28th, 1916. Referring to when Wu was last seen alive, Aston was able to confirm that on June 23rd, Sung clocked off at 5.41pm. Curiously, he did not report for work the next two days but was there on the 26th and the 27th. On that day, Sung was dismissed because of his bad timekeeping.

Arthur Grosvenor was Sung's landlord and he told the court that on the night of June 27th, the prisoner had come down-stairs with a candle in his hand and had asked if he could sleep with him. Sung claimed that he was very nervous about the murder in Warley woods and that this was keeping him awake. Grosvenor was also able to say that on the 29th, Sung had been to view the body at the mortuary and appeared to be much distressed when he returned, saying that Wu had been badly knocked about.

Sung admitted that he had been at the scene of the crime but that Jig had actually done the deed. Once it was shown that Jig was elsewhere at the time, and that Sung had tried to draw money from Wu's account, the jury took only nine minutes to decide that he was guilty.

The execution was originally fixed for November 11th but this was cancelled when Sung announced his intention to appeal. That appeal was heard on November 17th before the Lord Chief Justice, Lord Isaacs, and two colleagues who stated that there were 'no grounds for impugning the verdict or for criticising the summing up of the learned judge'.

At 8.00am on Wednesday, December 3rd, 1919, Djang Djing

Sung was hanged at Worcester by John Ellis who was assisted by Edward Taylor. It was the 12th and last execution of 1919, and the last ever at Worcester.

CHAPTER TEN

TWO AWKWARD PEOPLE

O N July 31st, 1920, Samuel Westwood married Lydia
Vaughan and immediately after the ceremony, they
went to live with Samuel's parents at 57 Bentley Lane,
Short Heath, Birmingham. Unfortunately, there was trouble
from the very beginning, not between Westwood and his new
bride, but between Lydia and her in-laws, especially her mother-
in-law.

Every week, Lydia would visit her own mother at 11 Cross
Street, Spring Bank, Willenhall, and tell her of the constant interference she was suffering from Mr and Mrs Westwood. In all that
time, Samuel accompanied his new wife only once, for he too
had problems with his in-laws and again it was the mother-in-
law, in his case Alice Vaughan, with whom there were particular
difficulties.

For some time, this situation persisted until finally, on
September 6th, on one of her visits to see her mother, Lydia
exclaimed, "I can't put up with it much longer. I shall have to
leave him. It's upsetting my nerves." This was perhaps just what
Alice Vaughan had been waiting to hear, for three days later, on
September 9th, she went to Westwood's house at Bentley Lane,

said that her husband had told her to go and fetch Lydia home
and returned to Cross Street with Lydia and her belongings. The
next day both Lydia and Alice were back at Bentley Lane to
collect the rest of her possessions. It seemed that the relationship
had floundered almost as soon as it had begun, due largely to the
interference of both sets of parents.

For his part, Samuel Westwood seemed to have done little to
save his marriage. He had been present on September 9th when
Alice had called to take Lydia home, but had made no move to
interfere. For a couple of days, no one made any attempt to save
the relationship.

On Saturday, September 11th, Alice Vaughan, her husband
George, and Lydia went to Walsall. They did not get back to
Willenhall until 8.00pm and it was then that Lydia said she
would like to see her husband. Alice wasn't too pleased about this
but finally agreed to accompany Lydia to the Wake's fairground
where Lydia thought Westwood was likely to be. Unfortunately,
they could find no sign of him and rather reluctantly, Lydia
began to walk back to Cross Street with her mother. It was now
about 8.45pm.

Lydia and Alice had to pass down Walsall Street on their way
home at it was there that, finally, they saw Westwood. Lydia was
pleased to see him and they fell into conversation in an attempt
to sort out their differences. All this time, Alice Vaughan
remained silent, until they reached the Prince of Wales Inn.

It was outside that inn that Westwood gently caught his wife's
arm and begged, "Come with me Lydia." They began to walk off
together, just a few paces in front of Alice who then heard
Westwood say, "Come with me anywhere. I will go in lodgings
or anywhere." Knowing that the only thing keeping her
daughter and Westwood apart was the interference of Westwood's parents, Alice knew that Lydia would almost certainly
agree to this and it was then that she suggested that before Lydia

finally made up her mind, she had better talk to her father. Lydia hesitated and within seconds, Samuel Westwood, fearful perhaps that he had finally lost his wife, drew out a penknife and stuck the blade in Lydia's throat. As Alice Vaughan cradled her stricken daughter in her arms, Westwood threw down the blade and walked off up the street.

Samuel Westwood made no attempt to escape. Some 60 yards from where Lydia lay was a police station and Westwood walked straight there and asked the first officer he saw, Constable Joseph John Thomas Brown, "Are you a police constable?" Brown replied, "Yes, what do you want?" and Westwood continued, "I've just stabbed my wife. She's down the road. I believe I've killed her."

Constable Brown took Westwood inside the station and handed him over to Sergeant Evan Henry Evans. After Brown had explained what Westwood had just told him, the prisoner was left with another officer, Constable Joseph Edward Wild, while Brown and Evans went to the scene of the stabbing. Lydia was still lying in the road, close to the junction of Walsall Street and Church Street. She had a deep cut on the right side of her throat and was still bleeding badly. Alice Vaughan, seeing the two officers, handed over to Constable Brown the penknife she had picked up after Westwood had walked off. Meanwhile, Sergeant Evans tried his best to plug the wounds and render first aid while Brown went to fetch Dr Dean. Once the doctor had arrived, and pronounced Lydia dead, she was carried into the police station as that was the nearest place where she might be left until the ambulance arrived to take her body to the mortuary.

Dr Henry James Dean arrived at Walsall Street at 9.00pm and after examining Lydia at the scene and announcing that she was dead, went to the police station to examine Westwood. Almost as soon as he saw the doctor, Westwood announced that he had taken some poison and, even though he showed no symptoms, Dr Dean administered an emetic which made Westwood violently sick.

Samuel Westwood made his first appearance before the magistrates on Monday, September 13th, when he entered the court with a broad smile on his lips. Sergeant Evans gave details of the arrest of the prisoner and he was then remanded to September 20th.

On the afternoon of the 13th, after the police court had ended, the inquest opened before Mr J.T. Higgs. George Vaughan, the dead girl's father, gave evidence of identification, stating that he had last seen Lydia alive at about 8.30pm on Saturday, September 11th when she left the house with her mother. Lydia had told him at the time that she was going to the Wakes Fair to find Westwood and he claimed that he had said to her, "Don't go. I shall never see you any more until you are a corpse. He is sure to do you in." Asked why he had said such a thing, George claimed that on a previous occasion, even before they were married, Westwood had said to Lydia that if he didn't have her, no one else would. Hearing this, Westwood shouted out in court that it was all lies.

Alice Vaughan told the court of the troubles Lydia had had with her in-laws and added that on September 9th, a little girl had arrived with a message from Lydia, asking if she could come home. After speaking to her husband, Alice had gone to fetch her daughter back to Cross Street.

Referring to the incident of Westwood taking poison, Constable Wild stated that after he had made this claim, Westwood produced a piece of newspaper on which was written the word 'Poison'. Wrapped up in this was a white powder and Westwood said that this was something he had taken from his work and was used for hardening tools. After the emetic had been administered and Westwood had recovered from its effects, he was placed in the cells. There, at about 9.40pm Westwood had said, "She left me last Thursday. I intended to do this the first time I saw them. I had had two half-pints of beer or I could not have done it." Some time later the prisoner had added, "They thought I was frightened to do it, but I have showed 'em. She was awkward, and I was awkward, and two awkward people don't get on together. We should have been all right if they had left us alone."

After hearing the medical testimony of Dr Dean, the court concluded that Lydia Westwood had been murdered by her husband and he was sent for trial on the coroner's warrant. On September 20th, the police court reconvened, Westwood now being represented by Mr Ernest J. Hall, while Mr Hedley Parham appeared for the Director of Public Prosecutions.

Alice Vaughan elaborated on the conversation between her daughter and Westwood. After grabbing her arm and asking her to go with him, Lydia had remarked, "I can't go with your mother; we can't agree." It was then that Westwood told her that he would go anywhere, even in lodgings if that was what Lydia wanted. Hearing this, Alice had grabbed her daughter's arm and said, "Lydia, come with me tonight." Even now Westwood was reasonable and said, "Well, I'll come down tomorrow for you then," and Alice had suggested speaking to Lydia's father first. Only then had Westwood produced the knife and plunged it into Lydia's neck.

Westwood reserved his defence and was sent for trial at the next assizes. These opened at Stafford in November and Westwood appeared before Mr Commissioner Young on the 19th of that month. The case for the prosecution was given by Mr J. Lort Williams and Westwood was defended by Mr T.P. Haslam.

In addition to the witnesses already mentioned, the prosecution called Rose Hannah Perry, who lived at 48 Walsall Street. At just before 9.00pm on September 11th, she was in the street and saw three people walking towards her. Although Rose could not hear what was being said, the young man, whom she had since identified as Westwood, was involved in a conversation with the younger woman when he suddenly took hold of her with his left arm around her neck. Rose then saw Westwood raise his right hand high above his head and, for the first time, she saw that he held a knife. Even as she watched, the hand came plunging down and the knife was thrust into the woman's throat. The woman collapsed as the other shouted, "Murder! Police!" Rose then saw Westwood walk off towards the police station as the older woman knelt by Lydia and tried to help her.

Samuel Westwood senior, the prisoner's father, identified the knife used to kill Lydia as one belonging to him. Only a couple of days before the attack, Samuel had seen his son using the knife to cut some leather so that he could repair his boots.

Dr Dean repeated his earlier evidence and added that the 'poison' Westwood had taken had now been tested and identified as Ferro Cyanide of Potassium, which was not in fact poisonous. He also described the single wound Lydia had suffered, explaining that the blade had penetrated down to the large blood vessels and the cause of death was loss of blood due to that wound.

Westwood went into the box to tell his own story. He explained that he had joined the Army in November 1915 and was sent to the trenches in France in February 1917. In March 1918, a shell exploded close to him and he was rendered unconscious. When he woke, he found himself in German hands and remained a prisoner-of-war until after the armistice had been signed in November.

Turning to the attack itself, Westwood said he remembered putting his arm around his wife's waist and knew that she would have come with him if his mother-in-law had not intervened. He did not remember drawing out the knife or stabbing Lydia and did not know what had happened until he found himself at the police station. Finally, he denied ever threatening Lydia in front of her father and claimed that he had not made the statement referred to by Constable Wild about intending to kill Lydia the first chance he got.

Dr Hamblin Smith, the medical officer of Stafford prison, stated that he had examined Westwood carefully and in his opinion, his war experiences might well predispose him towards losing his temper and acting violently at the slightest provocation.

The defence, seizing on this, suggested that Westwood had been sorely provoked and had acted on the spur of the moment without malice and as such, should only be found guilty of manslaughter. The jury, though, did not agree and after deliberating for just 15 minutes, they found Westwood guilty and sentenced to death.

An appeal was entered and this was heard on December 13th before the Lord Chief Justice, Lord Isaacs and Justices Bray and Shearman. The grounds of the appeal were that Mr Commissioner Young had referred to the fact that mere words were not sufficient to constitute such provocation as would reduce the charge to manslaughter, except in exceptional cases, and that this had meant that the jury were not properly informed. Giving the court's judgement, the Lord Chief Justice said that he believed that the summing up was actually in the appellant's favour, the jury had not been misdirected and that consequently, the appeal would be dismissed.

At 8.00am on Thursday, December 30th, 1920, Samuel Westwood was hanged at Birmingham by John Ellis and Robert Wilson. It was a busy day for the executioners of England with two other hangings: those of Mark Goodmacher at Pentonville and Edwin Sowerby at Leeds. There had now been 20 executions this year but even now, there was one more to come, Charles Colclough losing his life at the end of a rope on December 31st.

CHAPTER ELEVEN

OYSTERS AND BACON

THERE was something of an atmosphere at the Pheasant Inn, situated in Broad Street, Bilston, and a number of factors were leading towards an extremely unpleasant denouement.

To begin with, the man who held the licence, 48-year-old Elijah Pountney, had something of a drink problem. In addition to his duties at the inn, Pountney, who had once been a black-smith, worked as a labourer at the Tarmac Works. Elijah and his wife, 47-year-old Alice Gertrude Pountney, had been in the Pheasant Inn for some six years and during that time, Elijah had rarely been seen sober.

The couple had one son living with them, John Edward Pountney, but the real problem arose with the one other person who lived at the inn, a lodger named Edmund McCann, a brick-layer, who had been there for about six months, for Elijah Pountney had managed to convince himself that McCann was having an affair with his wife.

McCann was rather a large man and Elijah Pountney did not relish the thought of tackling him or attempting to throw him out so, on March 3rd, 1922, Pountney walked into Bilston police

station where he saw Sergeant Westbury. Pountney asked the
sergeant if he could send a man to the inn in order to eject a
lodger from the premises. Sergeant Westbury did not think that
this domestic dispute warranted the interference of the police,
and told Pountney that there was nothing he could do. To this
Pountney replied, "If he stays much longer I shall do her in.
Sergeant Westbury tried to calm the situation down and finally
Pountney returned home to his domestic concerns.

Some six weeks later, on Sunday, April 16th, Alice was in the
kitchen, peeling potatoes for the dinner. It was just before
2.00pm and John Edward Pountney saw his father go into the
kitchen and say something to Alice. John could not hear what
was said, but whatever it was, it must have upset and shocked
Alice for she turned to her husband and shouted, "What? In
front of my son?" Pountney had smiled at this and said calmly, "I
will say it in front of my son."

It, was at this point that one of the regular customers, Joseph
Henry Norton, shouted from the bar to ask what time Pountney
was closing. Pountney walked through to the bar and returned a
moment later, with Norton. Taking Norton into the kitchen,
Pountney pushed him towards Alice saying, "Kiss her Joe – it
might be the last time." Joseph Norton was deeply shocked at
this, turned to Pountney and said, "If that's it, I'm going home."

Once again Pountney smiled and apologised to Norton,
muttering, "Don't take offence; I don't mean anything." He then
left the kitchen again, only to return a few moments later, while
Norton was still there. Both Norton and John Pountney then
saw Elijah put his arm around Alice's neck. John thought that his
father was about to kiss Alice and turned away for a few seconds
and so didn't see exactly what happened next. He was surprised,
then, when he heard Norton cry out in alarm, and looking back
saw blood flowing from a wound in his mother's throat.

John Pountney ran forward to assist his mother while Joseph

Norton went to fetch a doctor. John assisted Alice out on to the verandah where she collapsed into his arms and died. As John cradled his mother's body, he saw his father wipe his blood-stained hands on a piece of newspaper before walking out of the inn.

A number of people saw Pountney running towards Bradley. Some minutes later, a group of youths, one of which was 15-year-old William Doughty, saw a man standing in the canal at Bankfield Road. The man was none other than Elijah Pountney and he was in the water up to his armpits, wedged between two boats, and apparently in some distress. The police were called and by the time Constable Percy Pidcock arrived on the scene, Pountney had been pulled from the water and lay unconscious on the canal side. Constable Pidcock applied artificial respiration and with some difficulty, revived Pountney before taking him to the police station where he was charged with murder. From there, since he was still suffering from the effects of his immersion in the canal, Pountney was taken to the Wolverhampton Workhouse Infirmary.

On April 18th, the inquest on Alice Pountney opened before Mr J.T. Higgs. Evidence of identification was given by John, the dead woman's son, and matters were then adjourned until Pountney was able to attend. On the same day, the police court proceedings were supposed to open but once again, since Pountney was still in hospital, an adjournment was ordered.

Pountney was released from the infirmary on April 21st when he appeared before the magistrates. Sergeant George Cartwright, who had accompanied Constable Pidcock to the canal side, gave evidence of Pountney's arrest and stated that in reply to the charge, Pountney had replied, "It is right; I have had cause for it." Pountney was then remanded for a week.

It was also on April 21st that the inquest reconvened and after hearing all the witnesses, the jury took just a few minutes to return a verdict of wilful murder against Pountney. Later that day, back in the police court, the owner of the inn, Mr F.E. Milward, had the licence of the Pheasant Inn transferred to himself and announced that his son-in-law and daughter would be taking over as soon as possible. Pountney's final hearing took place on April 28th, when he was defended by Mr Sharp. On that date he was sent for trial at the next assizes.

The assizes opened in July and Pountney's trial took place at Stafford on July 7th, 1922, before Mr Justice Shearman. The case for the prosecution was led by Mr Graham Milward, who was assisted by Mr F.T. Vachell, while Pountney was defended by Mr A.J. Long.

The only witness to the attack had been Joseph Norton who lived at 5 Sankey Street, Bilston. He explained that he had been in the tap room of the inn and after asking Pountney what time he intended to close, he was then taken into the kitchen and was told to kiss Alice. She had turned towards her husband, with the potato knife still in her hand and had said, "If it was not for the lad, I would." While speaking she had nodded towards her son and Norton had taken this to mean that if it were not for John, she would have stabbed her husband. Alice had explained to Norton why she was angry with her husband by saying, "Joe, he has accused me of going to have a baby and if he don't know, who should?"

Pountney had then left the kitchen but returned moments later and put his arm around Alice's neck saying, "Come here," as he did so. Without another word being spoken, Pountney pulled his other hand out of his pocket and Norton saw that he held an open razor. Before Norton could move forward to intervene, Pountney had drawn the blade across Alice's throat. Norton then saw John dash forward and shout for him to fetch a doctor, which he did.

The doctor who attended was Dr Charles Hope Waddell. After

seeing Alice at the Pheasant Inn, and pronouncing her dead, he had been taken to the canal side to minister to Pountney. When Dr Waddell arrived there, at about 3.00pm, Pountney had been revived and was lying on the ground. He smelt strongly of drink.

The next day, Dr Waddell performed the post-mortem on Alice and found a wound in her throat four inches long. That was the direct cause of death. There were no other injuries and Dr Waddell said that Pountney's suspicions had been unfounded, for Alice was not pregnant.

Sergeant Cartwright told the court that after being charged, Pountney had also referred to his suspicions about Alice and the lodger, Edmund McCann. Pountney had said, "They had been up before me having oysters and drinking beere and stout and when I got up and asked for my breakfast, was told the bacon was in the kitchen and to go and get my own. There is a bank book in the house and when I was going down the cellar for some beer, I heard her and McCann arranging to go away together and if she 'aint in trouble a post-mortem will prove it." He had also referred to his belief that Alice had been lending money to McCann.

Edmund McCann swore that there had been nothing going on between him and Alice Pountney. There had been no relationship, no intention to run away together and he had never borrowed money from Alice. Some time after he had first moved in, he had heard Pountney threaten his wife and say to her, "I'll do you in before the night is out." Pountney had then knocked her to the ground. McCann also confirmed that the couple were always quarrelling and that Elijah Pountney had been constantly drunk.

There could, of course, be no doubt that Pountney's hand had caused the death of his wife, so the only real defence could be that he was not responsible for his actions at the time. John Pountney said that his father had once been struck on the head at work and as a result had been off work for seven weeks. Once he had recovered physically, there had been a marked change in his father's manner and he had begun drinking heavily.

Edward Reynolds, Elijah's brother-in-law, confirmed that he had been 'funny in his ways' after the accident. He had become much more violent in his behaviour and Edward had once seen him take a running kick at Alice. At the time, Edward had remarked, "You may use her as a punching ball, but not as a football." That apparently was the level of his attempt to protect his sister.

To counter these suggestions that the head injury he had suffered some years before had affected his mental stability, the prosecution called Dr Hamblin Smith, the medical officer of the prison where Pountney had been held. He testified that Pountney had been under constant observation and he had seen no evidence of insanity. With that and the testimony of the other witnesses, the jury had no difficulty in returning their guilty verdict.

An appeal was heard on July 24th. Once again Pountney's head injury was referred to and the defence suggested that he had been so under the influence of drink and the weakness from his accident that he could not distinguish between right and wrong. Mr Long went on to say that Pountney should have been either found guilty but insane or, if he did not realise that what he was doing was likely to cause Alice's death, guilty only of manslaughter. It was also suggested that Alice provoked Pountney by pointing the potato knife at him and suggesting that if it were not for her son, she would use it on him.

Giving the court's judgement, Mr Justice Darling said that the matter of Pountney's mental state would be dealt with by the Home Secretary and was not a matter for the Appeal Court. Neither could he allow the proposal that Pountney had been provoked, as it would set a dangerous precedent whereby drunken people might well imagine themselves to be provoked and put this forward as a defence in future trials. The appeal was dismissed.

On the afternoon before he was due to die, Pountney was visited by a number of his relatives and friends who reported that he seemed to be resigned to his fate. At 8.00am on Friday, August 11th, 1922, Elijah Pountney was hanged at Birmingham by John Ellis who was assisted by Robert Baxter. A crowd of between 30 and 40 people had gathered outside the prison gates to see the notices of execution posted.

Ellis who was assisted by Robert Baxter. A. crowd of between 30 and 40 people had gathered outside the prison gates to see the notices of execution posted.

CHAPTER TWELVE

NO IDLE THREAT

ADA Taylor was a married woman, but Arthur, her husband had walked out on her in 1910, leaving her alone with her daughter, Jessie. Some 18 months after this event, a new man, John Fisher, came into Ada's life and in due course, he moved in with her and Jessie at 1 Back 27 Wright Street, Small Heath. The house was in Fisher's name, but all the furniture belonged to Ada.

The problems really began in 1922 when Fisher started a long period of unemployment. He was in and out of work for the next three years and spent much of that time on the dole. This led to financial problems which Fisher tried to solve by borrowing money from both Ada and her daughter, who were both in regular work. Those debts were rarely repaid and this caused many arguments between Ada and the man in her life and several times she told him to leave. Once, after such a request, Fisher had been heard to reply, "Not until I've done you in. Then I'll go."

On Sunday, October 25th, 1925, Jessie Dutton, Ada's daughter, rose at 9.00am. After she had eaten her breakfast, Jessie heard Fisher telling Ada that the previous Thursday, he had wanted to try out his luck, needed some money to do so, and in order to get it, had pledged a green tablecloth which belonged to Ada. Upon hearing this admission, Ada threatened that she would have some keys made and lock up her possessions in future. An argument developed and ended only when Fisher promised that he would get the tablecloth back from the pawnbrokers on Monday.

At 2.00pm Ada, Jessie and Fisher ate together, although the atmosphere between them appeared to be rather frosty. Soon afterwards, Ada said she was going to bed for a lie down, while Fisher sat in the chair, flicking the pages of a book. At 4.00pm Jessie went out to visit some friends. Fisher was still sitting with his book and Ada was in bed upstairs.

It was not until 9.55pm that Jessie Dutton returned to Wright Street and found that the door was locked. Although she knocked two or three times, and called out for her mother, no one stirred inside the house. Luckily, Jessie remembered that a neighbour had a key to her house and Jessie borrowed this and finally gained entrance.

As she walked into the house, Jessie saw that a light had been left on downstairs and her mother's shoes lay on the floor, implying that she had not left the house after all. Going upstairs, Jessie saw that there was someone in the bed, with the bedclothes pulled up over their head. Gently pulling back the sheets, she found that her mother was lying on the side of the bed nearest the window. Both she and the bedclothes were covered in blood. Jessie ran to her neighbours for help.

Charles Thomas Bullen lived at number 27 Wright Street and it was to his house that Jessie had first gone to borrow the key. Soon after Jessie had left, Charles heard her screaming for help from the yard at the back. He went out to see what the problem was and Jessie told him, "I believe he's done my mother in."

The screaming had also been heard by Sarah Ann Averne, who

lived at 26 Wright Street. She, too, ran next door to see what she could do and she and Charles Bullen went upstairs together. They saw Ada, lying on her back as if she was asleep. Jessie, of course, had pulled the sheets back a little and now Ada's head and shoulders were exposed. Seeing that there was little they could do to help, Charles and Sarah went back downstairs to comfort Jessie and send for the police and a doctor.

Constable Henry Lowe was on duty at the Coventry Road police station when he received information that a woman had apparently committed suicide at Wright Street. Lowe was sent, by Inspector George Lawrence, to investigate and found that he was dealing with a case of murder, not suicide. Constable Lowe notified his station and Inspector Lawrence was soon on the scene to take charge of the investigation.

In fact, very little investigation was needed, for at about the same time that Jessie Dutton was finding her mother's body, Constable Charles Bent was climbing on to a tram at Digbeth. Constable Bent, who was still in full uniform, had finished his duty for the day and was on the way to his home in Small Heath, but by pure coincidence, he happened to take a seat next to John Fisher.

As the tram approached Watery Lane, Fisher turned to Constable Bent and said, "I have done murder in Wright Street and I want to give myself up to you." Charles Bent cautioned Fisher and advised him to say no more until they reached Coventry Road police station. The two men alighted from the tram at the stop closest to Coventry Street and as Constable Bent escorted his prisoner to the station, Fisher gave him his name and address.

At the station, Charles Bent explained to Inspector Lawrence, what Fisher had said. Lawrence asked Fisher where and when the crime had taken place and when he heard that it was the address to which Lowe had just been despatched, his interest was further aroused. Fisher said that the crime had taken place at 5.30pm and Inspector Lawrence cautioned him again and advised him to remain quiet until he had verified his story. After visiting Wright Street and confirming with the doctor that the wounds could not have been self-inflicted, Inspector Lawrence returned to Coventry Street, shortly before midnight, and charged Fisher with murder. Fisher made a written statement explaining what had taken place.

Fisher appeared at the police court the following day, where the stipendiary magistrate was Lord Ilkeston. Details of the arrest were given by Mr M.P. Pugh, who was handling the prosecution case, and Fisher was remanded until October 29th. On that date, it was explained that the evidence could be heard on November 3rd. Another case had already been pencilled in for that date but the injured party in that case would not be well enough to attend court, so Fisher's case could be dealt with instead. He was remanded to November 3rd.

It was also on October 29th that the inquest opened, before Mr Isaac Bradley. Fisher was represented by Mr Philip Baker, and after hearing the evidence, the jury concluded that Ada Taylor had been murdered by Fisher. Just four days later, Fisher was back before the magistrates, by now having obtained legal representation, this time in the form of Mr Herbert Willison. Here it was explained that 56-year-old Ada Taylor had been married twice before she had met Fisher and that Jessie Dutton was a child from the first marriage. The rest of the evidence was heard and Fisher's statement to the police was read out, after which he was sent for trial.

The hearing of the murder charge at the assizes took place at Birmingham on December 4th, 1925, before Mr Justice Talbot. The case for the prosecution rested in the hands of Mr Sanderson, while Fisher was defended by Mr Douglas Jenkins.

Jessie Dutton told the court how she had discovered her

mother's body. Medical evidence at the inquest had shown that Ada Taylor had been battered and her throat had been cut. Jessie identified the knife found at the scene as one that belonged in the house and was normally kept in the table drawer in the kitchen. Turning to the day that Ada died, Jessie said that in the morning, Ada was washing some clothes and Fisher was helping her with the mangle. They seemed friendly enough at the time and there was no sign of strife between them.

Jessie then spoke of the book which Fisher had been holding after dinner. At one stage he flicked the pages but did not appear to be reading. Later he sat with the book on his lap for nearly an hour, never turning a single page. She had asked him if he was going to have a lie down, like Ada, but he told her he was going out to get some money, and when Jessie told him she was also going out, he suggested that she should take a key as he would be out late. To this, Jessie had said that there was no need as her mother would be in.

Talking of the details of the relationship between Fisher and Ada, Jessie said that Fisher had agreed to pay the rent of 7s 1d each week and had taken the rent book so that he could do so. He had refused to show the book to Jessie who suspected, after all the other financial worries, that the rent was in arrears. On Friday, October 23rd, just two days before Ada died, Fisher had said that he had won some money and was going to pay Ada all that he owed her and clear the rent book. The next day, he claimed that due to a death, he had been unable to draw the money but would probably be able to get it on the Sunday. On that Sunday morning, the family had breakfast together and it was then that Fisher mentioned the tablecloth he had pledged. Ada was upset but Fisher managed to convince her that once he had drawn his winnings, everything would be all right. Later that morning, Fisher sharpened the kitchen knives, which was something he did every Sunday. Jessie also told the court that although Fisher had sometimes threatened her mother with violence, she knew that Ada had not taken these threats seriously or she would not have continued to live with him.

Ada Taylor had suspected that the rent book was not up to date and this had certainly been the case. Austin John Edkin was the landlord's agent and he had first had dealings with Fisher in November 1924 when he gave him notice to quit the house in Wright Street, due to the rent arrears. Luckily, these debts were cleared in December and Fisher was given permission to stay on. On June 26th, 1925, Fisher was again given notice to quit as the rent had once more fallen into arrears. On August 26th, when no attempt had been made to clear these arrears, Fisher was summonsed to appear in court, which he did on September 4th. The case was adjourned for four weeks after Fisher was ordered to pay 14s 2d for the first two weeks and the balance of the debt over the last two weeks. No such payments were received and so a registered letter was sent to Fisher telling him that on September 25th, an ejectment order would be applied for. Fisher attended the court on September 25th to hear the order granted but judgement was given that it would not be enforced if the arrears were paid off by October 23rd. Mr Edkin was able to show that no rent or arrears had been paid since May 1925, and had it not been for the crime, the ejectment order would have been enforced.

William James Cafferey was Mr Edkin's assistant and he had been the gentleman who actually served the court summons on Fisher, stating that he had to appear on August 26th. The notice was served in the early evening and Fisher seemed most anxious that the neighbours should not hear what was taking place and so invited Mr Cafferey into the house. Once inside, Fisher seemed equally eager to get rid of him since Ada Taylor was due home from work at any time.

In addition to telling the court what she had seen when she

went into the bedroom on October 25th, Sarah Ann Averne also detailed other times that there had been trouble between Fisher and Ada Taylor. She had known the couple for 14 years and in that time she had often heard them quarrelling and once she had heard him threaten to cut off Ada's head.

On October 25th, Sarah had seen Ada at 2.15pm when the two women had a brief conversation outside their houses. At 4.30pm Sarah went into her back yard and, looking next door, saw Fisher arranging his tie. That was the last she saw or heard from next door until she heard Jessie Dutton screaming in the yard at around 10.00pm.

Dr Robert George Macdonald Ladell had been called to Wright Street by Sarah Averne and arrived there at 10.20pm. He certified that Ada was dead and stated that she had been so for about three or four hours. He noted a large transverse wound in the throat which had severed the windpipe and the main arteries. On October 26th, Dr Ladell, together with Dr George St Johnston, had performed a post-mortem. They found a four-inch long wound which had separated the trachea completely. Half an inch below this wound was a second, also four inches long, which although largely superficial, was deeper on the left side, indicating that the probable direction of the cut was left to right. On the front of Ada's chest was another superficial wound, below the right collar-bone. More damaging was a deep triang-ular shaped wound on the upper part of Ada's forehead, some two and a half inches above the right eyebrow. Underneath this wound the skull had been fractured. Both Dr Ladell and Dr Johnston stated that the wounds were probably not self-inflicted although this could not be totally ruled out. There was, though, no sign of a weapon near the body, which in itself seemed to remove any possibility of suicide. It also appeared that Ada had been knocked unconscious by a blow to the head as there was no sign of a struggle.

Inspector Lawrence said that after signing his statement, Fisher had told him where he would find the knife he had used, pointing out that it was 'the one with the broken handle'. Such a knife was found in the kitchen drawer and when Inspector Lawrence took this back to the police station and showed it to Fisher, he remarked, "That is the one." A few days later, Inspector Lawrence returned to the house and collected a walking stick which Fisher said he had also used to batter Ada as she lay in bed.

Fisher's statement was now given in evidence. In this he stated that he had been a general machinist by trade and had lived with Ada Taylor and her daughter for some years. He admitted that on October 25th he had sharpened all the knives at dinner time but he had taken care to especially sharpen the one with the piece missing from the handle as he had something on his mind. Fisher went on to say that normally, after Sunday dinner, he would have gone to bed for a nap, but on this day, he stayed in the kitchen instead so that he could watch Jessie, who was reading. His intention was to 'do her first', but before he had the opportunity to kill her, she went out. Frustrated in his original plan to kill both mother and daughter, Fisher then went upstairs and killed Ada, it then being about 5.45pm. Afterwards, he had gone back downstairs, washed the knife clean and put it back in the table drawer, before making himself a cup of tea.

Satisfied with his work, Fisher then walked into town and strolled about the streets waiting for the pubs to open. Once they did, he took a few pints in various hostelries until finally he had just 2d left in his pocket. With that last couple of pence, he got on to a tram intending to give himself up at the Small Heath police station but when the constable sat down next to him, he decided to give himself up to him instead.

The only hope for Fisher could be a defence that he had been insane at the time he killed Ada Taylor. Dr Hamblin Smith, the medical officer at Winson Green prison, testified that he had observed Fisher ever since his admittance on October 26th. Fisher had slept well, ate normally and conversed rationally and there was nothing to show that he was mentally disturbed in any way. Under cross examination, though, Dr Smith confirmed that Fisher had been discharged from the Royal Marines in 1900, suffering from epilepsy. Dr Smith also agreed that Fisher's claim that sometimes he had 'funny feelings', during which he had to do something wrong, was a possible sign of epilepsy and that worries over financial problems might well trigger a fit in such a person.

For the defence, Mr Jenkins called no witnesses but claimed that the absence of a motive showed that this crime had happened during some kind of fit. As a result, Fisher was not responsible for his actions and so was not guilty of murder. The jury retired at 12.25pm. An hour later they had still not reached their verdict and the judge adjourned the proceedings for lunch. In total, the jury deliberated for two and a half hours before finding Fisher guilty but adding a recommendation to mercy.

Asked if he had anything to say before the sentence of death was passed, Fisher said, "I would like to say a few words in favour of Jessie Dutton, the daughter, to prove that I have not an atom of jealousy against the girl. I idolised that girl. I worshipped her. I hope she lives a long and happy life and God bless her. That's all I want to say sir."

An appeal was entered and this was heard on December 21st before Justices Sankey, Salter and Swift. Once again, the main grounds were that Fisher had killed Ada Taylor during an epileptic fit and so this was not a case of murder. Giving their judgement as to why the appeal would be dismissed, the three judges said that they accepted that Fisher suffered from epilepsy, had financial worries and no motive, but there was ample evidence to show that he knew what he was doing and that the crime was premeditated.

On Tuesday, January 5th, 1926, John Fisher, who was by then aged 58, was hanged at Birmingham by William Willis who was assisted by Robert Wilson. No more than 50 people were present outside the prison gates at the time.

CHAPTER THIRTEEN

—⁂—

THE CANAL-SIDE KILLER

—⁂—

CHARLES Broomhead had enjoyed his night out with Olive Gordon Turner. The couple had known each other for some nine months but had been walking out together only for the last six weeks or so. Now, on Saturday, July 2nd, 1927, Charles had taken his lady to the picture house on Winson Green Road.

The film finished at 9.40pm and Charles began to walk Olive home to Ford Street, Hockley. As they passed the entrance to the canal towing path, 18-year-old Olive suggested they walk along the water for a change. Charles agreed and as they slowly strolled by the canal, he noticed two other couples standing close by the asylum wall. Soon afterwards, Olive stopped to pull up one of her stockings. It was then that a large powerfully built man approached them from the direction of Clissold Street.

The large man identified himself as a policeman and informed Charles and Olive that they were trespassing on private property. He asked them for their names and addresses, both of which were given, but when the policeman asked for written confirmation of those details, both Charles Broomhead and Olive Turner told him that they had no means of proving who they were, or where they lived. The policeman told the couple that they would have to accompany him to the police station. Olive was upset at this and pointed out that she was an orphan and begged to be released, but the officer could not be persuaded to let her go, even when Charles Broomhead stated that he would be happy to accompany the officer alone.

The trio had not gone far when the policeman made a suggestion that he might possibly be 'squared.' Charles took this to mean that if he handed over some money, the policeman might conveniently forget to take them in. The trouble was that Charles had little money on him. Feeling in his pockets, he brought out all the cash he had, four pennies. To this, the policeman thrust his hand into his own pocket, brought out three half crowns and said, "Fourpence is no use to me."

By now, Charles Broomhead had become convinced that the man he was talking to was not a policeman at all. As they walked towards Winson Green, they passed two more courting couples and Charles demanded to know why they had not been moved too. The policeman replied, "I've got two. That's enough for you."

Olive had started to cry by now, and again asked to be released. The policeman still refused but Charles Broomhead told Olive to ignore this and run off home. Olive turned sharply and ran back towards Clissold Street. The policeman dashed after her and Charles Broomhead also ran off in the same direction.

Although the policeman was bigger, Broomhead was faster and he was soon pulling past the policeman and catching up to Olive. No sooner had he done so, though than the officer grabbed Broomhead's waistcoat with his right hand, spun him around and crashed a heavy punch into the left side of Broomhead's face. Charles fell to the ground, badly dazed. He was down for only a few minutes but by the time he managed to pull himself to his feet, there was no sign of Olive or the policeman who had gone after her.

Naturally, Charles Broomhead searched high and low for Olive but soon realised that he would need some help. Running to Olive's home in Ford Street, Charles blurted out what had happened to James Henry Rooke, a man who was courting Olive's sister, and who would subsequently marry her. Together, the two returned to the canal and renewed the search, it now being close to midnight.

After some minutes, James Rooke found, on the canal bank, close by a doorway. a hat, fur and handbag and Broomhead saw to his dismay that they belonged to Olive. There was now no alternative but to call in the police. It was officers from the Birmingham force who early on the morning of July 3rd, recovered Olive's body from the dark waters of the Soho branch of the canal. She still wore her wrist watch and since this had stopped, at 11.41pm, the time of her death appeared to be pinpointed with accuracy.

Initially, the chief suspect in this crime was Charles Broomhead himself. However, after a police appeal had been made, a number of witnesses came forward who also spoke of a tall, powerful man, seen on the canal that night. Indeed, two witnesses were found who had actually seen him drag Olive away.

John Godfrey was a boatman who worked on the canal and he was on his boat from 10.30pm on July 2nd. Godfrey was near the Western Road bridge when he saw a muscular man, who seemed to be looking at a courting couple. From the man's size and bearing, Godfrey assumed that the man was a policeman and watched his actions for some time. Godfrey saw the tall man approach the couple, who were standing in a gateway. Something appeared to be said and the couple immediately walked away. The policeman followed them for perhaps 50 yards before stopping to stare at yet another couple. Godfrey saw the policeman walk back towards the bridge and stand there as if waiting for someone. He then went home, passing yet another courting couple on the way. He told them, "You'd better look out. I think there's a detective."

Of even more value was the evidence of John Edgar Whillock and his girlfriend, Doris Emeny. John and Doris had been to the Bordesley Green picture house and were walking back to Doris' house at 157 Winson Green Road, along the canal towpath. Close by the workhouse they saw a tall man talking to a woman who seemed to be with a shorter man. Although John and Doris could not hear precisely what was said, there was some conversation about money and the clink of coins could plainly be heard. John and Doris passed by this threesome but just a minute or so later, the girl they had seen came running breathlessly up to them and cried, "There's a fellow up there. He says he's a policeman, and he's after you as well as me. Run with me.

Upon hearing this, John Whillock and Doris Emeny had run with the young girl towards Clissold Street. Close by the bridge, the tall man they had seen before, caught up with them and turning to the girl, had said, "Come on, I want you." The young girl seemed to faint at this and the tall man grabbed her around the waist to support her. Whillock, though, was not a man simply to walk away from this situation and asked the tall man who he was and what he wanted with the girl. The man replied, "I am a policeman," and at this point, Doris Emeny had told John not to interfere. As they walked off; the policeman took the semiconscious girl off under the bridge. When they were shown a photograph of Olive Turner, both John Whillock and Doris Emeny agreed that this was the girl they had seen.

The time of Olive Turner's death seemed to be confirmed by two other witnesses. Florence Robinson, who lived at 20 Norton Street, was on the way home from a whist drive and passed over a bridge on the canal at around 11.35pm on July 2nd. She heard some terrifying screams from the canal side but assumed that they had come from a patient in the mental hospital nearby.

Frank Pritchett was in his bedroom in Brookfields Road at 11.40pm and he, too, heard a horrible scream coming from the canal.

Another witness was Caroline Leonard, who also lived in Brookfields Road. At the back of her house was an alleyway and this in turn was separated from the canal towpath by a high wall. At 11.45pm on July 2nd, she was looking out of her kitchen when she saw a man come over the wall and drop down into the alleyway. Caroline was able to describe him as tall, very broad and wearing a dark coat and a lighter coloured cap which he had pulled down to cover part of his face. A similar description was also given by Thomas Hill of 68 Peel Street. He had been walking down the canal on his way home from the Theatre Royal, at about 11.10pm. He, too, had seen a tall man talking to a young couple. The tall man wore a grey coat with a pin-head stripe and a lighter cap. The testimony of these witnesses, together with that of Charles Broomhead, gave the police a good description of the man seen with Olive Turner before she died. According to a statement they issued, the man they were looking for was: 'Aged about 40; five feet ten or an inch taller; well built; clean shaven; having dark hair; wearing a dark suit and a dirty light collar; a dark cap; walks somewhat splay-footed and has a rather swinging gait.'

On July 5th, the inquest on the dead girl opened before the city coroner, Mr Isaac Bradley. Only the most basic evidence of identification was given before matters were adjourned, but later that day, the police made the breakthrough they needed.

Detective Sergeant Albert Edwards had looked carefully at the description of the man who had been seen on the canal with Olive. This, together with his knowledge of a man who had once been a serving police officer, but who had now left the force, led him to suspect that he might know the identity of the man he was looking for. Knowing where this man worked, Sergeant

Edwards took Charles Broomhead to Kenyon Street where they positioned themselves outside Cannings factory. Between 6.00pm and 6.45pm, perhaps 90 men and boys left the factory and although Broomhead watched them all, he made no remark which indicated that he had recognised anyone. Then, just a few minutes later, a tall, well-built man came out. This man saw Broomhead and immediately dashed back inside the factory gates, only to reappear a minute or two later when he was positively identified by Charles Broomhead. The tall man was immediately taken into custody by Sergeant Edwards. Back at the police station, the man, who confirmed that he was 32-year-old James Joseph Power of 28 Heath Green Road, was interviewed and then charged with the murder of Olive Gordon Turner.

Power appeared before the stipendiary magistrate, Lord Ilkeston, on July 6th. Here the prosecution evidence was given by Mr M.P. Pugh, while Power was represented by Mr Herbert Willison who stated that of six witnesses who had attended an identification parade at the police station, only one had identified Power. As such, he felt that there was no case to answer and the charges against his client should be dismissed. The magistrate did not agree, and Power was remanded for a week.

The second police court appearance took place on July 13th and although the proceedings lasted only a few minutes, it was stated that other charges had now been preferred against Power. In addition to murder, Power had now been charged with impersonating a police officer and demanding money with menaces. These charges would be dealt with separately at future hearings.

Power was back before the magistrates on July 19th when the evidence on the charge of demanding money with menaces from Charles Broomhead and Olive Turner was heard. Detective Sergeant Edwards told the court that after being cautioned, in

Kenyon Street, Power had replied, "I was never near the cut that night."

Back at the police station, Power had explained that he had spent July 2nd at a cricket match at Cape Hill. He had been with a close friend of his, Jack Davis, and after the match had finished, they had spent the evening together in a public house. The two friends had finally parted, at the corner of Heath Green Road, at 10.45pm and Power had then gone home. When interviewed, however, Mr Davis had confirmed most of this story except that he claimed that he had left Power at 10.25pm, not 10.45pm. Power was then remanded again, this time until July 21st.

On July 21st, Power was again remanded and on his next appearance, on July 26th, a further remand followed, this time until August 3rd. On that date, the magistrates were informed that Power was now facing another charge, that of raping a woman on the canal side at Winson Green on May 23rd. Power was now represented by Mr P.W. Williams, who asked for the rape charge to be adjourned until after the murder charge had been heard. Mr Williams claimed that by bringing up this particular charge, the prosecution were trying to show that his client was in the habit of being on the canal side and molesting people. This would cause the jury to be prejudiced against Power and meant that he would be less likely to get a fair trial. The magistrate, though, felt that there were no grounds for postponing this or indeed any of the other charges and ruled that all matters would be proceeded with. Evidence was now heard on the rape charge.

At 10.45pm on May 23rd, Lucy Folks, a widow, had been walking along the canal towpath with the new man in her life, Thomas Pitt. A man they had subsequently identified as Power had come up to them and said, "You know who I am?" Pitt had replied in the negative, to which Power had said, "Well, I am a police officer. What are you going to do?" At first, Pitt was not sure what Power meant and asked him what he was talking about. It soon became clear that Power was suggesting that some money might help him forget that they were trespassing but Pitt had said, "I don't know what you mean. I am out of work and cannot give you anything." At this, Power took hold of Pitt's wrist, put an arm lock on him, and forced him to the ground. Power then grabbed Pitt by the throat, shook him and finally hit him so hard that Pitt was unconscious for two hours. Thomas Pitt finally staggered to his house at 1.30am, assuming that Lucy would have found her own way home. In fact, Power had grabbed Lucy and taken her under a bridge. Some distance further along the canal, he took her out of sight of the towpath and raped her. Lucy had not told anyone, not even Thomas, about this assault upon her until July 7th when they had read of the death of Olive Turner. Both Thomas and Lucy had attended an identification parade on July 13th, when they had immediately picked out Power as the man who had attacked them.

A further remand followed, until August 11th, when the evidence on the murder charge was heard. After this, Power was sent for trial on four charges: murder; demanding money with menaces; assault; and rape. That trial opened at Birmingham on December 7th, 1927, before Mr Justice Swift, and an all-male jury. Power was defended by Sir Reginald Coventry and Mr Williams, while the case for the prosecution was led by Sir Norman Birkett who was assisted by Mr W.E. Bousefield. The proceedings lasted until December 9th, and as was customary, only the most serious charge was considered, that of the murder of Olive Turner.

Charles Broomhead told the court his story of the encounter with the tall man on the canal towpath. In all, Broomhead was in the man's company for more than an hour and he was absolutely certain that the man now standing in the dock was the same person who had struck out at him.

Ivy Gordon Rooke was the dead girl's sister, and by now the wife of James Rooke who had helped Broomhead in his search. She reported that Charles Broomhead had called for Olive early on the evening of July 2nd. She had next seen Charles at around midnight when her grandmother, who also lived in the house in Ford Street, woke her to say that Charlie had arrived without Olive. Ivy's husband went out to help in the search and the two men did not return until 1.15am on July 3rd. Only now did Broomhead give any details about what had taken place on the canal, saying, "We were walking home along the canal side from Winson Green picture house. A fellow stopped her and said he wanted our names and addresses for trespassing. We gave them and the man said he was going to take us to the police station. We started to go there, but the man kept stopping and delaying us. We offered him money. I had only got four pence..." Broomhead went on to say that Olive had then offered the man some money but he (Broomhead) told her to run home. Olive did as he had asked but the man followed her and when Broomhead caught up with him, the man suddenly spun round and struck out at him.

After telling this story, Broomhead and Rooke had gone back out to search again and when they came back, Rooke was carrying the bag, fur and hat which Olive had with her when she first went out. Much of this story was backed up by James Rooke, who also said that when he had first seen Broomhead, at midnight, he was sporting a mark on his lip, which had bled.

John Whillock and Doris Emeny told of their encounter with Olive Turner. Whillock, who lived at 13 Tree Place, off Ostler Street, Ladywood, said that after Doris had told him to come away and not interfere with the policeman, they had walked off towards Winson Green Road. Along the way they saw a uniformed policeman in Aberdeen Street, and reported to him what they had seen. The constable told them to leave the matter in his hands, adding that he would be taking a walk down that way in about half an hour.

The problems for the prosecution came with the identity parade which John Whillock and Doris Emeny had attended. This parade had taken place on July 6th and Whillock had picked out two men, saying that it was 'between these two'. He had, however, selected Power first, and thought he was the most likely to be the man.

A more curious identification had been made by Doris Emeny. She had picked out a man who was not Power. As she turned away from the line up of men, though, someone had called out, "I believe Miss Emeny wants to say something else." She had then turned back and touched a second man in the parade, this being Power. Seeing that she had picked out two men now, Doris Emeny said, "It is either one or the other of these." Under cross examination, though, Miss Emeny had to agree that had she not been called back, she would not have picked out Power.

All of these three witnesses – Charles Broomhead, Doris Emeny and John Edgar Whillock – had stated that the man they saw on the canal had worn some sort of flower in his buttonhole. John Albert Blagdon Davis, confirmed that he and Power had been together in the Beehive pub on Cape Hill from 8.00pm until 10.00pm on July 2nd. They had consumed about five half-pints each and towards the end of the evening, a woman came into the bar, selling roses. He and Power each bought a small bud from her, for their buttonholes. Finally, Davis told the court that he had left Power at around 10.20pm or just a little later and at the time, Power was wearing a dark suit with a thin stripe, and a dark grey cap.

Joseph Pym was the gatekeeper at Cannings, the factory where Power worked and where he had been taken into custody by Sergeant Edwards. He testified that he had seen Power leave the factory but return almost immediately and say, "Oh Joe, about the keys." Joseph Pym had no idea why Power should be asking about the factory keys. It was something he had never done before in all the time he had worked at Cannings, so he said to Power, "What keys? Mr Ruthben brings the keys and he hasn't left yet." Power then simply bade him goodnight and walked out of the gates again.

Detective Sergeant Edwards told the court how he, Charles Broomhead and Detective Constable Hewins had gone to the factory where he had arrested Power, and how Power had then denied being anywhere near the canal on the night that Olive Turner died. After hearing the statements of the various witnesses, Sergeant Edwards had checked and shown that the man they had seen was not a serving police officer. He then came to the conclusion that the assailant might be someone who knew police procedure very well, such as a former officer. This was when he thought of Power, who had been discharged from the force for unsatisfactory conduct.

The early statements from the witnesses, especially that of Charles Broomhead, had referred to the tall man wearing a grey suit and Sergeant Edwards confirmed under cross examination that he had even gone so far as to dig up the garden at Power's house, in an attempt to find this grey suit. Power had only the one suit, and this was dark blue. Much was made of the fact that at subsequent police court hearings, the witnesses had now begun referring to a dark suit, rather than a grey one. Sir Reginald Coventry suggested that statements were being altered to fit the known facts, a suggestion which Sergeant Edwards denied vehemently.

Other witnesses were called who showed that Power was indeed in the habit of spending his time accosting couples on the canal towpath. Edward Morris and his young lady, Frances Lillian Atkinson, had been stopped on the canal side by a tall man, on

February 3rd. Both had attended the identification parade and picked out Power as the man. Even more telling was the testimony of Frank Hammond Hill and his girlfriend, Jessie Roper. They, too, had been stopped and Jessie had been most upset but the most valuable evidence was to come from Hill. He was a neighbour of Power's, living at 43 Heath Green Road, and had recognised Power when the incident took place. As Power put on his policeman's act, Hill had identified himself and asked him what he was doing. Power had remained silent for a few moments before saying that he was on some 'special duty'.

One of the final witnesses was Dr John Walker Cathles, who had been called to the canal when Olive's body had been found. He first examined Olive at 6.30am on July 3rd and believed that she had by then been dead for about seven hours. Olive's clothing was not disarranged and there was no sign of any sexual assault, she still being virgo intacta. There were some injuries on Olive's thigh, but Dr Cathles believed these had nothing to do with her death. Dr Cathles suggested that Olive might have been struck a single blow, since a blue discolouration was noted on her forehead, and then either fallen or been placed into the canal while she was unconscious, or semi-conscious. The cause of death was drowning.

In his closing speech for the defence, Sir Reginald Coventry again made much of the word 'grey' being dropped from Charles Broomhead's statements and of the fact that although there were something like 300 houses in Brookfields Road, only one man, Mr Pritchett, had apparently heard a scream. Sir Reginald suggested that this was nothing more than a case of mistaken identity and his client was not on the canal side at the time and so could not be guilty of Olive Turner's murder. The jury, though, did not agree and Power was found guilty of murder, the other charges being left on file.

Asked if he had anything to say, Power launched into an attack upon Sergeant Edwards, saying, "I still maintain that the jury and the witnesses have made an honest mistake. If it was not for the prejudice of a certain detective sergeant, I should have been found not guilty. I will tell you why.

"My Lord, it has not been brought forward for the defence that on the 28th of last month, that detective sergeant arrived at His Majesty's prison to serve some additional evidence on me. The prosecution today at any time did not put that evidence forward. When he served that evidence on me, a certain incident happened. You must remember, my Lord, I have been five months awaiting trial for wilful murder, and in order to provoke me to commit a crime he stoops down and picks up a poker and says, 'Go on, I will smash your brains out.'

"The governor of the prison and two officials can testify to it, and if it was not for the detective sergeant who has had it in for me since I left the police force, I should have been found not guilty."

The judge listened patiently to this outburst and then sentenced Power to death. After the dread words were finished, Power replied, "I quite understand that. I don't want any sympathy from you."

An appeal was entered and this was heard on the 12th and 13th of January, 1928. before Lord Hewart, the Lord Chief Justice, and two of his colleagues. Once again, the defence made much of the discrepancies in the evidence but the Lord Chief Justice stated that the opinion of the court was that there was corroboration of the statements made by the witnesses. The appeal was dismissed.

On Tuesday, January 31st, 1928, at Winson Green prison, which was situated less that 600 yards from the spot where Olive Turner had met her death, James Joseph Power was hanged by Thomas Pierrepoint, who was assisted by Robert Wilson. A crowd estimated at 2,000 strong, waited for the notices of execution to be posted on the prison gates.

CHAPTER FOURTEEN

THE MESSENGER

FOR 33 years, William Thomas Andrews had worked for Messrs W.M. Taylor & Co, a drapers of Potters Hill, Aston, finally reaching the position of head porter. Part of his duties each day was to walk to the National Provincial Bank at Six Ways, to bank the takings from the previous day's trading.

On Monday, July 21st, 1930, the chief cashier of the company, Lilian Alice Ward, made up the bank bag, as usual, at 1.35pm. Lilian placed £728 in £1 notes, £124 in 10s notes, £51 in silver and an odd 2d in copper, along with a single cheque for £5 5s, to make a total of £908 5s 2d. The bag of cash, along with the paying-in book, was then placed into the company safe and Lilian handed the key to Rose Millard, one of the clerks. Some half an hour afterwards, at around 2.00pm, Andrews took the key from Rose and collected the items from the safe and then returned the key. At the same time, another £4 in notes was also handed over, with a request for Andrews to get some change for the tills. It was 2.10pm when 63-year-old Andrews walked out of the offices on a journey he had been making for the last 25 years of his service with Taylors. The bank was just a few minutes walk away.

Charles Henry Dowd was a driver and on July 21st, he was steering his employer's van down Victoria Road. He drove past Six Ways and when he was about 75 yards away from Rifle Crescent, he noticed two men on the pavement. One man was quite elderly 'and short, while the other was taller and far younger. The younger man was holding the elder at the back of his neck and as Dowd watched, the man's other hand was raised and a vicious blow came down on to the old man's head, causing him to fall to the pavement. The young man then snatched up a bag from the ground. At the same time, a yellow car came out of Rifle Crescent and turned into Victoria Road, one of the doors flying open as it moved. The young man ran after this car, threw in the bag and jumped into the passenger seat as the car sped off away from Six Ways. Dowd tried to follow the vehicle but lost it in the traffic.

Ruth Matthews, a housemaid who lived at 1 Rifle Crescent, came out of her house at 2.20pm and went into the shop house, talking. A yellow car was parked outside the house and it opposite. She saw two men leaning against the railings of her was empty. When Ruth came back from the shop, she saw one of the men get into the car and drive into Victoria Road. There was no injured man on the pavement at the time.

Annie Blears, a widow, ran a shop from 23 Victoria Road and just five minutes later, at 2.25pm she looked through her shop door and saw a man lying on the pavement. Thinking he had fallen over and possibly hurt himself, Annie went out to offer what assistance she could. The man was lying on his left side, with his face pressed against the cold pavement and his hat still on his head. He wasn't moving and Annie tried to raise him by his right arm, as a man passing by tried to assist by lifting the injured man's head. Only now did Annie notice that blood was running from a cut on the man's forehead, just above his left eye. Recognising the old man as William Andrews, the chap who went to the bank for Taylors, she dashed back to her shop and brought a chair for the poor man to sit on. There was, however, no sign of the bank bag that Andrews should have had with him.

Constable Evan Hugh Jones was stopped by a motorist who told him that there had been an incident in Victoria Road, and also about a yellow car being involved. Jones got into the informant's vehicle and they turned down Lichfield Road. They couldn't find the car, so Jones went to the scene, arriving there at 2.50pm. William Andrews was still sitting on the chair but was deeply unconscious. Jones accompanied Andrews to the General Hospital where he was seen by the resident surgical officer, Dr James Gore. He noted that Andrews had a wound on the outer margin of his left eye, possibly caused by glass from his spectacles when he had fallen, and that there was a depressed area of bone on the left side of the head. That evening, Dr Gore operated in an attempt to repair the damage.

It was obvious that Andrews had been the victim of a robbery and that at least two men had been involved. A young man had been seen striking Andrews, and stealing the cash bag, and his accomplice had driven a yellow car in which they had made their getaway. It wasn't long before that car was found.

Margaret Fellows had been strolling down Claverdon Street when a rather dirty yellow-coloured car came speeding from the direction of Saltley Road. Margaret had to jump back on to the pavement to avoid being knocked down and as she caught her breath, the car stopped ten yards away and two men got out. The smaller man was carrying some sort of parcel and without a word of apology, the men ran a few yards further on and climbed on to a tram. Margaret, suspicious, contacted the police.

Once the report came in that a yellow car had been found abandoned in Claverdon Street, the police made the natural assumption that this was the same one involved in the robbery in Victoria Road. Constable James Brown attended and informed his station that the registration number of the vehicle was FH 3254.

It was a simple matter to trace the owner of that vehicle, a Morris Cowley four-seater, and he turned out to be Thomas Harold Young of 73 Holte Road. Young was a coal merchant and he told the police that at 12.30pm he had been at Rose Garage in Park Road when a young man said he wished to hire the car for an hour, possibly an hour and a half; to take two old people to Four Oaks. Young agreed to the transaction and accepted the princely sum of 5s as payment. Even more important, though, Young was able to give the police the name of the man who had hired his car: 23-year-old Herbert Charles Ridley. Unfortunately, when officers visited Ridley's lodgings at 120 Barton Street, they found that he had already left.

The investigation was not many hours old when the name of the second man involved in the robbery and assault was determined. Fanny Frances Jones lived in Windsor Street and at 2.45pm on July 21st, a man she knew knocked on her door and asked if he might use her outside toilet. Fanny handed over the key but to her surprise saw that there were two men who went into the toilet together, where they remained for three or four minutes. After they had gone, a curious Fanny Jones checked the toilet and found an empty bank cash bag. As soon as she heard of the bank robbery, she, too, contacted the police and reported that the man who had wished to use her toilet was 22-year-old Victor Edward Betts. Descriptions of both men were widely circulated, as were details of a £130 reward for information leading to their arrests.

Back at the hospital, despite the medical attention he received, William Andrews succumbed to his injuries and died at 7.10am on July 24th, without ever regaining consciousness. The inquiry was now a murder investigation but despite the best efforts of the police, no signs of Ridley or Betts could be found.

On July 30th, the inquest opened before Dr W.H. Davison. Mr D.L. Finnemore acted for Andrews' employers, expressed his deepest sympathy to the relatives and stated that W.M. Taylor & Co had wished him to add that William Andrews had been a, 'faithful and trusted servant for many years'. After medical testimony had been given as to the cause of death, the proceedings were adjourned until September 18th.

It was on August 6th that a motor accident near Chichester in West Sussex, led to the arrest of the two wanted men. A vehicle containing two men and two women was driven into a ditch and all four occupants needing treatment at the Royal West Sussex Hospital. A report was submitted to the police and as a matter of routine, the address where the two men were lodging, 20 Grand Parade, Brighton, was noted. Only later did the local police realise that the descriptions of the two men wanted by the Birmingham police, were very similar to those of the two who had been involved in the road accident. The search for Ridley and Betts now moved to Brighton.

The first man to be arrested was Herbert Ridley. It was 10.40pm on August 8th when Detective Sergeant Thomas Wells saw a man who fitted Ridley's description, in Grand Parade. Sergeant Wells stopped his man, told him he matched the description of a man wanted in Birmingham in connection with a robbery and murder and cautioned him.

Ridley did not deny that he was the man Wells was looking for. Ridley was then searched and the sum of £150 was found in his pockets.

Just 15 minutes after Ridley had been stopped, Constable Edward John Rowlands saw Betts on Grand Junction Road and stopped him. Betts made no comment when cautioned and initially offered no resistance to Constable Rowlands as he escorted Betts towards the police station. At Pool Valley, Betts did start to struggle but Rowlands held him firmly and he quietened down. Later that same evening, the lodgings at Grand Parade were searched and a further £230 found.

On August 9th, Chief Inspector Frederick Baguley and Detective Inspector Thomas Dillon, travelled down to Brighton to pick up both men and return them to Birmingham. Both made statements admitting that they had robbed William Andrews, Ridley saying that he had done nothing more than drive the car. Betts admitted hitting Andrews but claimed that this was only with his fist, and that the blow had only been a light one. On the train on the way back, Ridley made a further, verbal statement which was taken down by Baguley. Ridley said, "I was surprised when I saw the amount of money in the bag. It was like a fortune to me. I thought of sending some of the money home, but I thought they would think my wife was in it too. I read of the old man's death at Leeds. I have been spending money as fast as I could get rid of it and should have chucked it up after the holiday and have come home." Back at Birmingham, both men were charged with murder.

There were a number of police court appearances but the evidence did not begin to be heard until August 27th. Ridley seemed nervous in court and once or twice he looked to be in tears. Betts behaved indifferently and, if anything, revelled in his notoriety. The case for the Director of Public Prosecutions was detailed by Mr M.P. Pugh and both men were defended by Mr Herbert Willison.

The prisoners' movements after the attack were outlined and details given of two Bristol girls, May Morris and Beatrice Stone, who were on holiday in Brighton, and who Ridley and Betts had met up with, lavishing presents upon them and spending money freely.

There were too many witnesses to be heard on the one day and further hearings followed on August 29th and September 3rd. All the evidence had been concluded then, but there was another matter pending which required a further remand, until September 8th. Betts, in addition to facing the murder charge, was also charged with robbing Harold Charles Chalmers, a night attendant at a garage at Warwick Road, Greet. This robbery had allegedly been committed on June 22nd and his accomplice then had been one Frederick Lutwych and it was claimed that Betts had struck Chalmers over the head with a chair leg. On September 8th, all the details of that case having been given, Betts and Lutwych were sent for trial on the robbery charge. Minutes later Betts was back in the box, this time with Ridley, and both were sent for trial at the same assizes on the murder charge. Mr Willison then formally applied for bail for Ridley. The request was turned down, the magistrate, Mr J.S. Pritchett saying that he had never heard of such a thing when a charge of murder had been made.

The murder trial opened on December 4th, 1930, before Mr Commissioner E.A. Mitchell-Innes. The case for the Crown was led by Sir Henry Maddocks who was assisted by Mr M. Maurice Healy. Betts was defended by Mr Harold Eaden, while Mr A.P. Marshall appeared for Ridley. The proceedings lasted for two days.

One of the earliest witnesses was Emma Elizabeth Andrews, the widow of the dead man, who lived at 4 Barton's Bank, Aston. She stated that her husband had been a creature of habit. It was his custom to always go to the bank between 2.00pm and 3.00pm. On the day he was attacked, William had come home for his lunch at 12.30pm and returned to work exactly one hour later. By 2.00pm he was back home and left his umbrella, since it had now stopped raining. He had the bank bag with him at the time but this was nothing unusual. He had done the same thing many times before. Being a man who always followed the same routine, William invariably walked to the bank the same way and anyone who had observed him once or twice would know that he walked down Whitehead Road, along Rifle Crescent to Victoria Road and then on to Six Ways.

Confirmation that Ridley had hired the car used in the robbery was given by Thomas Young. The transaction had been witnessed by two men who were with Young at the time, Henry Hopkins and Albert Meads. Meads worked at the garage and even put half a gallon of petrol into the vehicle before Ridley drove it away. Both men had known Ridley for several months.

The man who had helped Annie Blears to lift the stricken William Andrews on to a chair was Arthur Simkiss, who knew Andrews quite well. Simkiss had been strolling along Victoria Road when he saw a man lying injured on the pavement. He had not actually witnessed the attack but must have arrived on the scene just a minute or two after it had taken place.

John William Cope was an investigation officer at the Aston Employment Exchange and he testified that both Ridley and Betts were out of work and claiming benefit. Ridley had last signed the register on July 18th and was due to sign again on the day that the robbery took place. Betts, who had been claiming since February 4th, 1929, had actually signed on at 11.50am on July 21st. This testimony proved, of course, that neither man should have been in the position to be carrying the large sums of cash they had at the time of their arrest.

After the court heard of the finding of the abandoned car and the empty bank bag, and details of the arrests in Brighton, the prisoners statements were read out in court. Ridley had said Betts had mentioned to him that he knew of an old man who walked down Rifle Crescent every day with a bag of money to take to the bank. Betts said that he intended to rob the man but needed some help and asked Ridley to drive the car. He had agreed after Betts had suggested that all he would do was push the man over and that no violence would be used.

On the appointed day, after hiring the car, Ridley had gone to

Six Ways where he met Betts, then drove around slowly until they saw the messenger. It had been Betts who got out of the car and struck Andrews, although Ridley claimed that he had not actually seen the blow. The next thing he saw was the bank bag being thrown into the car as Betts climbed into the passenger seat. Going to the lavatory in Windsor Street, the cash had been shared out.

From Birmingham, Betts and Ridley hitched a lift to London where they hired another car and drove back to Birmingham where Betts directed Ridley to a house which he said was his mother's. Ridley waited in the car while Betts spoke briefly to an elderly woman and then shouted that he had to go next door. Betts went around the back of the house and returned five minutes later, saying that they had to go as the police were looking for them. From there they drove back to London and then travelled on to Brighton.

May Morris, one of the two women Betts and Ridley had met on the south coast, said that she and Beatrice Stone had met the two men on August 3rd at 11.00am by the Palace Pier. They had all gone for a drive and the girls had gone out with the two men every day afterwards. On August 6th, after visiting Southsea, they had been returning via Chichester when Betts drove off the road into a ditch. After receiving treatment at the hospital, Betts had hired a car and chauffeur to take them back to Brighton. The next day, all four again went out in this hired car and to explain the amount of cash they were spending, Ridley said that his father, who was quite well-off had given him the money to pay for the holiday. As if to prove the point he bought May a gold watch for £20 and a diamond ring for £25.

Chief Inspector Baguley said that he had interviewed both men. Ridley maintained that he had not known that Betts was going to hit Andrews and Betts claimed that he had not used any weapon and had struck out only with his fists. Told that they would be placed into an identification parade, Betts said, "I don't want to be put up for identification." Ridley, too, stated his opposition. This of course, could well have been due to the fact that both men bore injuries from their car crash and knew that they would stand out immediately in any parade. Also, the fact that they had been injured had been reported in the newspapers.

Dr James Gore, in addition to treating Andrews at the hospital, had also assisted at the post-mortem after he had died. Andrews' skull had been cracked all the way round and this, together with an injury to the brain, had been the direct cause of death. The skull fracture had, in Dr Gore's opinion, been caused by an impact from a hard object but could certainly not have been caused by his fall to the pavement. Finally, Dr Gore stated that Andrews' skull had been slightly thinner than normal.

Professor Morrison had assisted at the post-mortem and he agreed with Dr Gore's findings as to the cause of death, adding that he believed that an oval-shaped object of some kind had been used to inflict the head injury. Under cross examination, Professor Morrison agreed that it might have been possible for the heavy application of a fist to have caused the fracture.

Professor George Haswell-Wilson, of the University of Birmingham's pathology department, had also worked on the post-mortem. The professor said that the object which had caused the fatal injury to Andrews' head had been quite small. It may have been a stone held in the hand, or equally, the curved end of a tyre lever, which had been found inside the abandoned car, might have been used to cause the injury.

In his summing up for the prosecution, Sir Henry Maddocks told the jury that 'both men had set forth with felonious intent and a death had resulted from a blow struck by one of them'. He ended by saying that since Ridley was a partner in this venture, he was equally guilty in the eyes of the law. For Ridley, Mr

Marshall said that his client had remained in the car and had not been a party to the attack upon Andrews and as such should be found not guilty of murder. Finally, for Betts, Mr Eaden asked for a verdict of manslaughter as his client had had no intention to kill.

The jury took one hour to decide that both men were guilty of murder and as the death sentences were read out, a woman in the public gallery was heard sobbing. Betts walked firmly to the cells below the court but Ridley appeared to faint and had to be assisted by a warder.

Both men appealed against their death sentences and these was heard on December 19th before Justices Avory, Swift and Charles. In Betts' case, the grounds were that the judge had mis-directed the jury with regard to the distinction between murder and manslaughter, and for Ridley, the claim was that the judge had not told the jury that to convict him of murder they had to be satisfied that he had gone out not only with the intention to rob, but also prepared to use or be a party to violence. Finally. the judge should have told the jury that they could find a verdict of murder against Betts and still decide that Ridley had only been guilty of manslaughter.

Dismissing both of the appeals, Mr Justice Avory said that Ridley knew that Betts was going to steal the cash bag and that in order to do so, violence might have to be offered to Mr Andrews so his defence failed on that point. As for Betts, the facts were not in dispute. He had struck Mr Andrews in order to rob him and was directly responsible for his death. The law defined that as murder and the sentence must stand.

A new execution date was set, and the governor of Birm-ingham prison prepared for a double execution. On December 31st, 1930, the Home Secretary announced that he had decided to advise the King to respite the capital sentence in the case of Ridley, who was now given penal servitude for life instead. At the same time, he announced that he had not found any grounds to interfere in the sentence on Betts, despite a petition which contained 12,000 signatures.

At 8.00am on Saturday, January 3rd, 1931, a crowd of several hundred people assembled outside Birmingham prison as Victor Edward Betts was hanged by Thomas Pierrepoint and Alfred Allen. As a nearby factory hooter sounded the fateful hour, the entire crowd fell silent and all that could be heard was the anxious barking of a dog.

CHAPTER FIFTEEN

CROSSED IN LOVE

JAMES Charles Payne, like so many of his countrymen, answered the call to arms when Britain declared war on Germany and her allies in 1914. During the hostilities, James was wounded and sent back to England to recuperate. He was admitted to hospital in Manchester and there he met a nurse, a native of Chorley, with whom he fell in love and married. By the early 1930s James and his wife, Jessie Payne, had been married 15 years and she had given birth to four children.

In 1932, Jessie and her family were living at 11 The Leys, Brockmoor, near Brierley Hill. It was at that address that they received a regular visitor in the form of 49-year-old Jeremiah Hanbury, who had been a friend of James Payne's for many years. Hanbury had been calling at The Leys for close on four years and James Payne thought there was nothing suspicious about these visits, even though Hanbury appeared to be very friendly with Jessie. James trusted both his wife and his close friend.

In early September, Jessie Payne told Hanbury not to call at her house any longer. This distressed Hanbury who, soon afterwards, spoke to James and asked him why Jessie had stopped him visiting her. James said he had no idea, to which Hanbury, somewhat cryptically, replied, "Well, this thing has to be cleared up first and last. If you will come down to your house sometime unexpectedly, you will find out for yourself. Go down and tell Jess what I have said."

Over the next few days, Hanbury elaborated on what he had said to James. He now claimed that he had been having an affair with Jessie for some time, but that she had now found herself a new man named Bert Eardley. Faced with this, Jessie admitted that she had had sex with Hanbury but that he had raped her. For his part, Hanbury now added that he had paid Jessie for sex and that in all probability, Eardley was now doing exactly the same. Then, finally, on October 8th, Hanbury met James Payne again and told him, "Your wife has been a bad woman. I can go home with your wife any time." James had heard enough and told Hanbury that it was time to forget the past and that they should all get on with the rest of their lives.

It was just after 2.00pm on Monday, October 17th, 1932, when Edith Elizabeth Harris, who lived at number 12 The Leys and was Jessie Payne's next door neighbour, saw Jessie shaking a tablecloth in her back garden. Just five minutes later, as Edith went out to look at her washing, she glanced over at number 11 in time to see Jeremiah Hanbury come out of the back door. Hanbury, who was bleeding from a wound in the throat, called to Edith, "Come on, I've done it now."

This encounter was also seen by Priscilla Edmunds who, although she lived at number 41, was in the house of a friend at number 46 The Leys. She was chatting to her friend in the back yard of the house, which was almost directly opposite the back of Jessie Payne's, and she saw Hanbury emerge from number 11 and speak to Mrs Harris. Priscilla thought that Hanbury had actually said, "You can go into her. I've done it." but there was no dispute over the fact that Hanbury's shirt was wide open, he was bleeding from his throat and there was also blood on his hands.

Maria Bates lived at 9 The Leys, but just after 2.00pm she was in the yard of her sister-in-law's house at number 10, which was also next door to Jessie Payne's house but on the other side from Edith Harris. When Maria saw Hanbury, she thought he looked wild, 'almost like a madman', and when she saw his throat wound, she screamed. It was perhaps this noise which caused Hanbury to start to walk rapidly away from the house.

At 2.15pm Louisa Phoebe Marsh was in High Street, Brock-moor, and as she strolled down the street she saw Hanbury walking towards her from the direction of The Leys. Louisa was shocked to see a man bleeding from the throat and stepped back to allow him to pass. As Hanbury dashed past, apparently oblivious to Louisa's presence, he was muttering to himself something which sounded like, "Jerry said revenge, Jerry's had revenge."

It was also in High Street that Hanbury was seen by James Henry Round and Edward Warwick Simpson, two men who had known him for many years. They were near the church when Hanbury approached them. James Round saw the state Hanbury was in and asked him what on earth he had been up to. Both men heard Hanbury reply, "I've done a murder." As he spoke, he jerked his head back towards The Leys and added, "Murder down there."

Hanbury had made his way to his home at 18 Newton and at 2.30pm he saw his neighbour, Alice Emery, who lived at number 17. Alice saw the condition that Hanbury was in and backed away from him. To this he muttered, "Alice, come here, don't be afraid, I'm not going to hurt you." Alice gingerly stepped forward and asked Hanbury what he had done to which he said, "I've killed Jessie with a razor, go and tell Sally and Lily." Alice knew the family well — Sally was Hanbury's niece and Lily was his step-daughter.

Jeremiah Hanbury did not stay long in his house and was soon off walking down the streets again. Constable William Kirkham was cycling up Hickman Road when he saw Hanbury walking towards him. Hanbury began to wave his arms as a signal for the officer to stop and when Constable Kirkham did so, he saw that Hanbury's jacket, waistcoat and shirt were wide open, his chest was covered in blood and he was bleeding badly from a throat wound. Constable Kirkham rendered first aid and after doing so, cautioned Hanbury that anything he said would be taken down in writing. Then, just as Constable William Henry Hazell, Constable Green and Sergeant George Herbert Lea arrived on the scene, Hanbury admitted that he had killed Mrs Payne. He was then taken to the Landfield House Institute at Wordsley, so that his wound could receive professional medical attention.

The inquest on Jessie Payne opened before Mr J. T. Higgs, the coroner for South Staffordshire, on October 19th. Hanbury was still receiving treatment and was unable to attend and for that reason, the proceedings were adjourned until November 2nd. Three days after this, on October 22nd, Jessie's body was laid to rest at Brockmoor and less than a week later, on October 28th, Hanbury made his first appearance at the police court before the stipendiary magistrate, Mr W. Pearson. Hanbury had a heavy bandage around his throat and claimed that he had no memory of the crime. Nevertheless, he was remanded until November 2nd.

It was on November 2nd that both the police court and the inquest reopened. At the inquest, only medical evidence was given before matters were again adjourned, until after the police court proceedings were complete. The magistrates, however, adjourned matters again, until November 7th, and it was only on that date that Hanbury was sent for trial.

The assizes proceedings opened on December 8th, 1932 before Mr Justice Humphreys. The prosecution case was led by

Mr C.B. Marriott, who was assisted by Mr Paul E. Sandlands and Hanbury was defended by Mr John F. Bourke and Mr G. Rogers. Hanbury pleaded not guilty, his defence being that he was insane at the time Jessie Payne died.

Alice Baker lived at 6 The Leys and she told the court that she had known Jessie Payne for 13 years, and Hanbury almost as long. Some time before October, she had been speaking to Hanbury and he had claimed that he had been sleeping with Jessie for the best part of four years, paying her for the privilege. He went on to say that Jessie had now found herself someone with more money and was selling her favours to this man instead. Ominously he had ended the conversation with, "I shall have my revenge on her and him." Just a few days before Jessie's death, on October 14th, Hanbury had again spoken to Alice and intimated that he loved Jessie so much that if she had asked him to murder her husband, he would have done so.

In addition to the witnesses already referred to, who had seen Hanbury either around Jessie's house, or in the street afterwards, Sarah Pratt, who was Hanbury's niece, had also seen him in Hickman Road at about 2.20pm on October 17th. At the time, Hanbury looked bewildered and seemed unaware of what he had done. Sarah also stated that several years before, Hanbury had once threatened to kill himself. His wife had died about three years before and Hanbury had lived alone ever since, his behaviour becoming rather strange over the years. Hanbury had told Sarah that he was involved with Jessie and after she had told him to stop coming to her house, Hanbury had said to Sarah, "She has thrown me over and I cannot forget her. I cannot sleep at nights, she is calling me all the while."

Hanbury had gone to Hickman Road after he had left his own house, for soon after Sarah had seen him, he was in the garden of 2 Hickman Road where he called out Elijah Watts, one of his oldest friends. Elijah saw the wound and asked Hanbury what he had done but he would only reply, "I've cut it." Elijah told Hanbury to remain where he was while he went for help, but as he ran off down the street, Hanbury followed him and it was then that he had waved down Constable Kirkham.

Evidence of the finding of Jessie's body was given by Frank Hill, who lived at 52 The Leys. He had heard a woman scream and had rushed out to see what the matter was. After speaking briefly to Mrs Harris, Frank had gone in to Jessie Payne's house and found her lying on the kitchen floor in a pool of blood. There was a severe wound in her throat and a razor lay just three inches from the right side of her head. Frank Hill stayed in the house until the police and a doctor arrived.

Constable Kirkham repeated the details of his encounter with Hanbury in Hickman Road. After being cautioned, Hanbury had made a somewhat rambling statement which was now read out in court. According to Constable Kirkham's notebook, Hanbury had said, "I killed Mrs Payne. I know I did some way. I had done one thing. I came out. I could not live without her. You remember what I was telling you about getting out of those children. She told a pack of lies. She has that. I know all about it. Never mind, if I do get hung I shall only get hung once. This job never ought to have happened. She's a wrong one. I have relieved the world of a word of trouble."

The rather curious mention of children was a reference to an accusation Hanbury had made earlier that Jessie Payne had been pregnant with his child and had procured an abortion. This matter had been investigated but no hard evidence could be found and the matter was dropped by the police.

According to Constable Kirkham, Hanbury had made a further statement in the ambulance on the way to the hospital. Then he had said, "Is she dead? I'll never tell lies. I was never a coward in my life. I always like to be straight with one another. I must have been off my bloody head when I went into that house. I don't remember now. I know I did it, but I don't remember what with." Later, at the hospital, Hanbury had spoken again, at one stage saying, "I don't know whether I used a razor or not to kill her. Is her knocked about a bit? From after two o'clock I killed her. I can't remember using razor. I don't know how I have done this."

Constable William Hazell had gone to The Leys with Constable Green. They made an inspection of the premises and saw, in addition to the large wound in Jessie's neck, a puncture wound on the right side of her forehead. Jessie had false teeth and her top dental plate was broken and protruding from her mouth. In addition to the razor found near the body, Constable Hazell also found a hammer, nine inches from Jessie's right hand. A hair on this hammer seemed to match Jessie's colouring. Finally, close to Jessie's head, the officers found a piece of skin and flesh apparently from a right forefinger. When Hanbury was examined later, just such a piece was missing from his finger, an injury he had obviously sustained when he had used the open razor on Jessie.

Dr Edgcume Wentworth Moore had first gone to 2 Hickman Road where Hanbury had been taken by Constable Kirkham. Hanbury had a wound three inches long in his throat and he had lost a lot of blood. After ministering to Hanbury and seeing him into the ambulance, Dr Moore went to 11 The Leys where he certified that Jessie Payne was dead. The following day, Dr Moore performed a post-mortem and noted that in addition to the seven-and-a-half inch wound in her throat, Jessie had sustained a fracture of the left parietal bone and one of the occipital bone. He was able to confirm that the hair on the hammer was indeed one of Jessie's and suggested that the blows from this weapon preceded the cutting of her throat. Referring to Hanbury's behaviour after the attack, Dr Moore said that loss of memory about recent events was a characteristic of certain forms of temporary insanity, as was talking about some dreadful event as if it was of no importance. This testimony was backed up by Dr Chesterfield Cook, who had examined Hanbury on November 28th. He confirmed that Hanbury appeared to be suffering from genuine loss of memory and agreed that this might be an indication of insanity.

Two doctors had intimated that Hanbury may not have been responsible for his actions, so the prosecution called Dr Hamblin Smith, the medical officer of Winson Green prison who said that he had observed Hanbury since his reception and had found no indications of either epilepsy or insanity. He believed that Hanbury had been fully aware of what he was doing when he took the life of Jessie Payne.

Constable Henry Pass was on duty at the infirmary on October 20th and had been told to guard Hanbury and note down anything he might say. Hanbury had started to make a statement, after he had been cautioned, and halfway through, fell asleep. When he awoke, he asked where he had got up to and then continued his narrative, finally having the document read over to him before he signed it. That statement was now read out in court.

Hanbury had begun by making a sort of will, in which he gave his Holy Bible to Elijah Watts and other property to his niece. He went on to detail how he had starting visiting Mrs Payne when he knew her husband, a driver for a transport company, had gone off to work. The first time he had done so had been with James Payne's blessing when his youngest son had taken ill with diphtheria and James had asked Hanbury to look after him while Jessie was out. When she returned, she came upstairs to the child's bedroom, and touched Hanbury intimately. They then made love in her room, for the first time, but the relationship had carried on ever since.

Some ten weeks before Jessie's death, she had seen Hanbury at his brother's house and called over to him, saying that she wanted a word with him. Back at her house, she told him that he had to stop coming to see her and he had come to believe that this was because she was seeing another man. Eventually he saw her with Bert Eardley and told James Payne what was going on and also threatened to tell Eardley's wife.

Moving on to October 17th, Hanbury said that he had his breakfast and spent the morning repairing some of his shoes. Later he heard that the Paynes had agreed to part and had a few drinks in a pub but had no recollection of going to Payne's house. The statement ended, "I cannot remember anything else. I don't know if she cut my throat or I cut hers. That's all I know about it."

Found guilty, Hanbury was asked if he had anything to say. He replied, "Well, your Lordship, I do not know anything about the crime at all. I can't remember nothing at all about it. That is all I have got to say."

On December 15th it was announced that an appeal would be lodged and this was heard on January 16th, 1933. The defence submitted that there was definite evidence of insanity. Several witnesses had described Hanbury as looking like a madman, he had spoken of the crime as if it were an ordinary event and Hanbury had invited several people to go and have a look at what he had done. Lord Hewart, giving the court's judgement, stated that he had admitted to a policeman that he had killed Jessie Payne and the motive for the attack was perfectly plain – that she had ended the relationship with him. The appeal was dismissed.

At 8.00am on Thursday, February 2nd, 1933, Jeremiah Hanbury was hanged at Birmingham by Thomas Pierrepoint, who had two assistants, Robert Wilson and Albert Pierrepoint. There were fewer than 30 people outside the prison gates at the time.

CHAPTER SIXTEEN

THE BURGLAR

CHARLES William Fox was a hard working man who did his best to provide for his family. A metal stripper for Bagnalls of Wednesbury, Fox also acted as a part-time collector for the National Clothing Company and every penny he earned went towards the upkeep of his wife, Gladys, and their eight-month-old son.

In August 1933, 24-year-old Charles Fox was working on the night shift at Bagnalls. As usual on this shift, he finished work in the early hours of Saturday, 26th August, but before relaxing for what was left of his weekend, he spent the latter part of that same day collecting money for the clothing company. It was not until 11.00pm that Charles and Gladys Fox finally retired for the night at their home, 8 Moor Street, West Bromwich.

The room was pitch black when a noise, which sounded like something being smashed downstairs, woke Gladys, who was quite a light sleeper. She shook her husband awake, told him that she had heard something in the kitchen and believed that there was someone downstairs. Charles Fox reached out for the candle near his side of the bed, struck a match and let the tiny flame flicker into life before setting out for the stairs, wearing only his undervest and shirt. As he reached the bedroom door, Gladys glanced at the clock and saw that it was 1.40am.

The stairs led directly down into the kitchen and as Charles slowly walked down them, Gladys took up a position at the top of the stairs and thought that the kitchen window was either open or broken, because a cold draught rushed up the stairs and stung her skin. Even as she called out, "Oh, look, someone's been in!" the same breeze snuffed out the candle plunging the room once more into darkness.

The last thing Gladys saw before the candle blew out was Charles heading towards the open window. By now she had moved to the third step from the bottom of the stairs and as she peered into the darkness, she saw the occasional flash of movement and heard the sounds of some sort of scuffle going on. Fearful as to what was happening, she ran back to the bed-room and called out, "Oh, come back up here."

Gladys was relieved to see her husband coming slowly back up the stairs, but this relief soon turned to horror as he gasped, "He's stabbed me." The truth of this statement was all too evident as Charles finally reached the bedroom and Gladys saw that there was a knife embedded up to the hilt, sticking in her husband's back. Gently she helped her stricken husband to a chair and he tried to reach out and take his wife in his arms but as he tried to speak, he fell to the floor and rolled off to one side, almost finishing up underneath the bed.

Gladys knew she had to get help, so she threw open the bedroom window and screamed for someone to come to her assistance. Then, even though she was fearful that the intruder might still be around, she ran down the stairs, out of the back door and along Lyng Lane where finally she found three men, two of whom were policemen, who escorted her back to her house.

Harold Richard Taylor was a printer who lived in Handsworth, but at around the time Charles Fox was being attacked, Taylor was in Price Street, close to the scene of the crime, when he heard a woman screaming for help. Taylor ran towards the screams and as he dashed across the railway bridge he saw a woman, Gladys Fox, with her head sticking out of her bedroom window, shouting that her husband had been stabbed. From Moor Street, Taylor dashed to High Street where he found two policemen, told them what he had seen, and all three went to the back of Moor Street where they were met by a hysterical Gladys Fox. When Taylor accompanied the officers to the kitchen of Gladys' house, he noticed, once the gas had been lit, that there was a great deal of blood on the floor, especially near the foot of the stairs.

Constable George Westwood was on duty in the High Street, with Constable Connor, when Harold Taylor told them that a woman was shouting that her husband had been stabbed. Gladys Fox was by then standing near her back door, fearful of going back into her house. Constable Westwood noticed that the middle pane of the bottom window of the house had been smashed, and some of the broken glass which lay in the small yard was bloodstained, implying that the intruder had cut himself when gaining entry. The window was quite small, suggesting that the burglar must have been a small man if he had managed to squeeze through it.

Going upstairs, Constable Westwood saw Charles Fox lying on the floor, half under his bed. Leaving Constable Connor and Harold Taylor to take care of Mrs Fox, Westwood went to a nearby telephone box and called out Dr Arnold. By the time Westwood and the doctor had arrived back at Moor Street, Sergeant Gibbs had arrived to take charge.

Sergeant Ernest Edgar Gibbs was on the scene at 2.10am and just ten minutes later, Dr William Bowyer Arnold arrived with Constable Westwood. Dr Arnold certified that Charles Fox was dead and only then did Sergeant Gibbs attempt to remove the knife from Fox's back. It took all the strength Gibbs could muster and after its removal, Dr Arnold made another examination of the body. He noted seven stab wounds in Fox's back.

The police investigation had not been in progress for long when a most curious fact came to light. On the same night that Charles Fox had been stabbed to death by a burglar, two other robberies had taken place close to Moor Street.

Robert Arthur Newton was a butcher who lived at 200 Bromford Lane, West Bromwich, with his wife, Elsie Maud Newton. Elsie had gone to bed at 1.00am on August 27th, leaving her husband to make sure that the premises were secure. Robert followed his wife to bed minutes later, and neither of them heard any noise in the night. Elsie did not rise until 9.45am and from the moment she went downstairs, she could see that something was wrong.

The back door of their house at Bromford Lane had a broken pane of glass which had been 'repaired' by means of a piece of cardboard. Someone had forced this cardboard to one side, opened the back door and had obviously been inside the house. The intruder, whoever he was, had stolen some money from the premises, a total of perhaps £7, but he had also helped himself to some milk and apparently used a needle and thread to repair some part of his clothing. Even cheekier than that, the man had helped himself to a shave using Robert's razor.

The police were called and Detective Constable Albert Smout arrived at the house at noon. He found a biscuit tin had been placed outside the back door of the premises so that the intruder could stand on it in order to reach through the cardboard and unlock the back door. This signified that the man must have been quite small as he needed this aid. Constable Smout took possession of the safety razor, the milk bottle and the needle and thread and returned to the police station.

Winifred Louise Randle was a schoolteacher who lived with her parents at 141 Bromford Lane. On August 26th, Winifred had taken a drive out to the seaside in her father's car, a maroon Jowett, registration EA 4545. At 4.00pm that evening, Winifred had locked the car away in a garage which the family rented, situated with others at the rear of number 170. Miss Randle did not return to the garage until 1.00pm on August 27th, when she found that someone had unscrewed the padlock and stolen the car. Once again it was Constable Smout who attended and Winifred told him that the car was easy to drive but was difficult to start except by using the starting handle.

It was perhaps reasonable to assume that the same man might well be responsible for the break-in at the butcher's shop, the stealing of the motor car and the murder of Charles Fox, since all three crimes had been committed during the early hours of Sunday, August 27th, and within a short distance of each other. For that reason, when a fingerprint was lifted from the milk bottle found at Bromford Lane and identified, the name and description of the man it belonged to were widely circulated in the newspapers.

The details were first published on August 28th and read, 'Stanley Eric Hobday, aged 21 years, height five feet five inches, brown eyes, dark brown hair, sallow complexion, slim build, a native of West Bromwich. His hair is brushed back with oil, he speaks very quietly and has a reserved disposition.'

The following day, August 29th, saw excitement in Cheshire when a man closely resembling Hobday was picked up on a charge of begging. The man was taken to Lymm police station and there was able to prove that he was not Hobday. So similar was he to the wanted man that, at his request, a senior police officer gave him a signed card to the effect that he was not so, just in case some other policeman should pick him up again.

On August 30th, the inquest on Charles Fox opened before

Mr Lyon Clark, but was immediately adjourned until September 30th to allow the police to complete their investigations. They did not have to wait for long.

It was around 7.45am on the morning of August 27th that Thomas Conlon, who worked on Manor Farm at High Legh in Cheshire, was in one of the fields on the Knutsford road when he heard a noise. Turning quickly, Conlon saw a maroon-coloured car turn a somersault on the road and finish the right way up on a grass verge. Conlon saw a man climb out of the car and, apparently unhurt, walk off towards Knutsford a few minutes later.

Shortly after this accident, Thomas Henry Flavell was driving his Riley car along the Knutsford to Warrington road when his attention was caught by a maroon Jowett on the grass verge on the left-hand side of the road. The back of the car was in a hedge and a man stood in front of the car, a map in one hand, his other hand dabbing at what looked like some kind of injury to his mouth.

By 8.00pm, news of this accident had reached Constable Robert Burgess Holland of the Cheshire police. Told that a car had apparently crashed near the Sowton Heath Smithy, Constable Holland went to the scene and noted the number of the car: EA 4545. A local garage proprietor, William Arthur Weston, was contacted and he towed the vehicle to his premises at 23 High Legh Road, Lymm.

When the car number was checked with the registration authorities, it became clear that the search for Hobday would have to move to Cheshire. In fact, he was to remain free for a few more days. It was not until 7.30am on August 30th, that Walter Barbour, a cowman from Rockcliffe near Carlisle, saw a man walking towards him as he took some cows to a nearby field. The man behaved suspiciously, putting a handkerchief in front of his face and turning away so that Barbour would not get a clear view of him. The cowman thought this so curious that when he got back to the farmhouse, he mentioned the incident to his employer, Mr James Watt, who in turn thought it strange enough to report to the police.

It was 8.40am by the time Constable William John Elder received the message from Mr Watt and he jumped into his car and began a search of the immediate area. At 9.10am, as he drove down a lane leading to Rockcliffe Marsh, Elder saw a young man who fitted the general description given by Walter Barbour. Elder stopped the man and asked him where he had come from, whereupon he replied, "West Bromwich." Asked for his name, the young man did not hesitate before answering, "Hobday," and when asked to confirm that he was Stanley Eric Hobday, he agreed. Hobday was immediately taken into custody, driven to Carlisle, and the Birmingham police were contacted.

Superintendent Charles Albert Clarke travelled from Birmingham to Carlisle that same day. On the way he stopped at High Legh, made an initial examination of the maroon Jowett car, and took possession of the vehicle's starting handle in the hope that this would link Hobday to its theft. Going on to Carlisle, Superintendent Clarke collected Hobday's clothing but it was not until the next day, August 31st, by which time the prisoner had been taken back to the Midlands, that he cautioned Hobday and charged him with the only crime to which he could so far be directly linked, the burglary at the butcher's shop in Bromford Lane. Hobday replied, "I'll say nothing yet."

Hobday appeared before the magistrate, Mr R. Beetlestone, in the police charge room at West Bromwich. He was remanded to Monday, September 4th, having been represented by Mr A.A. Millichip.

By September 3rd, the Jowett car had been transported to West Bromwich and here it was examined again, this time much more carefully, by Superintendent Clarke. Behind the back seat he found a small suitcase which could not have been seen until the seat was removed. At 11.45am he showed this case to Hobday, who admitted that it belonged to him, and when told that it had been found in a car reported as stolen, his only comment was, "That's funny." This, of course, had linked him to the theft of the car and he was charged with this second offence at 3.45pm.

Hobday again appeared before the magistrate, in the charge room, on September 4th when he was remanded until September 7th after a hearing lasting just three minutes. A third appearance in the charge room followed, by which time Hobday was also charged with murder. There were then two actual court appearances: one on September 14th and the final one commencing on September 26th. Here the evidence on the charges was heard over three days, the murder charge taking up all of the first two days and the two burglary charges being heard on the final day. The prosecution evidence was outlined by Mr Hedley J. Parham and at the end of the third day, Hobday was committed for trial on all the charges.

The hearing of the case of the Crown versus Stanley Hobday opened at Stafford before Mr Justice Talbot on November 14th, 1933. Over the three days of the trial, the prosecution was led by Mr W.G. Earengey and Mr Ralph Thomas. Hobday was defended by Sir Reginald Coventry and Mr A.J. Long and, as is customary, only the most serious charge, that of the murder of Charles Fox, was proceeded with.

One of the most crucial tasks for the police was to link Hobday to the knife which killed Charles Fox. The weapon bore a rather distinctive handle with coloured metal bands, was stamped, 'J. Clarke and Sons, Sheffield' and was a type known as 'Wasp'. Mr James Spinks, the manager of Clarkes, stated that this had been a fairly experimental line and only 20 such knives had been made. With such a small number, it was a simple matter to detail the shops to which the knives had been sent and Mr Spinks was able to say that six had gone to E.R. Routledge & Sons of Worcester Street, Birmingham; eight had been sold to Albert Brodie of High Street, North Finchley, London; and the last six had gone to Alfred Martin of High Street, Lewisham, also in London. Although Clarkes still made Wasp knives, they were now stamped 'Rogers, Sheffield' — only these 20 had been stamped with the Clarke's name.

Mr Spinks had also told the court that some knives, like the one produced in court, had zinc bands around the handle while others had brass bands. It was impossible to say how many of each type there were in that batch of 20, but usually the company sent out half zinc and half brass, so it was logical to assume that there were only ten knives with the zinc bands.

Two of the shops mentioned were in London but even so, those establishments were checked. One shop had sold none of the knives and the other had sold only a couple. It was, however, more reasonable to suggest that if Hobday had owned such a knife, he would have obtained it from the shop in Birmingham.

Ernest Rowland Routledge ran his shop from 12 Worcester Street and having examined his stock book, was able to say that he had purchased six 'Wasp' knives on March 23rd, 1933. Since he now had two knives left, one with zinc bands and one with brass, he must have sold four. Mr Routledge was unable to identify Hobday as the purchaser of any of those knives. There were, however, other witnesses who were able to say that they had seen Hobday with such a knife and since there were now, at most, just a maximum of four zinc-banded knives in Birmingham, that would be a most telling piece of evidence.

Gilbert Bertram Pursell was a 14-year-old schoolboy who occasionally camped out with some friends at an area known as Warstone Fields, West Bromwich. On August 20th, Pursell was at Warstone when a young man came and pitched his tent, a

Falcon, close by. At one stage the man even asked Pursell and his friends to keep an eye on his tent while he went to the shop. Later that day, Pursell saw the man cooking himself some bacon and tomatoes on a small oil stove and he used a knife to turn over the rashers in the pan. Pursell admired the knife and asked to take a look at it. The knife was exactly the same as the one produced in court and on September 2nd, Pursell had identified Hobday as the man he had seen on Warstone Fields.

Reginald Barlow was one of the friends camping with Pursell and he confirmed this testimony. He, too, had picked out Hobday at the identification parade on September 2nd, but had also picked out a knife from a collection given to him by the police. That knife was identical to the one used to kill Charles Fox.

Another camper had been James William Tinsley, but he pitched his tent at Warstone only on August 26th. He, too, saw a young man with a distinctive knife in a sheath on his belt. That same afternoon, the farmer who owned the field came and told all the campers to clear off. The young man with the knife packed his tent up into a small suitcase and left the field at 8.30pm. At the police station, James Tinsley had picked out Hobday as the man he had seen.

At 3.45pm on August 26th, Gladys Herbert and some of her girlfriends had visited Warstone Pool, close by the place where there were a number of tents pitched. Gladys had also visited the pool the previous Sunday and on both occasions she saw a young man who wore a knife in a sheath on his belt. She positively identified that man as Hobday and when the farmer came and told everyone to clear off, she heard Hobday remark, "I'm going home tonight in any case. Even if the farmer hadn't come, I was going home tonight." Gladys saw Hobday stuff his tent into an old battered suitcase and identified the one found in the Jowett car as the same suitcase. When that case had been opened by the police, it had contained, among other things, a

Falcon tent of the same type described by all these witnesses.

Two other witnesses had seen a young man either on Warstone Fields, or nearby, on August 26th, and both later identified Hobday as that man. Kitty Tinsley was another visitor to Warstone Pool and she saw Hobday, with his sheath knife, at about 3.30pm. Thomas Henry Westwood was sitting outside the Jubilee Colliery offices when a number of people came off Warstone Fields, having been told to leave by the farmer who owned the land. One of those who left was Hobday, and Westwood saw him again some time later, Hobday having by then pitched his Falcon tent in Hay Pit Wood.

As if all this testimony were not enough to link Hobday to the murder weapon, the prosecution also called witnesses to show that a sheath the police had found was also connected to the crime. Once the assailant had stabbed Charles Fox, he had no further use for the sheath and might well have thrown it away. A leather sheath had been found by seven-year-old Kenneth Godfrey Moreton, who swapped it with a friend for some toy boats. This friend, Glyn Howard Richards, had shown the sheath to his father, Gruffydd Owain Richards who, once he had read reports of the crime in his newspaper, took the sheath along to the police. This sheath had been examined by Luther Frederick Milner of Sheffield, who confirmed that his company had manufactured it and that it was a type made exclusively for Clarke & Sons.

Other evidence was now given to link Hobday to the house at Moor Street. It had been suggested that whoever broke the pane of glass to gain access to the house had cut himself in doing so. When Hobday had been picked up, he had complained of a sore arm and a medical examination, by Dr Archibald Hardy Macgregor McMullen, the police surgeon, had revealed a triangular-shaped wound on Hobday's left elbow, which might have been caused by broken glass. There was a cut in Hobday's coat which corresponded with this wound and the cut had been patched with cotton. That patch had been microscopically examined by the public analyst, William Thomas Rigby. He reported that the thread used matched that found in the needle at the butcher's shop at Bromford Lane.

Outside the house, in a small patch of soil, Superintendent Clarke had noticed a number of footprints, and plaster casts of these were taken by Detective Constable Robotham. These casts had now been compared with Hobday's shoes and appeared to match exactly.

Although no real evidence was called on the two burglary charges, some evidence did demonstrate that Hobday had been responsible for these crimes. Detective Inspector Frederick Cherrill of the Scotland Yard fingerprint bureau said that he had compared Hobday's prints with the ones found on the milk bottle at Bromford Lane. He had also examined the starting handle of the Jowett car and had also found a match there.

When Hobday had arrived back at West Bromwich he had mentioned to Detective Constable Smout that he could do with a shave. Hobday had been provided with soap, water and a safety razor and when he had finished, the hairs were sent for analysis. William Rigby was therefore also able to say that he had found two types of hair on the safety razor used at Bromford Lane. One had been very fair and matched the colouring of the shop owner Robert Newton. The other type was dark and matched that found on the razor sent to him by Constable Smout.

The time came for medical testimony to be given on the wounds suffered by Charles William Fox. Dr Albert William Wood was the police surgeon who performed the post-mortem. He described Fox as being just under six feet tall and said that the man had sustained seven stab wounds to his back. The upper four of these wounds were all the same size and were three-quarters of an inch from point to point. All would have caused extensive bleeding but none of these were serious enough to cause death. The fifth wound was the largest and lowest and the path of the blade had caused a puncture of the left lung which had consequently collapsed. This was the wound which led directly to Fox's death and was the one in which the knife had still been embedded when he died.

In case the defence should suggest that Hobday was not responsible for his actions in some way, one of the final witnesses for the prosecution was Dr John Humphrey, the medical officer at Birmingham prison. He testified that he had observed Hobday since September 7th and there had been no signs of insanity. Hobday was actually of above-average intelligence, although he had apparently been undisciplined and anti-social from a very early age.

The defence called no witnesses and in his summing up, Sir Reginald Coventry suggested that the Crown had simply not proved its case. The word 'Foreign' appeared clearly on Hobday's shoes and yet no such word could be seen in the plaster casts of the footprints found at the scene of the crime. The cotton used to darn Hobday's sleeve was a common type and there was no conclusive proof that this had been obtained from the butcher's shop in Bromford Lane. Even if Hobday had committed this burglary and the theft of the car, then his guilt in those crimes proved his innocence in the murder case since it was inconceivable that a man who had just killed someone should coolly go off and commit two burglaries, in one of which he shaved himself. Finally, Hobday was a small man and he did not have the strength to drive the knife into Charles Fox's back as his killer had done.

The jury took just half an hour to decide that the evidence, circumstantial though it was, pointed to Hobday's guilt and he was sentenced to death. An appeal was heard on December 11th before the Lord Chief Justice, Lord Hewart and Justices Avory and Branson. Here the defence argued that allegations that Hobday had committed other burglaries on the same night should not have been submitted to the jury. Further, at the trial it was suggested that Hobday had washed himself to remove traces of the conflict with Fox when it was plain that there had been no real struggle. Fox's killer, whoever he was, had attacked him from behind and it had been said that there would be little, if any, blood, on the killer.

Giving his judgement, the Lord Chief Justice said that the trial judge, Mr Justice Talbot, had been careful in his summing up to instruct the jury not to be prejudiced in any way by hearing about other possible crimes and the weight of evidence was such that they had rightly convicted Hobday of the crime. There was nothing in the appeal and the sentence of death would stand.

By 8.00am on Thursday, December 28th, 1933, a crowd of about 50 people gathered outside Birmingham prison as Stanley Eric Hobday, still only 21 years old, was hanged by Thomas Pierrepoint and his nephew, Albert. It was the ninth, and last execution in an English prison that year.

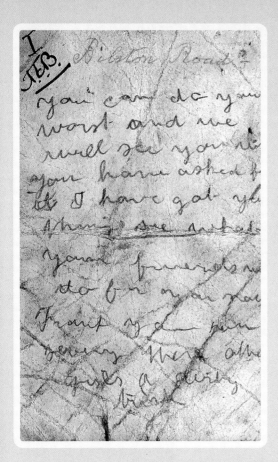

The postcard which Frank Greening sent to Elizabeth Ellen Hearne whilst she was in the Queen's Head pub. See Chapter 5. (Public Record Office).

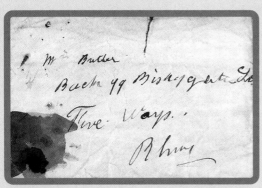

The letter *(above and right)* found on William Allen Butler and addressed to his mother, explaining why he had just committed murder. See Chapter 6. (Public Record Office).

Louis Van de Kerkhove who killed his lover in a hotel room. This picture is taken from his identity card. See Chapter 7. (Public Record Office).

The handwritten statement reads:

> ...off and almost cut the left leg off. then I dragged the body to a sewer culvert near by. ... took the head and clothes to the Hednesford Gasometer. reached home about 11.15 p.m. On Thursday afternoon I went to work and was met on the pit top by two of the Hednesford Police who asked me if I knew where my wife had gone, as she had not returned home since going out to meet me. after I left them I went over the common towards home. but at the corner on the Pott Rd I turned towards Hightown till I got opposite 3° pit turned on to the railway and walked along the line through Hednesford Station then turned towards the Mines Rescue Station over the commons to the place where I left the body. dragged it out and carried it to the Gasometer where I took the head. and forcing a two inch gas pipe down inside the body I lowered into the water remarking "Now you can go to Monty if you like." I left the place. reach home about 2.30 a.m.
>
> I swear this statement is true.
>
> Signed Henry Thomas Gaskin.
>
> 23 February 1919.
>
> Witness.
> J. Morrey.
> Act'g Supt
> 25 Feby 1919
>
> This is the Document marked "10" referred to in the examination of John Morrey.
> S. W. Morgan. Coroner.

The last page of Henry Thomas Gaskin's chilling statement, confessing to the brutal murder of his wife. See Chapter 8. (Public Record Office).

How the *Birmingham Mail* reported the case of Djang Djing Sung who battered one of his countrymen to death in order to steal his savings. See Chapter 9. (Birmingham Mail).

Newspaper clippings:

BOARD ... RECALLED.

AN E... IC CRICKETER.

...death took place yesterday, following an operation of Mr. William Ansell, who at one time played a prominent part in Birmingham life, though his later years were absorbed in business and he was not, as formerly, very much in the public eye. In his earlier days he was known as a successful and capable elementary schoolmaster and an enthusiastic participator and organiser in the national game of cricket. He was the leading spirit in the foundation of the Warwickshire County Cricket Club, and its inception was in a large measure due to his energy, zeal, organising ability and abounding enthusiasm.

The outstanding event in his career, however, was his sensational election to the Birmingham School Board in November, 1894. A few weeks before, he had retired from his position as headmaster of Bristol Street School and had purchased a manufacturing business at Aston. This left him free to seek election to the Board, from the services of which he had so recently

[Photo: Whitlock]
MR. W. ANSELL.

resigned. Coming out as the teachers' champion and an independent candidate, he achieved a remarkable success, occupying a commanding position at the head of the poll. He had an immense advantage over the other candidates by reason of the method of voting adopted in School Board elections. Mr Ansell's aggregate was almost wholly made up of plumpers of fifteen, whereas the supporters of the Liberal Eight and the Church party divided their votes with a view to securing the return of the whole of their candidates. Mr. Ansell's victory was a sweeping one, ... possessed enough votes and ...

SUNG ON TRIAL FOR M... OF MR. WU.

PLEA OF "NOT GUILTY."

REMARKABLE EVIDENCE AT THE WORCESTERSHIRE ASSIZES.

Before Mr. Justice Rowlatt, at Worcestershire Assizes, to-day, the trial took place of the Chinaman, Djang Djin Sung, who has been committed from the West London Court on a charge of murdering a fellow-countryman named Zee Ming Wu, in Warley Woods, near Birmingham, on June 23.

The prosecution alleged that Sung decoyed Wu to a lonely part of the park, and that after rendering him unconscious with a hammer, inflicted a number of stabs on the head and body with a glazing tool. It was suggested that robbery was the motive of the crime.

Public interest in the trial was considerable, and there was a packed court when Sung took his place in the dock.

Mr. A. Powell, K.C., and Mr. A. E. N. Jordan were for the prosecution, and the Hon. R. Coventry for the prisoner. The lack of knowledge of English by the prisoner led to interpretations by a Chinaman, who, in response to the Clerk, stated "he had no guilt." The accused, diminutive and dejected, told the interpreter that he could not understand English. He sat with fol...

...AL ELECT...

CONTESTS IN 27 BIRM... PROBABLE.

SIXTEEN LABOUR CANDIDA...

Increased activity is being shown in political and labour circles in Birmingham with regard to the municipal elections, but so far as the general public is concerned there is an extraordinary amount of apathy. In some cases great difficulty has been experienced by the political parties in securing nominations as candidates. Thirty councillors will retire at the end of the present month, and it is anticipated there will be contests in 27 of the wards.

The councillors who are not coming before the voters again are: Messrs. S. Issett (Acock's Green), J. E. Williams (Aston), E. T. Everton (Balsall Heath), A. J. Kelley (King's Norton), A. W. Auster (Ladywood), H. E. Goodby (Lozells), D. T. Timins (Northfield), J. W. Kneeshaw (Rotton Park), A. H. Close (Selly Oak), and A. W. Heath (Sparkhill).

It would appear probable that in the Edgbaston Ward Miss Clara Martineau (Unionist) will not be opposed, and at the moment there is no opposition to the retiring representative, Mr. Gibbs, in the Moseley Ward, and Mr. Poole, in St. Paul's Ward. At Northfield Mr. A. J. Leeson has been approved as the Unionist candidate, in succession to Mr. Timins. Mr. Leeson has been already a member of the City Council as a representative for Harborne. In Rotton Park Ward Mr. Kneeshaw, who is now a travelling emissary for the Independent Labour party, does not seek re-election, and there will be contests there between Mr. C. Chance and Mr. Simmonds, the Labour nominee. Mr. Chance is a son of the late Mr. Alexander Chance, and has an active association with important industrial undertakings.

In the Duddeston Ward, which was formerly represented by Mr. Yoxall, who becomes the Unionist nominee at King's Norton, vice Mr. Kelley, resigned, Mr. J. F. White will be brought out as a Unionist candidate, and here a three-cornered fight is in prospect, as the Independent party intends to nominate Mr. N. Dean, and the Labour party Mr. Sawyer. The Unionists are apparently content to lose a seat in Acock's Green, where Mr. Issett, the retiring representative, does not seek re-election, and Mr. S. J. ... is to be brought forward as an Independent candidate, whilst Mr. F. Atkin is the Labour nominee. ...Mr. G. Perry, who was returned as an independent ... ...himself ... he Lab... party. ...

N... below

THIS ... re... introducing... wear gar...

The id... at the be...

They ... it into e... of the ... were ...

The letter written by Sung from Brixton prison, explaining to the magistrates that he was not guilty of murder. See Chapter 9. (Public Record Office).

> Brixton Prison
> 17. 7. 17.
>
> Your Worship,
> I am very sorry that this has occurred. to tell the truth — he Ding Jig was the man who killed Lee Ming Wu.
> I never touched him at all, I am married & have one child 8 years old in China, I am also a business man & have never had any trouble before, this is the first time. he Ding Jig called me to go for a walk in the Park,
> I cannot understand English very much. Will you please be very lenient with me, as I want to go back to my wife & business & my mother who is very good to me.
>
> Djang Djin Sang
>
> The Justices
> West London Police Court.
>
> P.S. Last Saturday I quite forgot to say that he Ding Jig was the man who did the murder, am very sorry but I could not understand what was being said. I want to see him again
>
> P.P.S.

How the *Midland Counties Express* reported the case of Samuel Westwood and his victim, Lydia Westwood. See Chapter 10. (Midland Counties Express).

ALLEGED MURDER ... OUNG WIFE

EYE-WITNESS'S STORY AT THE INQUEST.

The "wake festival" at Willenhall this year, which is being celebrated as usual with a fair on the grounds in Walsall-street, was marred on Saturday night by the alleged murder of a young married woman.

The deceased is Lydia Westwood, aged 24 years, who on the Saturday before August Bank Holiday, just six weeks ago, married a keysmith named Samuel Westwood, aged 26, who lived at 25, Bentley-lane, Short Heath, with his parents. Like many another couple starting in life, they were faced with the shortage of houses, but the young husband induced his wife to share his parents' home, and she remained there until Thursday last, the 9th inst.

Differences had arisen, and the young woman sent for her mother, with whom she returned to her former home. Her parents are named William and Alice

going home with him." Her daughter sadly wanted to speak to her husband, however, as she complained that "they had been scandalising her, and she wanted to have it out."

PRISONER SMILES BEFORE THE MAGISTRATES.

The prisoner, Westwood, was brought before Messrs. S. Lister and J. R. Mattox at Willenhall Police Court on Monday morning, on a charge of murdering his wife by stabbing her with a knife.

He entered the Court smiling, and afterwards turned and scrutinised the large number of persons sitting in the gallery. Observing someone he knew he nodded very familiarly in that direction. He was respectably attired in a grey suit, but wore no collar, his shirt being open at the front. He is of light build, with light wavy hair brushed back from his forehead, and is clean shaven.

Superintendent Tucker informed the Bench that he only intended offering formal evidence to justify a remand.

Sergeant Evans stated that at a few minutes

Police-constable ... Saturday night ... was in the police station when prisoner ... and asked if he was a police ... ness replied in the affirmative ... and asked what he wanted. He said, "I have just stabbed my wife. She is down the road, and I think I have killed her." Witness took the man into the charge-room to Sergeant Evans, and, leaving him in the custody of Police-constable Wild, went with the sergeant to the junction of Walsall-street and Church-street, where they found the woman lying in the road bleeding freely from a wound on the right side of the throat. He was handed a knife by Mrs. Vaughan, and found that the blade was wet with blood.

PRISONER'S ADMISSIONS.

Police-constable Wild stated that when he searched prisoner he found in his possession a piece of newspaper containing a white powder, and prisoner said, "I have taken poison." Witness asked "What poison?" and prisoner pointed to the packet found on him. Witness asked what it was, and he said, "It is some stuff I have had from where I have worked. It is used for hardening tools." The doctor subsequently administered an emetic.

At 9.10 the same night prisoner said, "She left me last Thursday. I intended to do this the first time I saw them. I had had two half-pints of beer, or I could not have done it. A little time later he said, "They thought I was frightened to do it, but I have showed 'em," while still later he remarked, "she was awkward, and I was awkward, and two awkward people don't get on together. We should have been all right if they had left us alone."

PRISONER'S WISH.

At this stage prisoner expressed a wish to see "Lydia," and showed some signs of emotion.

The Coroner: You mean you would like to see her before she is buried?—Yes, sir.

Sergeant Evans repeated the evidence given at the police court, and added that when Westwood was brought into the charge-room he appeared pale and excited, but quite sober.

MEDICAL EVIDENCE.

Dr. Henry J. Dean said the woman was dead when he arrived at the police station, the cause of death being due to hemorrhage from a wound in the right side of the throat. Witness was told that Westwood had taken poison, and he went into the charge-room to him. The doctor said, "What have you done?" and he said, "I have taken poison." Witness asked why, and he said, "Because I have killed my wife." Witness said the man did not appear to be suffering from poison, but he gave him an emetic and he vomited. He was not under the influence of drink. The wound in the woman's throat was about 1½in. in depth by the side of the windpipe, and in the region of the big blood vessels.

In reply to the foreman of the jury as to whether the prisoner was collected and realised what he was saying and doing, witness said he was quite calm, and answered his questions most collectedly.

The Coroner summed up, and said any question of the state of the man's mind would be inquired into hereafter.

The jury retired, and upon their return, Mr. Cartwright (the foreman) intimated that they were agreed that the deceased was murdered by her husband (Samuel Westwood), and a verdict of "Wilful murder" was returned against him.

The Coroner thereupon committed him for ...

FROM ANY MANFIELD BRANCH—
BIRMINGHAM, NOTTINGHAM, DERBY, SHEFFIELD, and throughout LONDON and United Kingdom.

IF NOT NEAR A BRANCH, send P.O. for sample pair, or write for descriptive list to Postal Department, 38 & 60, ST. PAUL'S CHURCHYARD, LONDON, E.C.

CLARK'S

with its delightful ... provement on the old style ... ets, 1/- tins and small packets.

...AM CUSTARD (pure cane ... where the sugar difficulty is ... ets 1/9, small packets 3d.

CHILDREN LOVE IT!

...M CUSTARD

IN SECRET.

...P OF ... ...AMPTON.

TRADES COUNCIL DISCUSS BEATTIES IN PRIVATE.

Wolverhampton Trades ... ... day ... ning discussed ... ...ent (Coo...

The canal where James Joseph Power accosted Charles Broomhead and Olive Gordon Turner. See Chapter 13. (Public Record Office).

The bridge where Power seized his victim. See Chapter 13. (Public Record Office).

Olive Gordon Turner. Was her life taken by James Power, or was he framed by the police as he claimed? See Chapter 13. (Public Record Office).

The entrance to the Soho branch of the canal. See Chapter 13. (Public Record Office).

The Soho branch, where Olive Turner's body was recovered. In the centre of the picture, on the left bank of the canal, can be seen the doorway where her belongings were found. See Chapter 13. (Public Record Office).

The doorway where
Olive's belongings were
discovered. These were
removed by Charles
Broomhead and
subsequently replaced by
the police so that this
picture could be taken.
See Chapter 13. (Public
Record Office).

Mr Justice Avory
who sentenced
Butler to death and
was involved in the
unsuccessful
appeals of Greening,
Betts and Hobday.
(Popperfoto)

CHAPTER SEVENTEEN

THE WALKING STICK

JANE Turner had been living apart from her husband, Arthur, since June, 1939. She was a woman who was rather too fond of drink, and had known John Franklin, who lived at 44 Holmes Buildings on Farmer Street, for four or five years. In due course, he took pity on her and offered her a home with him in return for her acting as his housekeeper. Unfortunately, Jane's intemperate habits did not improve in her new residence and John Franklin warned her about her behaviour. So it was that when she returned home drunk at 10.30pm on the night of Thursday, March 27th, 1941, Franklin refused her admittance. Reluctantly, she walked off into the night but by 6.20am the next morning, she was back at Farmer Street trying to gain access to John Franklin's home. When she was again refused permission to go inside, she tried to force her way past Franklin but he managed to keep her out, gave her what few possessions she had, and told her to be on her way. Ten minutes later, John Franklin left for work. He did not see Jane Turner again.

Percy James Puddepha was the licensee of the Bell licensed house on Bristol Street, Birmingham. At 9.00pm on March 28th, one of his regular customers, 45-year-old Eli Richards, came into the bar in the company of an elderly woman. For a time, Richards and his friend were quiet enough and enjoyed a glass of mild ale together but just after 'time' had been called, Richards was involved in an argument with a soldier. Richards' language became rather choice and he was asked to leave the Bell.

That argument with the soldier had been seen by two other men who knew Eli Richards well. The first of these was Herbert Pedley who was the foreman of the ICI Metals factory at Selly Oak, the same establishment where Richards worked. Pedley had first gone into the Bell at 8.50pm on March 28th and saw Richards and the woman come in together at 9.00pm. Richards, who walked with a pronounced limp, had his walking stick with him and as he sat down, Pedley bought both Richards and his companion a drink.

After the argument, Pedley saw Richards and the woman leave together and thought that although both were showing the effects of drink, neither could actually be described as drunk. Pedley left the Bell soon afterwards and outside, saw Richards, still with the woman, standing at the tram stop at the corner of Bromsgrove Street. After a few minutes, the number 71 tram pulled up and Pedley saw Richards and the woman get on together, before boarding the same car himself. As the tram made its way through the streets, Pedley fell into conversation with Richards, who told him that he was taking the woman to Cotteridge, to stay with one of his relatives. It was around 10.45pm when Richards and his lady friend got off the tram at Pebble Mill Road. As he climbed down from the car, Richards bade Pedley goodnight and said he would see him in the morning at work. Pedley reminded him to be there by 6.00am.

The other witness to the pub argument had been James Gaffney, a labourer of 288 Great Colmore Street. After Richards had been told to leave the pub, he had asked Gaffney to buy him two bottles of ale, knowing, of course, that Percy Puddepha would refuse to serve him personally. Gaffney purchased two bottles of Amber Ale for is 8d and handed them over to Richards as he left the Bell.

When Richards and the woman alighted from the number 71 tram at Pebble Mill Road, a transport inspector, William Edwin Ward, got off with them. Ward saw Richards limp towards the number 36 tram and heard him shout, "Wait for an old soldier." Ward climbed on to the same tram, noting that it was then 10.47pm. Inspector Ward also saw Richards and the woman leave the number 36 at Kitchener Road, at 10.51pm and at the time, they seemed to be getting on quite well.

Robert Francis Farman and Frank Walsingham were two members of the Home Guard and were on duty at the Bourneville chocolate works from 10.30pm on March 28th. At around 11.30pm the two men heard a woman's scream, coming from the direction of the public baths, so they made their way down Bourneville Lane to see what the problem was. Between the baths and a lodge, Farman and Walsingham saw a man and a woman standing together and heard a distinct moan come from their vicinity. Farman noticed that the man was carrying a stick and as Frank Walsingham asked what was going on, the man replied, "It's all right chum, we've had a drink." He went on to explain that he and the woman had been put off the tram at the wrong stop and were looking for Linden Road, where he could get a night's lodgings with a relative. The woman, though, did not seem too keen to go with her companion and said, "If you are taking me anywhere you are taking me back to Small Heath where you've dragged me from." After some consideration, though, she changed her mind and told Farman that she would go to Linden Road if he came with them. Farman and Walsingham then escorted the couple to the corner of Franklin Road and Maryvale Road. There the couple walked off together towards Linden Road, after being admonished by Farman not to argue anymore. It was then around 11.40pm.

At 4.45am the next morning, Kenneth Hewitt, a chocolate moulder, was on his way to the Bourneville works and passed down Franklin Road. There on the left-hand footpath, he saw the body of an elderly woman, her clothing disarranged. Hewitt ran to Stirchley police station and reported what he had found. Ten minutes later, Inspector James Dunnicliffe was at the scene. He saw that the woman had received injuries to her face and head, and appeared to be already dead. The woman's face was covered in blood and she was bare from the naval to the tops of her stockings. Between the woman's legs, by her left heel, was a broken bottle neck, with the cork still in place and off to one side was a walking stick. The woman's false teeth lay in the gutter nearby and just inside the park railings to the side of the body, Inspector Dunnicliffe found the bottom part of the broken bottle, which was clearly labelled 'Amber Ale". Just a few yards away from this bottle were a pair of women's knickers, presumably torn from the body now lying on the pavement.

At 5.50am, Detective Inspector George Brown arrived at Franklin Road. A leatherette shopping bag had also been found, close by the woman's head, and this contained personal items, including an identity card, which showed that the dead woman was 64-year-old Jane Turner. That identity was confirmed when Jane's daughter, May Moseley, saw the body at the mortuary.

Police enquiries soon found two more witnesses who might help to pinpoint the time that Jane Turner had died. Albert Edward Vaughan lived at 50 Franklin Road and he told officers that he had gone to bed at 10.50pm on March 28th. Just after midnight, he heard a scream coming from the direction of the allotments and just 30 seconds later, this was followed by a much fainter scream. This had also been heard by William James Witts, who lived at number 120, although he put the time at just before midnight. Mr Witts had not looked at his watch but put the time by the fact that soon afterwards he heard a train pass in the distance and knew this was an express which he always heard at this time. Neither Albert Vaughan nor William Witts had thought to investigate these screams.

It was not long before the two Home Guard men came forward. Their mention of a tram led to Mr Ward speaking to the police and eventually officers were able to trace Jane Turner's movements back to the Bell public house, which in turn gave them the name of Eli Richards. At 12.45pm on March 30th, Inspector Brown and Detective Sergeant Neil Campbell visited Richards at his lodgings at 106 Castle Road.

Richards was told that a body had been found and that he fitted the description of a man seen with the woman shortly before she died. He replied, "I know nothing about it," and denied being the man who had been drinking with her in the Bell. Inspector Brown saw that Richards had some scratches on his face and asked how he had received these. Richards claimed that he had fallen off a tram the previous night, and had lost his stick at the same time. Despite these denials, he was taken to the police station to attend an identification parade.

In the police car Richards changed his story and admitted that he had indeed been in the Bell on the Friday night, with a woman. He went on to say that they were later seen by two Home Guard men, who took them to Franklin Road. There the woman started to argue with him, so he walked off and left her there. At this point, Inspector Brown cautioned Richards and advised him to say no more until he reached the police station where he could make a full written statement if he wished.

Once they had arrived at Newton Street, Richards did indeed make a written statement. In that document, he detailed his early life. He had been married and divorced and said that he had served in the Great War from 1915 until 1918 but had injured his leg in May 1940 after he had re-enlisted and been sent to France. After returning to England, he had been admitted to Alderhey Hospital in Liverpool and had used a stick ever since.

Coming out of hospital at Christmas 1940, Richards had gone to live with his brother, David, before moving to his present lodgings. The statement continued, 'I have been working at the ICI Selly Oak about six weeks. I went to work at 6.00am last Friday morning and I finished at 2pm.

'I went straight home and had my dinner. I went out between five and six and I went down town to see a man about some overalls …I went round to the long bar, by the Market. I stopped there. I had some ale there and I didn't come out of there before nine, and coming into Bromsgrove Street I met this lady. She asked me if I would pay for a drink for her, and then I went with her into the corner public where the buses run down for Stretford Road. She had a stout and I had a glass of ale.

'She then asked me to go down Ashted Row and I went with her and we had a drink in a pub there. We came back up Bromsgrove Street and we went into the Bell at the corner of Great Colmore Street, and we had a drink there. I give *(sic)* a soldier the money to get me two Amber Ales there and I brought them away in my pockets. We come out of the Bell and got on the tram. I give the woman the two bottles of ale and she put them into her bag. We got off the tram at the corner of Pebble Mill Road and Bristol Road and we walked to the bottom of Pebble Mill Road and got on the tram for Cotteridge. We wanted to go to the top of the hill at the Cotteridge, but they put us off the tram at the British Oak. We went straight up the Cotteridge Road and we went from there to Bourneville Lane. She started arguing the point in Bourneville Lane and two Home Guard men came up to us, and I told them we wanted to go to Linden

Road and they walked us to Franklin Road and said, "Go straight up Franklin Road and it will take you into Linden Road." The two Home Guard men left us on the corner and they went back. Me and the woman walked along Franklin Road. She wanted a drink and I told her to get one of the bottles of ale out of her bag. She got one of the bottles of ale out of her bag and drunk (sic) it. She got the stopper off the bottle by putting it on the top of the railings. I had a drink out of the bottle after her, and I emptied it. There was another bottle left in her bag. She started to argue with me again and I said, "Are you coming with me or going back?" and I turned to walk away, and she said 'Ain't you going to leave me a drink?' So I give her half a crown and I walked away. When I left her she said, "I am going back into the town." I never saw her after that.'

Richards went on to say that from Franklin Road he had walked to his brother's house at 215 Linden Road, but had been unable to rouse anyone in the house so slept in his bomb shelter until the morning. At 6.00am the next morning, he awoke, went home to his lodgings and went to bed.

Referring to the scratches on his face, Richards repeated that he had fallen against a hedge when he got off a tram in Bourneville Lane and had lost his stick in the gutter at the same time. He went on to describe his stick as a rosewood one from Australia and would recognise it again as he had sawn a short piece off it so that it was the right length for him.

After this statement had been made, Richards was searched and Inspector Brown found a pocket handkerchief, covered in blood. This was explained as coming from the injury when Richards fell into the hedge, and had to wipe some blood from his forehead. Richards' lodgings were visited by police officers and they found a shirt and a pair of underpants which had recently been washed. More important, small pieces of glass were still adhering to the underpants and it appeared that these fragments might have come from the broken beer bottle found near Jane Turner's body. All this was more than enough for Inspector Brown. Richards was charged with murder.

On March 31st, Richards made his first appearance before the Birmingham stipendiary magistrate where the prosecution evidence was detailed by Mr M.P. Pugh. Richards was represented by Mr Arthur Hall Wright who made no objection to a remand until April 8th. On that date, all the evidence having been heard, Richards was sent for trial at the next Birmingham assizes.

That trial took place before Mr Justice Stable and a jury of ten men and two women. The proceedings opened on July 21st and during the two-day hearing, Richards was defended by Mr Richard O'Sullivan and Mr A.E. James. The case for the Crown was led by Mr St John Field, who was assisted by Mr T. Norman Winning.

Horace William Jackson lived at 106 Castle Road on the Weoley Castle Estate and was distantly related by marriage to Richards. He confirmed that Richards had come to live with him at the end of February, 1941. On the day that Jane Turner died, Jackson had gone to work at 6.30am but an hour and a half earlier, had woken Richards so that he could get ready for his own job, and at 5.30am Richards had left the house.

Jackson returned home at 6.30pm but by midnight, Richards had still not come in. Deciding he could wait up no longer, Jackson locked up the house and retired for the night. The next morning, he left for work at 6.15am but when he got home, at 2.30pm, Richards was in the house and in bed. Jackson noticed that Richards' face was scratched and when he asked him where he had been all night, Richards had made no answer.

Dr Edward William Parsey had arrived in Franklin Road at 5.25am on March 29th and pronounced life extinct. At 7.30am he had been joined by Dr James Mathewson Webster, who started his own examination at 7.48am and said that Jane had

been dead for about eight hours. Later that morning he performed a post-mortem at the mortuary. Dr Webster said that in
life, Jane had been addicted to excessive amounts of alcohol but
the direct cause of her death had been multiple injuries and
cerebral contusion. Jane's ribs had been fractured and bruised on
both sides and a wound on the side of her head showed that
some blunt object had been used to strike her. Neither the stick
nor the broken bottle found at the scene showed any evidence of
bloodstaining but either could have inflicted the injuries
observed.

Turning to his examination of the prisoner, Dr Webster stated
that the scratches on Richards' face might have been caused as he
described, by a fall into a hedge, but they could equally have
been the result of an attack from Jane's fingernails. More impor-
tantly, the blood found on Richards' handkerchief was Group 'A'
which was the same as Jane's. Richards' own group was 'O' so it
could not have come from him.

One of the final witnesses was Dr John Humphrey, the medical officer of Winson Green prison. He said that Richards was
illiterate but able to give an account of his family history.
According to that, Richards had both a brother and a sister who
suffered from epilepsy, although there was no evidence of any
insanity in the family. Richards had been blown up at Ypres in
1916 and invalided home but had returned to France in 1917,
although he had suffered with his nerves ever since. In 1936,
Richards had fallen down in the street and as he had been
unable to speak, had been taken to the police cells as a suspected
drunk. From there he was sent to Dudley Hospital where he
spent two months in treatment. Since his admission into prison,
Richards had shown no sign of insanity or even of a volatile
temper.

When giving his own testimony, Richards pointed out an
indentation in his forehead. For the defence, Mr O'Sullivan

asked his client to explain what this was and Richards stated that it was a war wound and that his doctors had advised him not to drink as he would not be able to stand it. Richards went on to say that as a result of this wound, he did not know what he was doing after a bottle of beer.

The jury were out for 35 minutes and after being found guilty and sentenced to death, Richards again protested that he was innocent. An appeal was heard on September 4th, the grounds being that the prosecution had not supplied enough evidence to preclude the possibility of manslaughter. The judgement of the court was given by the Lord Chief Justice, Lord Caldecote, who stated that he saw no way in which the jury could have reached any other verdict on the evidence, and consequently the appeal would be dismissed.

On Friday, September 19th, 1941, Eli Richards was hanged at Winson Green by Thomas Pierrepoint, who was assisted by Stanley Cross. It was the seventh execution in this year.

CHAPTER EIGHTEEN

ABSENT WITHOUT LEAVE

AT about 10.45am on Wednesday, September 21st, 1941, Kitty Lyon, who was just 18 years old, left her home at 10 Union Street, Walsall and walked to 81 Tantarra Street, the house where her close friend, Violet Richards, lived. The two girls decided to go for a stroll together, possibly to find some blackberries along the way.

Kitty and Violet walked to Rushall Church and from there cut across the footpath to a railway tunnel, known locally as a cattle arch, which led into the fields nearby. As the girls approached the arch, they saw a young soldier, wearing his battledress, but without a hat, standing on the path by some bushes. Without acknowledging the man, Kitty and Violet passed him and headed towards the fields.

Suddenly a loud report rang out and Violet felt a sharp pain in her chest. As she staggered a few steps, Violet saw Kitty run off up the footpath, only to be followed by the soldier who soon caught Kitty and held a gun up to her face. Another shot was fired and as Kitty Lyon fell to the ground, Violet saw to her horror that the soldier was coming back towards her. She lay helpless as the soldier began to beat her about the head. She slipped into merciful unconsciousness and when she awoke, just a few minutes later, the soldier had vanished, along with Violet's handbag.

John Short lived at 101 Barnes Street but on this particular Sunday, had taken a stroll to the Park Lime pits. It was at some time between 11.00am and 11.30am that he was walking down the footpath near the church when he heard two shots coming from the direction of the fields near the cattle arch. Looking in that direction, John Short saw a soldier and a girl apparently struggling on the footpath and noticed that the man was hitting the girl about the head, with something that he held in his hand.

Even as Short took in this scene, the soldier looked in his direction and, seeing that he was being observed, stopped his attack upon the girl and ran off around a corner of the pathway. John Short dashed over to the cattle arch and after passing through it, found Violet Richards sitting on the footpath, her face smothered in blood and her left hand holding her chest. Short reassured her before running for assistance to his brother-in-law, Leonard Eric Smith.

Even before these two men could return, David Bickley, who had been walking from Rushall Church to Daw End, strolled through the same cattle arch. He put his time of arrival there at 11.20am and he, too, found Violet sitting on the footpath, obviously injured. David lifted the girl on to some grass nearby and as he did he noticed a second girl lying in a small furrow near a large tree. This was, of course, Kitty Lyon and it seemed clear to Bickley that she was beyond help.

Both Kitty and Violet were admitted to the Walsall General Hospital where they were attended to by the casualty house surgeon, Dr Werner Paul Hirsch. By now it was 12.35pm and Kitty was pronounced dead on arrival, Dr Hirsch noting that she had by then been dead perhaps 30 minutes. There was a single bullet wound, just behind her right ear, but Kitty had also bled from her left ear, possibly due to the damage inflicted when the bullet had passed through her brain.

Violet Richards had a wound on the outside of her left shoulder blade. This was an entry wound, caused by a bullet and the corresponding exit wound was in her breast bone, on a level with her second rib. There were also a number of wounds to her head which had caused a compound depressed fracture of the skull. Dr Hirsch counted eight other wounds on the left side of her skull, two on her forehead, and 12 smaller wounds on her head. Violet also had had two teeth knocked out and both her forearm bones were broken.

A police appeal for witnesses soon showed that quite a few people had seen the soldier, close to the cattle arch, on the morning of September 21st. James Doughty lived at 105 Daw End Lane and had walked through the cattle arch at 10.50am that morning. There was a soldier, standing with his back to the footpath, close by the large tree. Doughty said, "Hello," to the young man, who replied in kind. Significantly for what was to happen later, Doughty, and indeed all the other witnesses, said that there was only one soldier near the arch.

Some time later, at about 11.00am, Evelyn Neal walked through the archway, and she also saw the soldier standing just off the footpath. Some time in the next 15 minutes, Frederick Alexander Griffiths passed through the arch on his way to Rushall Church. The soldier was now leaning on a fence at the side of the footpath. As Griffiths drew near to him, the soldier got down from the fence and walked through the arch before turning left and heading into the fields for a few steps.

Harold Cooper was another man who walked through the cattle arch on September 21st. He, too, saw the soldier and noted that at the time, he had his hand thrust into his right trouser pocket, which appeared to be bulging as if something was being concealed there. Finally, William James Devine reported that he had seen the soldier standing some distance from the large tree, looking up at a signal on the railway. William Devine also noticed that the soldier wore an arm badge which he thought was two crossed flags.

Other people reported seeing a hatless soldier, but not near the archway. Thomas Thomas was walking up Cartbridge Crescent into Cartbridge Lane at some time after 11.40am. As Thomas walked on to the bridge, he saw a soldier coming down Cartbridge Lane, from the direction of the cattle arch. As he approached the bridge, the soldier caught hold of something from under his battledress and flung it to the left where the object, whatever it was, fell into a ditch by the railway line. The next day, a police search was made in that area and Constable Charles Jones recovered a service revolver from the ditch.

At about the same time as Thomas was walking on to the bridge, Horace Arthur Wilson was walking down Cartbridge Lane, towards Lichfield Road. He, too, saw the soldier and watched as he came around a bend in the road and dropped something. The soldier quickly retrieved what Wilson saw was a woman's handbag. The same soldier, still carrying the handbag, was also seen by Daisy Robinson who lived at 18 Cartbridge Lane. She was looking out of her front window at the time and saw him run off after he had picked up the bag from the ground.

All of these witnesses were able to supply descriptions of the soldier they had seen. So it was that the police knew that they were looking for a man 'aged 23; five feet seven inches tall, medium build, with a wild look in his eyes.' It wasn't that much to go on so the local officers called in the assistance of Scotland Yard and Detective Chief Inspector Arthur Davis and Detective Sergeant Powell were sent to Walsall.

In fact, it was another matter which brought a young soldier into police hands and would eventually lead to him being interviewed about the shooting of Kitty Lyons and Violet Richards.

Arthur Peach was a 23-year-old private who had enlisted at Lichfield on December 10th, 1939. On May 8th, 1940, Peach had been sent to King's Lynn in Norfolk and from there to various camps, finally ending up at Tavistock, in Devon. In September, Peach had gone absent without leave and once this had been brought to the attention of the police, they had gone to Peach's parent's house at 45 Green Rock Lane, Bloxwich.

It was 2.30am on September 22nd, when Sergeant Charles Smith called at Green Rock Lane to find Peach lying on a couch downstairs. Smith informed Peach that he held a warrant for his arrest as a deserter from the Army. To this, Peach replied, "I was going back in the morning if you hadn't come."

Taken to the police station, Peach was held in the cells, prior to his transfer back to his unit. It did not take long, though, before Chief Inspector Davis realised that this soldier fitted the general description of the man who had shot the two girls near the cattle arch. Peach was asked to explain his movements on September 21st. According to his statement, he had risen at 9.00am on the 21st, but had not left his house until 10.30am when he walked along the canal to the Barley Mow public house. On the way he had seen some Home Guard men on manoeuvres near Goscote Hill Farm and from there had walked directly home, arriving there at 12.15pm. He knew nothing of the shooting of the two women.

The next day, September 24th, the inquest on Kitty Lyons was opened before Mr J.F. Addison. Identification evidence was given by Mary Maud Lyon, the dead girl's mother and medical evidence was given by Dr A.B. Davies, the police surgeon. The proceedings were then adjourned until October 23rd, to give the police time to complete their enquiries.

In the meantime, the police were investigating Peach's movements since he had left his unit, and in due course they spoke to Frank Cowlishaw, the landlord of the Alma Inn on Bentley

Lane, Walsall. Frank remembered Peach coming into his pub at 12.40pm on September 17th. At the time, Peach was wearing a revolver in a khaki holster and bore an arm badge with the initials 'S.P.' emblazoned upon it. Peach had explained that this meant 'Special Police' and he was down in Walsall to 'fetch a chap'.

Another witness was John Stephen Wilcox, a friend of Peach's for many years. He told Chief Inspector Davis that on September 18th, he had been in the Cottage pub at Coalpool when Peach came in. It was then around 9.20pm or perhaps a little later and the two friends had fallen into conversation. Wilcox had also noticed that Peach was carrying a revolver in a holster and was wearing the 'S.P.' arm badge. Wilcox asked Peach what the letters stood for and Peach had told him too that they meant 'Special Police'. That was why he was allowed to carry a revolver.

At 10.00pm Peach and Wilcox left the pub together and Wilcox again asked him about the gun. Peach pointed out that it was a Webley .45 and even unloaded it and allowed Wilcox to examine it for himself. Back at Wilcox's house, he showed the weapon to his father, before returning it to Peach who then went home.

Further police inquiries revealed that a gun was missing from Peach's camp in Devon. In his first interview, Peach had denied having any gun with him when he left Tavistock. On October 3rd, armed with this new evidence, Chief Inspector Davis interviewed Peach again. At first, Peach denied any knowledge of the gun but finally he made a written statement admitting that he had taken the gun from the stores at King's Lynn. It was never made clear why Peach lied about which of his camps he had stolen the gun from.

The statement began, 'I want to tell the truth about a .45 Webley and six revolver bullets which I showed to my pal John Wilcox, at his address where he lives, on Thursday night the 18th

September, 1941, when he took the revolver and bullets upstairs and showed them to his father.

'I took this revolver from the weapon training stores of the 11th Battalion, South Staffs Regiment, at Kings Lynn, I had been put in charge of the store by Captain Ardagh ...I picked up some pistol ammunition from some place, I don't remember where. This ammunition fitted the revolver.

'I picked up a Special Proficiency badge when I was cleaning one of the huts out at Tiverton (another of Peach's camps). When I deserted and came home I sewed this badge with the letters 'S.P.' on, on my left sleeve. I sewed it on with white cotton. I sewed some white wool over the letters 'S.P.' to make them stand out more.

'When I used to come to Walsall I used to tell my friends that I was in the Security Police and used to wear the pistol in a khaki-coloured web holster on the left side of my belt. Attached to the pistol was a khaki lanyard which I wore round my neck.

'I bought a brass signaller's badge in an Army outfitters shop at Tiverton. I paid a shilling for it. I put this on the top of my left arm beneath the Divisional signs.

'I deserted from my Regiment at Whitchurch Camp near Tavistock on Monday, 8th September, 1941... I bought a ticket at Tavistock station and travelled to Exeter. I then jumped a lorry from Exeter to Bristol. I got off at Bristol, asked the way to the by-pass leading towards Gloucester. I travelled through Cheltenham and came through to Birmingham on a lorry.

'After I had been at home a week, my father told me that I should have gone back but I did not do so.

'I want to tell you how on Saturday night, I went to meet my girl and I lost my revolver. When I came home I brought my overcoat with me. I never wore it at all but on the Saturday evening, the September 20th, 1941,1 took my overcoat with me when I went to Newport Street to meet Winnie Grice. In the pocket of the overcoat, I had the revolver in the holster. After I had met her and seen her home at about 10.30pm I went to the bus station, Walsall. I was carrying my overcoat. I know the revolver was in the overcoat.

'I stood there about ten minutes and I put my overcoat with the revolver in the pocket on the rails. I went to the lavatory about 40 yards away but it was shut and I came back. I felt in my pocket for a cigarette but there were none there and I thought they must be in my overcoat. When I went to my overcoat it was gone. The revolver was in the pocket of the coat when I lost it.

'I have already told you in my other statement where I was on Sunday morning, September 21st, 1941, when two girls were shot at by a soldier, on a footpath near a cattle arch leading from Rushall church to Daw End. I know this footpath quite well, but I have not been along there since I have been in the Army. that is since the December 10th, 1939.'

At 6.00pm that same night, Chief Inspector Davis saw Peach again and told him that a palm print had been found on the gun recovered from the ditch by Constable Jones. Peach was asked if he consented to his palm prints being taken. Not only did he say that he didn't but he made a further short statement which was taken down and then signed by him. This referred to the various badges he had worn both officially, as part of his regimental identifications, and those that he had sewn on himself. Since he had absented himself, Peach had removed his badges and one of these, he now admitted, had been two crossed flags as described by William Devine.

On October 4th, Peach was placed in a line up of 11 men. Eight potential witnesses viewed the men and seven of those witnesses picked out one of four other men. Only one man, Horace Wilson, picked out Peach. The next day, Peach made two further statements. In the first of these, Peach stated that he had been told that the police had found no trace of anyone who might have stolen his overcoat and the revolver which was inside it, from the bus station. Peach now said that no such theft had taken place, but that he had sold the gun to a civilian on the Friday night, for a total of seven shillings. Peach claimed that he had never seen this man before, did not know his name or address and would be unable to identify him. In his second statement that day, though, Peach finally admitted that he had been at the cattle arch when the two girls were shot.

In this statement, Peach said, 'On the 9th of September, 1941, I was waiting for a bus on the Bridge, Walsall. I got into conversation with a fellow whom I'd never seen before. I was wearing a .45 Webley revolver which he became interested in. He was waiting for the same bus as me, it would then be about 11.00pm. Before the arrival of the bus he offered to buy the revolver from me, but I would not sell it to him. He boarded the same bus as me which as near as I can remember went at about 11.35pm. I was walking down Bloxwich Road on the 11th of September when I met the same fellow He was then dressed in khaki, the first time having met him in civilian clothes. I walked a distance of about 200 yards with him and he asked me if I had changed my mind about selling him the revolver. I was with very little money at the time and I agreed to sell it him. I asked him if he would meet me at a place called the Forest brickyard at about four that day, he said he would. I was there at the place I mentioned but I did not see the fellow. I took the revolver back home and after having my tea went down into the town and stopped there till about 11.30pm. I did not see the fellow again till about the 15th of September, when I met him while walking round the park in Lichfield Street. He asked me again about selling him the revolver. I again said I would sell it him if he would like to come to my home and buy it, but he would not come. He asked me if I would be in Walsall on the following Sunday morning and I told him I didn't know. He said that if I was I could meet him outside the public house called the Hardin at Coalpool at 10.30 in the morning.'

Peach said that he met the man as arranged and sold him the gun and the ammunition for seven shillings. The man then asked Peach where he was going and after being told that he was going for a walk, the man said he would accompany him as he wanted to try the gun out. The two then walked into the fields towards Rushall church. Peach's statement continued, 'We were walking down a footpath towards a cattle arch and he said it would be alright if he tried it there. He then loaded the revolver and stood by the cattle arch with it. I asked him if he was going to fire it and he said yes, when these two women have passed, and I noticed that two girls were coming under the bridge. I believe they had just passed under when I heard a shot fired and one of the girls cried out that he had hurt her. I asked him what he had done, he said the gun has gone off. I saw one of the girls suddenly drop to the floor and I said you have hit her. I went up to her and he suddenly started to fire again. I believe he did try to shoot me, and I loosed the girl and started to run away. I was running the same direction as we came when I noticed that I had still got hold of the girl's handbag which I picked up when I tried to get the girl to her feet.'

In the rest of the statement, Peach referred to dropping the bag as he ran down Cartbridge Lane, and picking it up again. He ended by saying that the other soldier, the one who had done all the shooting, was called Jock and from his badges, appeared to be in the Pioneers. Peach claimed that he was about 25 years old, around 5ft 8ins tall, clean shaven and weighed about 11 stone. The man also had a tattoo of the word 'Mother' across the fingers of his hand and when it was pointed out to Peach that the word 'Mother' had six letters, not five, Peach recalled that the first five letters were on one hand and the final 'R' was on the other hand. The police thought this highly unlikely.

On October 6th, Peach was taken back to the railway arch where he pointed out the spot where 'Jock' had stood when he shot the two girls. Later he was taken to Cartbridge Lane where he pointed out the place he had dropped Violet Richard's handbag. Later that same day he was charged with murder and appeared in the Walsall police court where he was remanded for three weeks.

On October 23rd, the inquest reopened but was immediately adjourned pending the outcome of the criminal proceedings against Peach. The second police court appearance took place on October 27th but it was not until November 4th that the evidence was heard, Violet Richards now being out of hospital, although she was accompanied by a nurse in court. Here, Mr G.R. Paling appeared for the Director of Public Prosecutions while Peach was defended by Mr A.V. Haden. The hearing took two days and on November 5th, Peach was sent for trial on three charges: the murder of Kitty Lyons; the wounding of Violet Richards with intent to murder; and the theft of Violet's handbag.

The trial of Arthur Peach opened on November 24th, 1941, before Mr Justice MacNaghten. The proceedings lasted until November 26th during which the case for the prosecution was led by Mr A.J. Long, who was assisted by Mr Ryder Richardson. Peach was defended by Mr John F. Bourke and Mr W. Field Hunt.

Some of the early evidence detailed how the gun used had been traced to Peach. Colour Sergeant Edward Foran Courtnay stated that he had received a Webley revolver from an officer in March 1941 and had handed this weapon in to the stores in Devon. He checked the stores once a week and the fact that the gun was missing came to his attention at the end of July. Courtnay confirmed that he had seen Peach in the stores from time to time.

Lance Corporal Robert Harrison was in charge of the stores and confirmed that the Webley Mark VI revolver, number 263097, was deposited there on March 15th, 1941. On July 17th, when Harrison took some leave, the gun was still there but on July 25th, when he returned, it was missing and he reported the matter to Sergeant Courtnay.

Private Peter Sells had taken over the stores while Harrison was on leave and he said that one day, Sergeant Courtnay had taken out the gun while checking the stores, leaving the weapon on the right-hand side of a table. Sells had then left the stores for a couple of hours and when he returned the gun was no longer on the table. At the time, he assumed that the sergeant had placed the gun back into the cupboard where it was normally kept, but subsequent events indicated that this was the most likely time that it had been stolen.

William Watson was a private in Peach's unit and in July 1941, he was in detention for a minor military offense. Peach was also in detention and the two talked while they were there together. Peach told Watson that he had a .45 revolver at home and said he might also be able to get one for Watson. The suggestion had been turned down, Watson seeing no reason why he would want a gun of his own.

The gun found in the ditch had been examined by Robert Churchill, a firearms expert based in Orange Street, Leicester Square, London. He noted that both vulcanite grips were broken and that a piece found at the murder scene fitted one of the grips. The trigger guard had been bent to such an extent that the gun could no longer be fired until it was removed. After conducting various test firings, Mr Churchill was able to confirm that this gun was the one used to kill Kitty Lyons.

Winnie Grice lived at 12 Newport Street, Walsall. She had known Peach since February 1941 and they had been walking out together for some months. In late July, Peach had been home on leave and she had noticed that he was wearing a revolver, something he had not done before.

Turning to the day of the shooting, Winnie said that she had been out that day but returned at 5.55pm to find Peach waiting for her at her house. That night, she, Peach and one of her girl-friends went to the pictures, getting back to her house at around 9.00pm. As Winnie went into her house, her father told her that two girls over the fields had been shot and she had dashed back out to tell Peach, who laughed.

Dr James Mathewson Webster, the director of the West Midlands Forensic Science laboratory in Newton Street, Birmingham, had performed the post-mortem on Kitty Lyons, and had been assisted by Dr Davies. Both reported that Kitty had been a well nourished girl, 5ft 3ins in height. There was a single puncture wound on the right side of Kitty's head, just behind her ear and a .45 bullet had been recovered from inside the skull, close to the left petrous temporal bone. At the time this bullet entered Kitty's head she was standing with the side of her head at almost a complete right angle to the axis of the bullet's flight. The wound showed evidence of powder burns indicating that it was a contact, or near contact discharge. Death was due to laceration of the brain, caused by the path of the bullet, and would have been almost instantaneous.

Peach stepped into the witness box and repeated his story about the other soldier doing the shooting. For good measure he also claimed that while being interviewed by the police, he had been subjected to violence from Chief Inspector Davis, who had slapped his face and pulled his hair.

The jury considered that all the other witnesses had been correct and that there was only one soldier at the cattle arch on that Sunday morning. Peach was found guilty and before passing the sentence of death, the trial judge remarked, "The jury are convinced, as I think anyone who heard the evidence must have been convinced, that the story that you were accompanied by another man at the cattle arch on September 21st, is untrue." Peach showed no signs of emotion as the death sentence was passed, and left the dock without comment.

Peach's appeal was heard on January 14th, 1942, before Justices Humphreys, Wrottesley and Croom-Johnson. The grounds were that the judge had misdirected the jury in regard to Violet Richard's testimony. The judge had said that Violet was a truthful witness but he should have said that she might well have difficulty with her memory since she herself had admitted that her recollection was somewhat blurred. The court ruled that there was more than sufficient evidence to uphold the conviction and consequently the appeal was dismissed.

On Friday. January 30th, 1942, Arthur Peach was hanged at Birmingham by Thomas Pierrepoint and Henry Critchell. There were no signs outside the prison that anything unusual was taking place inside the prison walls. No crowd gathered, no demonstrations for or against capital punishment were made and there was no one to read the execution notices as they were posted on the gates just after 9.00am.

CHAPTER NINETEEN

A LITTLE SECRET

ON February 28th, 1924, Harold Oswald Merry, who was then 22 years old, married at Bromsgrove register office. His new wife, Florence Sylvia Merry would live happily with her husband until early September, 1941, and before they encountered difficulties, she would bear Merry five children whose ages, by 1942, ranged from one to 14 years. The trouble arose when Merry started paying attention to another woman, 27-year-old Joyce Dixon, and after just a few weeks, they became lovers.

Joyce had not had the easiest of lives. She had suffered from mental problems which had seen her receiving medical attention between July 1931 and September 1938, but she seemed to have responded to that treatment and had been relatively free from trouble for more than three years. Indeed, for the past three years, she had managed to hold down a job as a shorthand typist at the Austin Aero works in Birmingham. That was where she had first met Merry, for he worked at the same factory, as an aircraft inspector.

Merry and Joyce first began passing the time of day in May, 1941. By July, they had started talking properly to each other and their first date took place in August, when Merry took Joyce to the cinema. The couple certainly got on well together and it was clear that she was deeply in love with this new man in her life. Unfortunately, at least during the early part of their relationship, Merry had told Joyce that he was a single man, even though he had never obtained a divorce from his wife. It was not until they had been walking out for six weeks, that Merry confessed that he was a married man, but by then, Joyce had fallen totally for him and chose to ignore what he had said.

At the end of September, 1941, Joyce Dixon had a week's holiday from work. Until then, of course, if Joyce wished to speak to Merry or send him a message, she merely had to seek him out at work. Now she was unable to do so and so she sent Merry a letter, to his home address, 205 Hewell Road, Redditch. This letter, written in a strange hand, was opened by Florence Merry on a Thursday morning and the result was that she refused to cook for Merry, or have anything to do with him, from that moment on.

The following Sunday, Merry went to visit his sister at 44 Mount Pleasant, also in Redditch, but when he returned home that night, he found the doors locked against him and Florence refused to grant him admission. Somewhat dejectedly, Merry went back to his sister's house where he stayed the night. For some time, Merry continued to live with his sister, although he was allowed back into his house to see his children. It was not until March 19th, 1942, that Merry returned home to live at Hewell Road.

By the early part of 1942, the relationship between Merry and Joyce had grown so strongly that it was common knowledge at the factory where they worked, that there was something going on. Tongues began to wag and the gossips began to spread rumours around the works. Things got so bad that Merry suggested to Joyce that they go away to London for the weekend. Joyce readily agreed, especially when Merry added that he thought they should get engaged. However, in order to do so, Merry would have to do the proper thing, speak to Joyce's mother and ask her permission.

Kate Elizabeth Dixon did not approve of her unmarried daughter going to London and sharing a hotel room with a man, but an engagement had been mentioned, so finally she agreed. What Kate could not know, was that the real reason for this weekend away was so that Merry could get a hotel receipt, show that he had booked in with another woman, and thus obtain a divorce from his wife, leaving him free to marry Joyce.

On Saturday, March 21st, 1942, Merry and Joyce travelled down to London and booked into a hotel at 36 Bloomsbury Street, where they were given room 14. Later, for their comfort, they were moved to room 8 and rather than stay for just a weekend, the couple remained at the hotel until Friday, March 27th. Merry obtained his receipt on a hotel letterhead but this was from a sister hotel, the 46 Hotel. Still, he thought it would be evidence enough to get him his divorce.

On that same day, March 27th, Merry and his lover returned to Birmingham, getting to New Street station at 4.00pm. Merry was owed some wages from his work and said he would join Joyce at her home later. She went directly back to her mother's house at 8 Rowen Way, Northfield, where she walked straight into a grilling.

What Joyce could not know was that while she had been away, her supervisor had called on Kate Dixon and told her that the man Joyce was seeing was married. Kate was furious and told Joyce that she could not see Merry again. When, some time later, Merry called on Joyce as he had said he would, it was made plain that he was no longer welcome in the house. That night he and Joyce parted at 9.15pm.

Joyce Dixon had no intention of giving up Merry and met

him the next day, by arrangement, at New Street station at 10.00am. They spent the day together, first visiting Walsall and then Wolverhampton. They finally said their goodnights at 10.00pm.

On Sunday, March 29th, Merry again met Joyce at the station, this time at 4.30pm. Kate Dixon may well have suspected that her daughter was still seeing Merry but there was little she could do about it. What may have been a concern on Kate's part turned to real worry, though, when her daughter did not return home that night.

It was 7.30am on March 30th when one of Joyce's younger brothers, Norman, telephoned an older married brother, Victor Oliver Dixon, who lived at 69 Willow Road, and explained that Joyce had not come home. At Norman's request, Victor went around to where Joyce worked and once he had discovered that neither Joyce nor Merry had come in that day, Norman went around to Merry's house, where the door was opened by Florence. Victor explained the problem and asked to speak to Merry, but even as Florence shouted upstairs, "You're wanted," Victor heard some strange gurgling noises coming from one of the bedrooms.

Victor Dixon rushed upstairs and found Merry with an electric flex around his throat, trying desperately to throttle himself. Victor tore the flex from Merry and demanded to know what had happened to Joyce. To Victor's horror, Merry confessed to killing his sister. Without delay, Merry was escorted to Redditch police station where he repeated his claim to Sergeant Albert Morris, who was informed that on the way, Merry had admitted that he had strangled and drowned Joyce in a pool in the fields at the back of her house. Later that day, he took the police and Victor Dixon to a pond where Joyce Dixon's body floated face down in the water. Merry was taken back to the police station and charged with murder. He was then searched and a notebook was found. On one page of that notebook was written, 'So goodbye to you all, we are terribly in love with each other.' Also found was a piece of paper on which Merry had written, 'Joyce and myself have been living as man and wife, hoping I should be able to get a divorce from my wife. We found it impossible to carry on, so we decided to die together. For God's sake forgive her; she is so happy now she knows we are going to die together.' The note was signed by both Merry and Joyce Dixon.

His first appearance at the police court took place on March 31st, when matters were adjourned until April 2nd. On that date, the prosecution evidence was given by Mr Ross, while Merry was represented by Mr H. Baker, who made no objection to a further remand. The inquest on the dead woman opened the same day but was adjourned until July 29th, by which time it was hoped that the criminal charge against Merry would be completed. The final police court hearing took place over two days, starting on April 23rd, and by this time Mr M.P. Pugh had taken over for the prosecution and Mr Herbert Willison had become Merry's representative.

On July 17th, the trial of Harold Merry opened at Birmingham before Mr Justice Croom-Johnson. Merry was represented by Mr John F. Bourke and Mr G.T. Meredith, while the case for the prosecution was led by Mr Paul F. Sandlands, who was assisted by Mr A.P. Marshall. The trial lasted for two days.

The most telling piece of evidence was Merry's own statement to the police. In this he explained that after they had met at New Street station on March 29th, Joyce had told him that after what had happened, she thought her mother was losing her love for her. From the station, they had walked to Broad Street, hoping to have a bite to eat in a restaurant there, but it was closed so they went into a park where they could talk in private.

Joyce was upset and said that she could not carry on much longer. Merry had replied, "Well, what shall we do about it?" Joyce had no answer, saying only that she knew that since 'they could not now get married, it would be better if they died together and they then discussed the possibility of Merry killing her and then himself. This ended when Merry wrote out the suicide note and after Joyce had signed it, he added his own name to the bottom.

From the park, the two lovers walked back to Broad Street where they had a cup of tea at a cafe, leaving at 7.50pm. From there they caught a tram back to where Joyce lived, arriving there at 8.55pm. They stayed in the street talking until, at 9.45pm Joyce and Merry decided that they should carry out their suicide plan. They began walking across the fields and on the way, Merry remarked, "I will kill you first and I promise you faithfully I will die with you."

Eventually, they came to a stile in a fence and it was here that Merry took his necktie off and tried to strangle Joyce. After some time, she fell to the ground, with blood coming from her mouth. Merry dropped her through the railings on to the other side of the fence but Joyce was still conscious and kept groaning, "I love you, I love you".

Merry had no idea exactly what had happened next, for the next thing he remembered was coming to in a pond some five minutes later.

He put the tie around his own throat, pulled it tight and fell forward in the water. The cold water shocked him back to full consciousness and Merry then made another attempt to kill himself, but again failed. He spent the entire night standing in the cold water and it was not until early morning that he left to walk home. He finally got, back to Hewell Road at 7.10am and told his wife that he had fallen into a brook. She seemed to be satisfied so he went upstairs, took off his clothes, had a bath and then lay down on the bed. It was then that Victor Dixon knocked on his front door.

The problem for the prosecution was that since making that confession, Merry had withdrawn it. Now he was claiming that the first part was still true – they had made a suicide pact and he had tried to strangle Joyce. This attempt did not succeed and Joyce remained conscious throughout. This seemed to bring Merry to his senses and he said that they should go to her mother's house to clear everything up. Joyce refused to move, so Merry walked off alone, thinking that she would follow him. After a few minutes, when Joyce had not caught up with him, Merry returned, only to find Joyce floating in the pond.

It seemed, though, that Merry's original story was closer to the truth. Constable Joseph Potter had attended the scene, a pond in an area known as Turves Green, at 2.30pm on Sunday, March 30th. At the time, Joyce's body was floating some 18ft from the edge of the pond but there were signs of a struggle near the stile Merry had referred to. Further, there were drag marks running from the stile to the edge of the pond.

Dr James Mathewson Webster had performed the post-mortem on Joyce's body. He stated that there was a large amount of chickweed and mud all over the body which was that of a plump, well-made young woman. There was a red ligature mark around Joyce's neck which was broader on the left side where the ligature might have been knotted or crossed. The ultimate cause of death was asphyxia by drowning, but she had first been brought near to death by strangulation.

The jury had no difficulty in returning a guilty verdict and Merry was sentenced to death. An appeal was heard on August 26th before Justices Humphreys, Hilbery and Tucker where the defence put forward three main grounds. The first was that the judge had misdirected the jury as to the manner in which they should consider Merry's explanation of the tragedy. Second, that the judge had allowed improper cross examination of Merry as to his acquisition of a wedding ring, and finally that the judge had criticised the defending counsel for declining to open his defence until all the Crown witnesses had been called to give evidence. The judges considered all these points but finally ruled that there had been no misdirection and the appeal was lost.

On the morning of Thursday, September 10th, 1942, three men died on an English gallows. In London, Samuel Dashwood and George Silverosa were hanged at Pentonville for the murder of a pawnbroker, while at Birmingham, Harold Oswald Merry was executed by Thomas Pierrepoint who was assisted by Henry Critchell.

The junction of Rifle Crescent and Victoria Street, where William Thomas Andrews was attacked by Victor Edward Betts. The shop is the one run by Annie Blears and the house on the corner, with the railings, is the one where Rose Matthews lived. See Chapter 14. (Public Record Office).

Victoria Road, where Betts and Ridley made good their escape. The car parked just inside Rifle Crescent is in the same spot as their car was parked. See Chapter 14. (Public Record Office).

The house at 11 The Leys, where Jeremiah Hanbury murdered Jessie Payne. The house is the one towards the back of the picture. See Chapter 15. (Public Record Office).

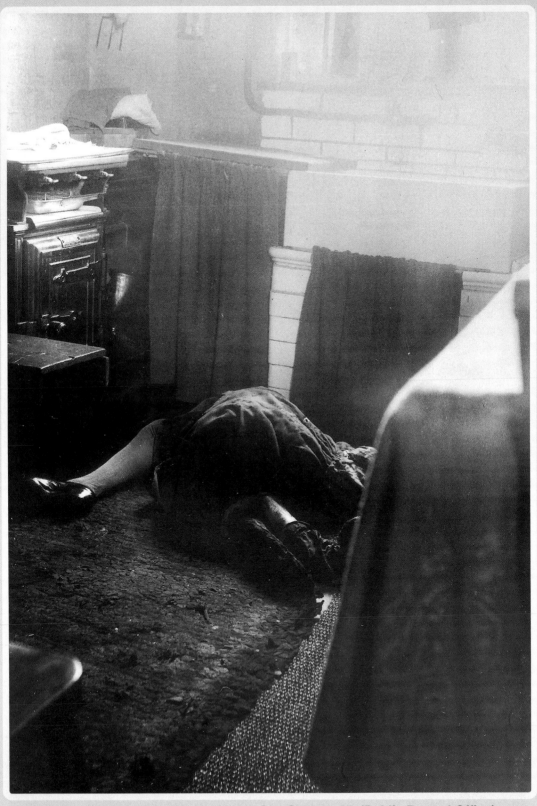

Jessie Payne lying dead inside her home. See Chapter 15. (Public Record Office).

The rear of the house at 8 Moor Street, West Bromwich, where Charles and Gladys Fox lived. To gain entrance, Stanley Eric Hobday had removed the middle pane of glass in the bottom of the large window. See Chapter 16. (Public Record Office).

Inside the kitchen of 8 Moor Street, where Hobday stabbed Fox whilst his wife, Gladys, stood on the third stair. See Chapter 16. (Public Record Office).

The lane down which Hobday made good his escape and where the police met a hysterical Gladys Fox after her husband had been stabbed. See Chapter 16. (Public Record Office).

(above left) **The maroon Jowett car which Hobday stole after he had killed Charles Fox, and which he subsequently crashed. Notice the damage to the roof;** *(above right)* **A side view of the Jowett, registration EA 4545. See Chapter 16. (both Public Record Office).**

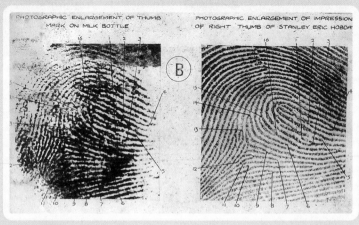

One of the police comparisons of Hobday's fingerprints. See Chapter 16. (Public Record Office).

Lord Hewart, the Lord Chief Justice, who presided over the unsuccessful appeals of Power, Hanbury and Hobday. (Hulton-Getty)

The body of Jane Turner as it was discovered in Franklin Road. See Chapter 17. (Public Record Office).

A closer view of Jane Turner's body. Note the walking stick lying in the road. See Chapter 17. (Public Record Office).

The cattle arch where Arthur Peach shot two women. Violet Richards was found near where the two small square markers are situated to the right and Kitty Lyon's body lay close to the large tree, and is shown by the larger marker. See Chapter 18. (Public Record Office).

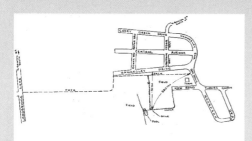

A police map of the area where Harold Oswald Merry killed Joyce Dixon. See Chapter 19. (Public Record Office).

Vera Clarke who was murdered by William Quayle. See Chapter 20. (Public Record Office).

Inside the kitchen at 132a Bath Row, where Vera Clarke met her death. The cellar door referred to in the story is to the extreme left, just before the banister. See Chapter 20. (Public Record Office).

The front of the bombed-out house at 12 Spring Vale, where Vera's body was finally discovered. See Chapter 20. (Public Record Office).

The rear of the house at Spring Vale. Vera Clarke's body was buried under rubble in the far corner of the room downstairs. See Chapter 20 (Public Record Office).

The Birmingham Mail

7·30 EXTRA

N°. 26,636   A   THURSDAY, AUGUST 2, 1951   LIGHTING-UP TIME: 9.59 p.m.—4.26 a.m.   **2d**

BAN ENDS G. 14
rial rder
HANGES

d on August 14 by 951, which removes nd lock-outs, and se the place of the , to which disputes y the Minister.

new Order was given Rohena (Minister of "wards explained its rrespondents.

ral requirement on s and conditions of

L MISSION LD UP

Message from arriman

PORTED FER"

t had been d Stokes. k with us in a s after new of ts were

ing the ature of a an.

Lady Godiva Returns

Coventry's Lady Godiva, Miss Ann Wrigg (left), renewed acquaintance with the horse she rode in the city's pageant, Willoughby Warrior, at to-day's Horse Show at Coventry. With her is Miss Kitty Bates, who rode the horse to-day in a show competition.

Cinema Wins Appeal Against Quota

DEMAND NOT PRACTICABLE

A decision of great importance to cinema exhibitors throughout the country was given in Birmingham to-day, when the Recorder (Mr. Paul Sandlands, K.C.) allowed an appeal by Ladywood Pictures, Ltd., of Lombard House, Great Charles Street, against a conviction and sentence imposed by the city Stipendiary Magistrate.

The company had appealed against a conviction for not showing 25 per cent. of Br...

Body of Birmingham Schoolgirl Found in Yard

FOUL PLAY SUSPECTED —POLICE

Following the discovery of the body of 11-year-old Sheila Ethel Attwood in a Corporation yard at Caversham Road, Kingstanding, to-day, Birmingham police state that foul play is suspected.

Sheila, one of a large family living at 36, Caversham Road, was a pupil at Burlington Road School, Aston, and had been missing since last night. Crowds of schoolchildren and anxious parents crowded the road this afternoon as police officers carried out their enquiries.

Mrs. E. Brooke, of 33, Caversham Road, told "The Birmingham Mail." "I knew Sheila well. She was a nice little girl. I often saw her taking some of her brothers and sisters down to the Finchley Road Park, where they went paddling.

"I last saw her two days ago, when she said 'Hello.'

"Then, last night, as my husband and myself returned home from work in a local public house, at about 11 o'clock, I met Mrs. Attwood, who told me Sheila was missing.

"I spent most of the night searching the neighbourhood.

"I was cooking lunch to-day when Mrs. Ford, who lives at No. 22, opposite me, came running to my gate. She told me and Mrs. Attwood she had found Sheila in a Corporation yard at the bottom of her garden.

"She had seen her legs as she went to hang out washing."

Paddling Together

Ten-year-old Dorothy Allan, of 28, Caversham Road, told "The Birmingham Mail." "I last saw Sheila at 2 p.m. yesterday. We were paddling together in the pool in Finchley Park.

"At four o'clock she said she wanted to go home, and I walked down the road with her. But when she got to her gate she said she was going back to the park, and disappeared along the road. That was the last I saw of her."

The parents of Sheila have eight other children, the eldest of whom, Albert (aged 19), is deaf and dumb.

Professor J. M. Webster, Home Office pathologist, is to examine the body.

In an official statement, the police said that at 12.35 a.m. to-day it was reported to them that the girl had been missing from her home since ... o'clock last night. Enquiries were made in the district and at 11.55 a... to-day the girl's body ... the rear of 32, Cave...

YOUTH SOUGHT IN BRISTOL

New Developments in Burton Murder

MISS MULLEY DIED FROM HEAD WOUNDS

Police enquiries into the murder of Miss Winifred Mulley, 52-year-old headmistress of Burton-on-Trent Girls' High School, whose body was found in her bedroom on Tuesday, switched to-day to Bristol.

Detective Superintendent J. N. Black, who, with Sergeant Bryce, of the Yard, has taken charge of the investigation, stated to-day that they wished to interview a youth between the age of 16 and 18 who bought a ticket for Bristol at Burton-on-Trent railway station early on Tuesday morning.

The youth caught the 12.52 a.m. fast train and was seen to alight at Temple Meads station, Bristol, shortly after 4 a.m. but then completely disappeared.

Seen by Porters

His description is: Aged 16 to 19, 5ft. 8in to 5ft. 10in. in height, thin build, pale faced, clean shaven, light hair, wearing a dark suit—probably dark blue or brown—no hat, and carrying no luggage. Bristol police have been issued with the description of the youth who, said the Yard officer, could possibly be a deserter from one of the Services. He paid for his ticket in Treasury notes.

Three porters have told the police that they saw a youth on Burton station early on Tuesday... The youth the p... week is not with ... sleeping school ...

A view of the yard

A view of the yard in which the girl's body was found. The body was lying behind the hedge over which the policeman is looking.

H.R.G. LETTER RECALLED

Mentioned Another Murder

Two children have been murdered recently. Christine Butcher (aged 7) was found strangled in Home Park, Windsor, on July 10. Five days later Brenda Goddard (aged 6) was found strangled in a copse behind her home at Camden Crescent, Bath.

An anonymous letter postmarked "Birmingham, July 11, 5.30" was received by Brenda Goddard's foster mother.

It said: "Dear Mrs. Pullen. I want to say how sorry I am for what I did to your daughter. I don't know what made me do it, but it is too late now. But I can say within the next two weeks they will find my body somewhere. Yours truly, H.R.G.

"P.S. There may be another murder within that two weeks."

The letter was received by ... Pullen on July 22.

M.P. TELLS (PERJURY NO

Commons Men of Child's Death

BOARD CRITICISED TWO DOCTORS

An M.P. stated in the Commons to-day that he had a letter from a Coroner's juryman alleging that perjury was committed at an inquest held at Bradford in private on five-year-old Eileen Cunliffe, who died from burns after being taken to three hospitals before being admitted.

Mr. P. McLeavy asked the Minister of Health what action he propose to take with respect to the board concerned arising from the ver at the inquest.

Mr. H. Marquand (Minister Health): I have asked the R Hospital Board to ensure th nearly understood by each als concerned ...

How the Birmingham Mail reported the killing of Sheila Ethel Attwood, who was dumped after she had been murdered by Horace Carter. See Chapter 23. (Birmingham Mail).

Doreen Bell, the girl who was David Keasey's fiancée and who came upon the scene of his murder soon after Dennis Howard had fled the shop in Wolverhampton Street. See Chapter 25. (Mirror Syndication).

CHAPTER TWENTY

RUNNING ERRANDS

ON Friday. May 5th, 1943, Ada Clarke, who lived at 49 Essington Street, Ladywood, returned home from work at 6.30pm as usual. To her surprise, however, she discovered that her eight-year-old daughter, Vera, had not returned home from her school in Piggott Street.

Vera had been home for lunch that day and had returned to her classes at 1.10pm. Now Charles James Clark, the missing girl's father, went to visit some of his daughter's friends and they confirmed that she had left school with them at around 4.30pm. Janet Blount, a nine-year-old who lived at 32 Essington Street, said that she had walked home with Vera, who had her skipping rope with her. Vera, though, had never arrived back at her home and so, at 7.10pm Charles Clarke reported his daughter missing.

Although the police had been called, Mr and Mrs Clarke still continued to search for Vera. On the morning of May 6th, the distraught parents went to her school and spoke to her teacher, Mr Reginald Milton London. He had heard that Vera Clarke had not returned home the previous night, and had already spoken to another of the children he taught, 13-year-old Dorothy Beatrice Binnion. Although Dorothy was a few years older than Vera, she knew her quite well and Dorothy had told Mr London that at around 5.00pm on May 5th, she had seen Vera Clarke standing on the doorstep of a house in Bath Row. Any thoughts that Dorothy might have been mistaken were soon dispelled when she told Ada and Charles Clarke that the girl she had seen had been carrying a skipping rope in her hand.

At 9.00am on May 6th, Mr London, together with the Clarkes and Dorothy Binnion, walked to 132a Bath Row, the house where Dorothy claimed to have seen Vera the previous evening. The door was opened by the occupier of the house, 52-year-old William Quayle. Mr London introduced himself and said, "We are making enquiries about a little girl who is missing from school since last night. She was seen on the doorstep of this house. Do you know anything about her? These are her parents and this girl saw her here last night."

Mr Quayle said that he had not seen any little girl on his doorstep. On May 5th, he had locked up his house at 5.00pm and this was the first time he had opened the door since. Mr London then turned to Dorothy Binnion and asked her to confirm that when she saw Vera on the step, the front door of the house was wide open, contrary to what Quayle had just said. Dorothy said that was indeed the case, so Mr London asked if he could possibly search the cellar of the house.

Quayle seemed more than happy to oblige and invited the group to inspect his cellar. The door, though, was apparently locked and Quayle suddenly recalled that it was bolted from the inside. The only other way in was through a grating in the street, so the party trooped back outside to watch Quayle make a great show of attempting to lift the rusty iron grating. There was no way he could budge it and it seemed clear that no one could have gained access to the cellar the previous day. Nevertheless, the fact that Dorothy had seen Vera here meant that the matter would have to be passed on to the police. Reginald London told

Quayle this and asked him if he would still be at home in the next few minutes as the police would certainly wish to talk to him. Quayle replied, "I shall be here. I shall wait all day for them. I've got nothing to be afraid of." With that, he closed the door and his four visitors returned to the school on Piggott Street.

The police were told about this sighting of Vera and at 9.55am Sergeant Cyril Smith returned to Bath Row with Ada Clarke. Quayle had said he would remain in the house, but there was no answer when Sergeant Smith knocked on the door. Smith then tried the cellar grating for himself and found it quite easy to move. The officer climbed down into the cellar but on walking up the steps which led into Quayle's kitchen, he found that the door was bolted against him. However, on that same cellar door, hanging on a hook, Sergeant Smith saw a child's coat. He took this back up to Mrs Clark, who immediately identified it as belonging to her daughter. Smith now had a valid reason to force an entry into the house. Taking out his truncheon he smashed a pane of glass and finally gained access to 132a Bath Row. Of Quayle there was no sign.

A full-scale search was launched and a description of Quayle circulated to police officers throughout the city. Just a few hours later, at 1.15pm, Detective Sergeant James Carpenter saw Quayle in Broad Street, recognising him from the description. Sergeant Carpenter stopped the man, confirmed that it was Quayle and informed him that he wished to interview him about a missing girl. Quayle said, "What are you talking about? I don't know anything about a little girl." Sergeant Carpenter escorted Quayle to Ladywood police station where he was told that a child's coat had been found at his house. Quayle would only say, "How should I know how it got there?"

Even as Quayle was being interviewed at the police station, at around 3.10pm, Charles Clarke visited the house in Bath Row and there he saw a rope on one arm of a chair. What looked like nothing more than an old washing line had been knotted in a rather unusual way and Mr Clarke recognised this as his own work. In his hand he was now holding the skipping rope Vera had had with her when she left school on May 5th, further evidence that she had been inside this house.

Quayle was interviewed by Detective Inspector William Anderson who told him about the finding of the skipping rope. At 4.00pm Quayle made a written statement. In this, he detailed his movements of the previous day, saying that he had been in town but had arrived home at about 4.30pm. He claimed that he had then had a nap, in one of the chairs, until about 5.30pm, when he made some tea. At 5.40pm, Quayle had left his house and gone to Fisher & Ludlow's factory where he worked as a company policeman, but on arrival he found that he had toothache so asked if he could take the night off. Permission was granted and Quayle left work at 6.15pm. Instead of going straight home, he had a couple of beers in a pub in Sherlock Street, later travelling to another couple of pubs and not leaving the last one until closing time at 10.00pm. By 10.30pm, Quayle was asleep at home and did not wake until 6.00am. His statement went on to refer to the visit of Mr London and the Clarkes, after which he went into town.

He ended by denying any knowledge of the missing girl and said he had no idea how her coat and skipping rope came to be in his house.

Inspector Anderson knew that there was much more to find out from Quayle and sent him down to the cells while the investigation continued. It was not until 9.30pm that Quayle was brought back to the office for a further interview. There were three police officers present in the room, Inspector Anderson, Sergeant Carpenter and Superintendent Richardson, but they had hardly begun to question Quayle when he volunteered, "You want to find her, don't you?" A caution was administered and Quayle went on, "I'll take you. I don't know the name of the spot but will show you the way."

Quayle and the three police officers, together with Professor James Mathewson Webster, climbed into a police car and were directed, by Quayle, to a bombed-out house at 12 Spring Vale. Quayle took them to the back of the house and in the rubble-filled room stopped, pointed to a pile of bricks, and muttered, "There." Professor Webster carefully lifted some of the bricks and soon revealed the almost naked body of a small girl. Vera Clarke had been found.

Quayle had not finished though. Even as the rubble was being cleared from Vera's body, he said, "I brought her down in my truck. I'll show you where I left it." The 'truck' was in fact a hand-cart and Quayle took the police to Vere Street where he had abandoned it. Later he took Sergeant Carpenter to Benacre Street where he pointed out a piece of coarse cloth, adding, "That's the cloth I covered her with in the truck." From there, Quayle was taken back to the police station where he made a second written statement.

In this second document, Quayle admitted that his first state-ment had been untrue. He went on, 'I have been drinking heavily the last few days. About half past four to five o'clock on Wed-nesday afternoon, the 5th May, I had just come in the house when I saw the little girl in the street. I asked her to go for some potatoes for me and I gave her 3d to get them. She came back into the house with them a few minutes later. Something came over me. I can hardly remember, but I seemed to rush at her all at once. I must have strangled her I suppose. I left her on the rug in the kitchen, and I hardly knew what I was doing. I did not inter-fere with her. I locked up the house and went to the works and asked them to let me off duty as I had toothache. I got permission to be off that night. I then called in several public houses and had quite a lot of drink between six o'clock and closing time.

'I went back to the house at about half past ten, and must have fell (sic) asleep in the chair in the kitchen. I must have woke up about four o'clock in the morning. I made some tea. I then stopped in the house and between half past eight and nine o'clock two men and a woman knocked at the door. They asked me if I had seen the girl, as she was seen near my house at five o'clock the night before. I told them, "No." They said the police would be coming down.

'As soon as they had gone I put the girl in the truck and wheeled her away to the bombed house near the Bristol Road where I took you to.

'I want to say I took the girl's clothing off in the house before I moved her. In the bombed house I covered the girl over with bricks so that she would not be seen.

'I left the truck in a street near at hand, where I showed you, and threw the cloth I had covered her with on some bricks in another street nearby.

'I have very little recollection of what I did to the girl in the house. I am sorry it has happened. It is all through the drink and the wife leaving me.'

Having been charged with murder, Quayle first appeared before the magistrates on May 7th when the prosecuting solicitor, Mr M.P. Pugh, requested a remand until May 11th. On that date a further remand followed, this time for two weeks, and on the same day, the inquest on Vera opened before Dr W.H. Davison. This was also adjourned, until July 21st by which time the criminal proceedings should have been concluded.

Quayle's next court appearance was scheduled for May 25th but then Mr E.B.M. Conway for the defence explained that his client had been seriously ill in the prison hospital and consequently was unable to attend. Matters were adjourned until June 8th, a further remand following to June 17th, when the evidence was heard and Quayle was sent for trial.

William Quayle faced that trial at Birmingham on July 12th, 1943, before Mr Justice Wrottesley. For the defence, Mr Richard O'Sullivan was assisted by Mr T.R. Whittingham, while the Crown's case was put by Mr Arthur Ward and Mr John F. Bourke.

William Abbotts, who was just ten years old, lived at 2 St Martin Street, Ladywood, and he, too, had known Vera quite well. On May 5th, at around 4.45pm, he had been standing at the junction of Bishopsgate Street and Bath Row and like Dorothy Binnion, he had seen Vera standing on the doorstep of 132a Bath Row, but William had seen Vera actually talking to Quayle. He saw Quayle hand something over to Vera and said that it looked like a large piece of white paper. Quayle folded this paper up and Vera put it under her arm before running off up Bishopsgate Street towards William Street. Some minutes later, William saw Vera return with some sort of parcel and go in to number 132a.

This testimony fitted with that given by Winifred Rose Dooling, who on May 5th, was helping her sister in the green-grocer's shop she ran at 94 Bishopsgate Street. It was around 4.50pm when a little girl fitting Vera's description came into the shop and asked for three pounds of potatoes. Winifred served the child, wrapping the potatoes in the large piece of white paper she had brought with her. Having been shown a photograph of the dead girl, Winifred was sure this was the one she had served on May 5th.

Evidence was now called to show that Quayle had indeed asked for the night off on May 5th. John James Cronin was another of the works policemen at Fisher & Ludlow's factory and he swore that at 6.30pm on May 5th, Quayle had reported for work in uniform but had asked to speak to his immediate boss, Mr Bland, on the telephone. After the conversation with Mr Bland was finished, Quayle told Cronin that he had been given permission to go home, and left the factory.

Frederick Charles Bland was a sergeant in the works police and confirmed that Quayle had worked there since March 6th. On May 5th, Quayle spoke to him on the telephone and explained that he had had some teeth removed and didn't feel too well. Mr Bland said that he could go home if he wished.

Medical testimony was given by Professor Webster who said that he had found the body of Vera Clarke underneath a pile of rubble in a recess at the back of the bombed house at 12 Spring Vale. There was a ligature around Vera's neck but this was loose. There were other such ligatures around the child's waist and both ankles. Vera was naked except for her two socks and her left shoe and there were obvious signs that she had been raped.

On May 7th, Professor Webster performed an autopsy, assisted by Dr Walter Pemberton Fooks. They agreed that Vera had died from asphyxia, due to strangulation by the ligature. When Vera's clothing had been found, Professor Webster examined them and stated that all the items, except for an overcoat, blouse and a pair of knickers, had either been cut or torn up the front in order that they might be removed more easily. There were no seminal or blood stains on any of the girl's clothing indicating that the removal had occurred before she was violated. Quayle's clothing was also examined and the only stain found was a small semen stain on the fly of his trousers.

The defence called no evidence, preferring to suggest that this was not the act of a normal person and this, allied to the fact that there was no malice aforethought should suggest a verdict either of manslaughter or guilty but insane. The testimony of John Humphrey, the medical officer of Birmingham prison, seemed to confirm that Quayle was perhaps suffering from some sort of mental imbalance. Mr Humphrey testified that on his reception at the prison, Quayle had been found to be carrying two pieces of tin in his socks. On May 20th, Quayle had complained of severe abdominal pains and soon this developed into hypostatic pneumonia, which was why he had been unable to attend the magistrate's hearing. The prisoner grew very ill and an X-ray revealed several foreign objects in his abdomen including an open safety pin. Once he had started to recover, Quayle had admitted that he had swallowed these objects in an attempt to kill himself and thus avoid the trial.

Having heard all this evidence, the jury returned the expected verdict of guilty and Quayle was sentenced to death. No appeal was entered and just over three weeks after the trial had ended, on the morning of Tuesday, August 3rd, 1943, William Quayle was hanged at Birmingham by Thomas Pierrepoint and Alexander Riley.

CHAPTER TWENTY-ONE

THE HOLLY BUSH MURDER

ON the afternoon of Sunday, November 21st, 1948, 14-year-old Joan Mary Marney left her home at 75 Sidcup Road, Kingstanding, to visit the Odeon cinema at Perry Barr. Joan set out with two of her schoolfriends but, at the end of the show, she left with a young soldier she had met and who said he would see her home. It was a journey that little Joan Marney never completed.

Joan's father, John Marney, became anxious about his daughter when she had not returned home by midnight, and reported her missing to the police. A search was launched but no trace of Joan was found.

At 11.45am the next day, Bertram Rennie, a male nurse, was walking across Sutton Park when he saw what looked like a handbag, some eight yards from the Banner Gate entrance. Going over to investigate further, Mr Rennie saw that the object was indeed a handbag but even as he stared down at it, something else caught his eye. There, just a few feet away, beneath a large holly bush, was the body of a young woman. Joan Marney had been found, just a mile from her home. She was lying with blood and bruising on her face and the corner of her plastic mackintosh thrust into her mouth.

The police spoke to Joan's friends and obtained a detailed description of the soldier she had been seen with at the cinema. As it happened, though, the police operation did not even have time to get into full swing, for at 10.00pm on November 22nd, the same day that Joan's body had been discovered, an 18-year-old soldier, James Farrell, of 4 Bevis Grove, Dornington Road, Kingstanding, walked into Steelhouse Lane police station and gave himself up as an absentee from the Army. The officers who interviewed him noticed that he fitted the description of the wanted soldier in the murder case and soon afterwards, Detective Inspector Thomas E. Medley travelled to Steelhouse Lane from Sutton Coldfield, to interview Farrell. He and Detective Sergeant Buchanan, arrived at 11.00pm. They told Farrell who they were and cautioned him and when questioned about the death of Joan Marney, Farrell readily admitted that he was responsible. He made a full written statement, and was formally arrested and taken back to Sutton Coldfield police station where he was again cautioned and then charged with murder. Farrell replied, "I have already told you about it."

The following day, November 23rd, Farrell made a brief appearance at the Sutton Coldfield magistrates' court. He was dressed casually in a brown sports jacket and grey flannel trousers and appeared composed. After evidence of arrest, and a few details of Joan's movements had been given, Farrell was remanded. The hearing lasted just five minutes.

The inquest on Joan opened before Mr C.W. Iliffe, on November 27th. Evidence of identification was given, John Marney, the dead girl's father explaining that Joan had turned 14 the previous April and was the youngest of his three daughters. He said that Joan was very well developed for her age, but as far as he was aware, she had never had a boyfriend. Professor J.M. Webster gave details of the injuries Joan had suffered and confirmed that the cause of death had been violent asphyxia, caused by manual strangulation. Asked if he had any questions to put to the witness, Farrell replied, "I did not use my fists on the girl. I did not punch her in any way." The inquest was then adjourned sine die.

Three days later, on November 30th, Farrell made his second appearance before the magistrates, when he was represented by Mr Roderick Baker. For the police, Detective Inspector Medley said that they were not yet ready to proceed and asked for a further remand. Mr Baker made no objection.

It was not until Thursday, December 16th, that the final hearing took place at the magistrate's court. Here the evidence for the prosecution was given by Mr J.F. Claxton who explained that Farrell was stationed at the RASC, depot at Broughton, not far from Preston, Lancashire. He had left his unit on Friday, November 19th, arriving home at 10.00pm. Farrell did not have permission to leave Preston, and had been posted as an absentee since 6.00am that same day.

On December 20th, a police officer called at Farrell's home and after speaking to the young man, advised him to return to Lancashire at his first opportunity. Farrell's father, Nathaniel, urged his son to follow this course of action, but James Farrell could not be persuaded. He decided to ignore the advice he had been given, and remained at home. Farrell's father had even threatened to escort his son to the police station but even this did nothing to persuade his son to report back to his unit.

On the day that Joan Marney died, Farrell had gone to the cinema to meet his brother, but when he failed to arrive, Farrell fell into conversation with Joan. They seemed to get on well and Farrell got on the bus with her and rode to her home in Sidcup Road. For some minutes they stood chatting outside and were seen by a number of witnesses, at around 7.30pm. It was the last time Joan was seen until her body was found in the park the next morning. Having heard Farrell's statement read out in court, the magistrates sent the prisoner to face his trial.

The case of the Crown versus James Farrell took place at Birmingham on March 10th, 1949, before Mr Justice Lynskey and a jury of 11 men and one woman. The case for the prosecution lay in the hands of Mr Paul Sandlands and Mr C. Shawcross, while Farrell's defence was led by Mr R.C. Vaughan, assisted by Mr Geoffrey Lane. There was no attempt to deny that Farrell was responsible for the death of Joan Marney, but the defence put forward the theory that he was insane at the time of the crime, and therefore not responsible for his actions.

One of the most important pieces of evidence was Farrell's own statement to the police. After being told that he fitted the description of a man seen with the dead girl, he had hesitated for a few minutes and then said, "Yes, it was me. I took her to the park and then strangled her." In his long written statement, Farrell had gone on to say that Joan had told him that she was 17 and a half and after talking to her outside her home, he had suggested that they go for a walk together. Joan had agreed, providing that she was back home by 9.30pm. Farrell said that he had felt disagreeable because his younger brother had not met him at the cinema as arranged and even as he and Joan walked off, he made his mind up to do her some harm.

After arriving in the park, Farrell said that he and Joan sat in a shelter and he started kissing her. His written statement continued, 'I took her by the arm and walked her into the wood. She said she wanted to go home. I pushed her down and continued to make love to her. She began to struggle and cry and said, "I thought this would happen. I shall report you when I get home."

'I thought I might get into trouble. I put my left hand on her throat and kept kissing her so that she could not get her breath. I put my right hand on her throat and pressed with all my force. She began to make choking noises, and I knew then I must have finished her off.'

Professor Webster, the Home Office pathologist, stated that Joan had not been sexually interfered with, however, blood on her face showed that she had been struck. There were also abrasions on both of Joan's legs and part of her plastic raincoat had been forced into her mouth to gag her. In addition, Professor Webster had examined Farrell's clothing after his arrest. He had found strands of hair on the battledress and these were of the same type as Joan's.

Nathaniel Farrell told the court that his son had been a problem ever since he had left school. He was, 'undisciplined, unruly and strong-headed'. Nathaniel went on to outline the events that took place in his home on the day before Joan was killed. On Saturday, November 20th, he had returned home at 6.30pm to find James semi-conscious in front of the gas stove. The gas tap had been turned on but the supply had run out, thereby saving his son's life. Nathaniel opened all the doors and brought James around. Once the boy was sufficiently recovered, Mr Farrell had asked him why he had tried to kill himself and James had replied, "I have been such a rat to you and my brother that I thought this was the best way out." Even as this evidence was being given, though, Farrell turned to the judge and shouted out in court, "I deny that, sir." Nathaniel Farrell also explained that his wife, James' mother, had been in the Lodge Road Asylum for the past three and a half years.

The defence called no evidence, Mr Vaughan preferring to rely on his summing up to put the case for his client suffering from insanity. At one stage he said, "This young man is suffering from some disease of the mind which is aborting the normal processes of thought and reasoning. He was so imperfectly able to balance between right and wrong, so completely callous and indifferent to the consequences of what he was doing, that he is to be considered as one who cannot differentiate between right and wrong." The jury did not agree. Farrell was found guilty and sentenced to death.

On March 19th, it was announced that the execution had been provisionally fixed for March 29th, pending the possibility of an appeal being entered. In the event, no such application was made.

At 9.00am on Tuesday, March 29th, James Farrell, who had turned 19 since he had been sentenced, was hanged at Birmingham prison by Albert Pierrepoint who was assisted by Harry Kirk. A future assistant hangman, Syd Demley, observed the proceedings as part of his training.

A crowd of about 50 people had gathered outside the prison gates and at the appointed hour, one woman knelt down on the pavement and began to pray. After the notice of execution had been posted on the gates, an elderly man shouted, "Down with capital punishment. It's inhuman. It's a disgrace to our civilisation." It was to remain so for the next 15 years.

CHAPTER TWENTY-TWO

NO EXCUSES

ALTHOUGH 49-year-old William Arthur Watkins was a married man, he was separated from his legal wife and, by the beginning of 1951, had been living for five years with a woman named Florence May White. They already had a three-year-old son and Florence was now heavily pregnant with their second child.

On Sunday, January 21st, 1951, during the early hours of the morning, Florence White gave birth to a healthy boy at her home, 6 Back 69, Clifton Road, Balsall Heath, Birmingham. The neighbours, who of course knew all about Florence's condition and that she did not have long to go, asked after her and were told by Watkins that the doctor and midwife had both visited them in the night, that Florence had given birth, and that mother and child were now doing well. There was something curious about Watkins' attitude, though, and he seemed to be reluctant to let anyone look at the new arrival. The neighbours grew suspicious and this in turn led to a telephone call to the local police station.

Detective Sergeant Black arrived at Watkins' house on Monday, January 22nd, and said that he had received a report that a baby had recently been born at the house and he wished to check after its welfare. By now Sergeant Black had already checked with Watkins' doctor, the local hospitals and the mid-wife and found that no one had attended Florence White at Clifton Road, so Watkins had been lying to his neighbours. Watkins, though, made no attempt to hide what had happened and immediately announced that the child was dead.

Having spoken to both Watkins and Florence, Sergeant Black discovered that almost as soon as the child had been born, Watkins had taken him from his mother, telling her that he was going to give the baby a bath. He left the bedroom, only to return a few minutes later to inform the new mother that her child had died. According to Florence, Watkins had told her that as he was washing his son, the baby had slipped out of his hands, fallen into the water and before he could pull him out, had drowned. Sergeant Black asked to see the body and Watkins took him into the bathroom and pointed to a pillowcase still floating in a bath of water. The body of the unnamed child lay inside the pillowcase, head down. Black told Watkins that he would be taken to the police station for further questioning.

Watkins persisted in his story that the death had been accidental, but could offer no reasonable explanation as to how the baby had ended up inside a pillowcase. As a result, in the early hours of January 23rd, he was charged with wilful murder. Later that same day he made his first appearance before the magistrates where the basic details of the case were outlined by Mr M.P. Pugh. Watkins was granted legal aid and remanded until January 31st.

On January 31st, a further remand followed, this time for eight days. His next court appearance took place on February 8th when he was again remanded, but later that day, the inquest was opened and after medical evidence had confirmed that the child had drowned, the proceedings were adjourned until March 22nd.

The final magistrate's hearing took place on February 15th, when Watkins was defended by Mr J.H. Alderson. Florence White testified that when Watkins had returned to the bedroom alone, he had announced, "I've done it. The baby is dead." He had then explained that it had all been a terrible accident.

Sergeant Black told the court that Watkins had made a full statement at the police station, part of which read, "We had made no arrangements. I lost my head and did not know what to do. I went to bathe it and it slipped and dropped into the water. I have not slept since. If I drowned the baby, I did it in a panic."

The trial of William Watkins opened at Birmingham before Mr Justice Finnemore on March 15th, 1951, the case for the prosecution being put by Mr R.T. Paget. The trial lasted for two days and Watkins, who was very deaf had to have parts of the evidence repeated to him by a warder who stood next to him in the dock.

Sergeant Black told the court that throughout his interview, Watkins had never wavered from his suggestion that this had all been a terrible accident. Before he made his written statement he had said, "I was helping her. I got a bowl of water and was bathing the baby. It slipped and I let it drop into the water."

Florence White repeated her story of Watkins taking the child and then reporting to her that it had died. Under cross examination, though she admitted that during her pregnancy, Watkins had been most attentive and had urged her to go to a pre-natal clinic and to see a doctor, but she said she had been too ill to do so.

Medical testimony was given by Dr James Mathewson Webster, who said there were no external marks of violence on the body apart from a small bruise on the nose which might have been caused during the birth itself. He confirmed that the cause of death was asphyxia due to drowning.

It was for the jury to decide if this was an accident or whether Watkins, concerned that he could not afford to feed another child, had deliberately murdered his son. In his summing up, Mr Justice Finnemore said, "If this man was washing the baby and it fell into the bath how would it have got head first into the pillowcase? If he put the baby into the pillow slip before it went into the water, it must throw very grave doubt on to his story that he was washing the child properly at the time of the accident."

The judge, though, was scrupulously fair to Watkins and towards the end of his speech, referred to the possibility of alternative verdicts. He concluded, "If his own story was true, the child had fallen into the water and he had taken no steps to rescue it, but had left it in the water. In view of this, the jury might think that at the least, Watkins was guilty of manslaughter."

The jury had therefore three possible verdicts: murder, manslaughter or simply not guilty. They took two and a half hours to decide that the only verdict they could find was that Watkins was guilty of murder. He was sentenced to death, to which he made no comment.

On March 24th, it was announced that a provisional date for the execution had been set for April 3rd, although this would be postponed if Watkins announced his intention to appeal. In the event, he decided not to exercise that right, preferring instead to rely on the possibility of a reprieve. On March 31st, though, the Home Secretary said that having considered the case carefully, he could find no reason to recommend His Majesty to interfere with the due course of the law.

At 9.00am on Tuesday, April 3rd, 1951, William Arthur Watkins was hanged at Birmingham by Albert Pierrepoint, who was assisted by Harry Allen. A crowd estimated at 50 strong, which included two of Watkin's former workmates, waited outside the prison gates at the time. It was only the third execution of 1951, a year that would see 14 men hanged on English gallows.

CHAPTER TWENTY-THREE

THE PSYCHOPATH

AT 5.45pm on the evening of Wednesday, August 1st, 1951, Sheila Ethel Attwood, an 11-year-old schoolgirl, went out to play with some of her friends, close to her home at 36 Caversham Road, Kingstanding. When Sheila, normally a most reliable girl, did not return home that night, her worried parents contacted their neighbours and a search party was organised. By 11.10pm, when no trace of the child had been found, the police were called in.

The police hunt continued long into the night but it was not until 11.25am on August 2nd that Sheila was finally found, and then it was a neighbour, Ada Ford living at number 32, who saw Sheila's body at the back of a privet hedge which separated her garden from waste land belonging to Birmingham Corporation. Mrs Ford was hanging out some washing when she caught a glimpse of the child's legs. She ran screaming into the street where she encountered another neighbour, Mr Gray, and told him what she had seen. The police were called and Sergeant Hancock, taking a closer look, saw a string was knotted around the little girl's throat. A subsequent post-mortem performed by Professor James Mathewson Webster, showed that she had been strangled manually as well as by means of the ligature. Sheila had also been brutally sexually assaulted.

As a matter of routine, all the neighbours were interviewed by police officers. Mrs Brooke, who lived at 33 Caversham Road, said that she had known Sheila, one of a family of nine children, very well indeed, but she had last seen her two days before when the child had said, "Hello," to her. On the night of August 1st, Mrs Brooke and her husband, who both worked in a local public house, were on their way home after closing time when they had run into a tearful Violet Attwood, Sheila's mother, who told them that her daughter was missing. They had immediately joined in a search, but without success.

Another witness was ten-year-old Dorothy Allen, who lived at 28 Caversham Road. At 2.00pm on August 1st, Dorothy and Sheila were paddling together in the pool at Finchley Park. By 4.00pm, Sheila had had enough and said that she was going home. The two girls walked back to Caversham Road but when Sheila reached her front gate she announced that she had changed her mind and wanted to go back to the park. Dorothy did not go with her and the last she saw of her friend, she was skipping off up the road heading off back towards the park.

One of the many people interviewed by the police was a man who lived at 34 Caversham Road, next door to where Sheila's body had been found. Horace Carter was a 31-year-old labourer at an engineering factory in Witton. It was around 4.30pm on August 2nd when Detective Superintendent Davies, Superintendent Molloy, and Detective Chief Inspector Harris visited Carter at his place of work and told him that they wished to talk to him about the death of Sheila Attwood. Since the factory was hardly the most conducive place to hold such an interview, the officers told Carter that they would drive him home where he could be questioned in private. Carter replied that he knew nothing about the matter and his conscience was clear but he would happily accompany them. Throughout all this time he appeared to be almost laughing but he was largely silent as the police car made its way along the streets of Birmingham. Suddenly, though, as the vehicle sped along Tame Road, Carter was overcome with emotion and said, "I never really intended to hurt the girl."

Carter was immediately cautioned that anything he said would be taken down and might be used in evidence, but he continued, "If you will take me home, I'll show you how I did it and where she is." Later he made a full written statement at Kingstanding police station admitting that he was responsible for the girl's death, whereupon he was charged with murder.

On August 3rd, Carter appeared in court before Mr J.F. Milward, the stipendiary magistrate. Carter was not legally represented and when his means were inquired into, he was offered legal aid. Carter, who seemed to be totally disinterested in what was going on about him, replied, "I don't think it's worth it." Nevertheless, he was informed that if he subsequently changed his mind, a solicitor would be appointed to advise him. After hearing evidence of Carter's arrest, Mr Milward adjourned the proceedings for a week to allow the police to continue their investigation. Throughout the short hearing, Carter had smiled broadly. Further appearances followed on August 10th, August 16th, August 24th and August 31st.

Carter was back in court on September 6th, for what was his final appearance. By this time he had indeed changed his mind about legal representation and Mr H.E. Wynschenk appeared on his behalf. The evidence for the prosecution was detailed by Mr M.P. Pugh. The main body of the prosecution's case was Carter's own detailed confession. In this he admitted that on August 1st he had asked Sheila into his house, giving her some sweets to entice her. Once inside number 34, Carter took the girl upstairs where he assaulted her. The statement continued, 'Fearing that she would talk, I got a pillow, shoved it under her head and after that I knelt on her arms and then whipped the pillow from underneath her head, and shoved it over her face.

'She struggled for a bit, so to finish her off more quickly shoved my fingers round her throat. After that she ceased struggling, but she was still breathing, so I decided to use string.

'She was still breathing so I got some cloth and my handkerchief and tied them around her mouth and her nostrils. I turned her down on her face on the bed and there she died.

'I tied her arms behind her back and then tied her legs and I left her in a praying position.' Carter went on to say that soon afterwards, his brother-in-law, Frederick Pearce, who lived with him, returned home and he left Sheila's body upstairs until Frederick had gone out. Once it had gone dark, Carter finally carried the body out of the house. Taking a pair of ladders from his shed, he climbed over the privet hedge. Before leaving the body where it would subsequently be found, Carter removed the gag from Sheila's mouth, took the string off her legs and arms and threw them into his dustbin. The statement ended, 'I am glad it is all over.'

Evidence was also given that after Carter had been taken to his house by the police, he showed them the bedroom where the crime had taken place, pointing out some of the string he had used. Later, he lifted the lid of the dustbin and pointed out the rest of the string and the handkerchief he had used to stifle Sheila's cries. It was also brought to the attention of the court that when Sergeant Hancock had viewed the body, a pipe and mackintosh belt were found nearby. Both these items had been shown to belong to Carter.

Frederick Pearce, Carter's brother-in-law and the man who shared his house, told the court that Carter had pestered him all evening, trying to find out what time he was going out. Eventually Pearce left at 8.20pm and stayed out until 9.30pm.

After hearing all this testimony, the magistrate had no difficulty in sending Carter to trial at the next assizes.

The case of the Crown versus Horace Carter was heard at Birmingham on December 12th, 1951, before Mr Justice Cassels and a jury of nine men and three women. Mr Walker Carter appeared for the prosecution, while the prisoner was defended by Mr Richard Elwes.

There could be no doubt that Carter was responsible for Sheila Attwood's death and his only possible defence could be one of insanity. Chief Inspector Harris read out the statement Carter had made at the police station, but under cross examination admitted that he had also inquired into the prisoner's family background. He had discovered that Carter's elder brother had been certified insane in 1934, although he was subsequently discharged from the asylum in 1941. In addition, his sister, Lily Carter, had been placed under supervision as a mental defective in 1932 and had remained so until her death, also in 1941.

Dr William O'Connor was the superintendent of a mental home in Staffordshire and he had examined Carter a number of times. Dr O'Connor testified that in his opinion, Carter had a psychopathic personality and showed no regard for anyone with the possible exception of his mother. Carter had admitted that while he was in the Army he had attempted to commit suicide by shooting himself in the chest and when asked why, had replied that it was 'something to do with the weather'. Dr O'Connor continued by saying that Carter was completely indifferent to his own fate, or to the death of anyone else. He had no idea of right or wrong and no sense of guilt or social responsibility. Mr Justice Cassels asked Dr O'Connor if Carter was actually certifiable, but the doctor replied that, based on the evidence of his interviews, he was not.

To counter this testimony, the prosecution called Dr J.J. O'Reilly, the medical superintendent of Winson Green prison, and Dr John Humphrey, the principal medical officer of that same establishment. Both men stated that they believed Carter was perfectly sane, knew what he had done was wrong and was therefore responsible for his actions.

It was for the jury to decide if Carter was sane or not and it took them just 15 minutes to decide that he was and therefore guilty of murder. No appeal was entered and on December 30th the Home Secretary, Sir David Maxwell Fyfe, announced that there were no grounds for interfering with the sentence and Carter would not be reprieved.

Horace Carter did manage to see in the New Year, but only just. He was hanged at Birmingham at 9.00am on Tuesday, January 1st, 1952, by Albert Pierrepoint and Syd Demley. One of the small knot of people who had gathered outside the prison gates to read the notices of execution was Detective Chief Inspector Harris, who had arrested Carter within three hours of Sheila Attwood's body being discovered.

CHAPTER TWENTY-FOUR

RAPID JUSTICE

AT 8.30am on Tuesday, May 31st, 1955, a Jamaican, 46-year-old Corbett Montague Roberts, walked into the police station at Newton Street, Birmingham and asked to speak to a policeman. Detective Sergeant Worrall was detailed to speak to Roberts and was shocked to hear him announce, "I have done my wife in."

After hearing this, Detective Chief Inspector Frederick Renshaw and other officers went around to Roberts' home at 113 Frederick Road, Aston. There they found the body of 41-year-old Doris Acquilla Roberts lying on the floor by the bed. She was suffering from extensive head wounds which appeared to have been inflicted by a hammer. Chief Inspector Renshaw returned to the police station and charged Roberts with murder. He replied, "I am guilty."

Roberts appeared before the magistrates that same day, May 31st, Mr M.P. Pugh, for the prosecution, explaining that Roberts and his wife had lived in a ground floor bed-sitting room at Frederick Road. After describing the finding of Doris' body and Roberts' subsequent charge, Mr Pugh requested a remand until

June 2nd. Roberts was asked by the clerk of the court, Mr W. Pratt, if he had anything to say, whereupon he replied, "I am guilty." Asked again by the chairman of the bench, Alderman J.C. Burman, if he wished to make a statement, Roberts would only say, "I am in your hands." He was asked if he wanted legal aid but said, "No, I am guilty. I am not causing any trouble. I am guilty."

This determination to offer no defence was repeated at the second hearing on June 2nd, before the stipendiary magistrate, Mr J.F. Milward. Once again Roberts was asked if he had anything to say when a further remand was requested by the prosecution. He replied, "I leave myself in your hands." Mr Milward now inquired of Roberts why he had refused legal aid, to which Roberts said, "I am not interested because I am guilty." In fact, Roberts seemed more interested in his property than in defending himself on the capital charge, for he then asked the court if he could have some of his property from his bed-sitting room as he wished to give it away to people he knew. It was explained that the room had been sealed by the police but if Roberts wrote down which items he wished to donate to which people, the matter would be attended to. A remand was granted, to June 9th, and on that date, a further adjournment was ordered, this time until June 17th. Further remands followed until June 24th and then to June 28th, when the evidence was finally heard.

According to Mr Pugh for the prosecution, Roberts and his wife had rented the bed-sitting room some 18 months before. There were apparently many quarrels between Roberts and Doris and once she had left him, although she returned after a few days. Eventually, the other tenants in the house complained to the landlord about the constant arguments and in May, Roberts was told that he would have to vacate the premises.

The Roberts' had two daughters and one of these, a married

woman named Carmen Brown, lived in Handsworth. On May 31st, Corbett Roberts had gone to visit his daughter there, but the door was opened by the landlady, Mrs Thomas, and Roberts told her that he had killed his wife. Roberts asked to see Carmen but Mrs Thomas, possibly fearful of what might happen, had advised him not to wait. Roberts had tried to reassure the woman by saying, "I am not going to kill her. I am going to tell her to live happily." Soon afterwards, Roberts had walked to the police station, handed over his front door key and announced that he had killed his wife.

Chief Inspector Renshaw explained to the court that he had found two bloodstained hammers at 113 Frederick Road, one of which was broken in the shaft. He went on to report that after being cautioned back at the station, Roberts had said, "I killed my wife this morning at about 20 minutes to eight. I hit her on the head with a hammer. There had been some trouble between us for some time. Last year I had been wrongly accused of stealing money. Last Friday my cousin, Selwyn Serchwell, told me that my wife and my brother-in-law had told the police that it was me.

"I mentioned to my wife about this money on Sunday morning and we had a fuss over it. After that she says she is not depending on me for anything because she has her house. I talked to her about the same matter this morning and she says it is me who stole it. I get out of bed to go to work and I have some breakfast.

"My wife began to talk about the same matter and I could not enjoy my breakfast and threw it into the bucket and prepared to leave her to go to work. There was some money on the table which was my weekly expenses to work, and she took it. I said in a passionate way, 'Please let me have that money.' She said, 'You have to kill me this morning for that money. You are not getting it.'

"I said, 'If I don't have money to keep me, where shall I get it?' She refused to give it to me. I threw my lunch bag and overalls down and picked up a hammer in the room. I hit her on the head once and she drop. I keep on hitting her on the head with the hammer. Then the hammer broke. I take another hammer and hit her again, and it goes through her skull. I change my clothes and go to my daughter's lodgings where I say I come to tell Carmen I kill her mother, but the landlady would not allow me in to see her."

Having heard this evidence and Roberts' statement, the magistrates ordered that he stand his trial at the next assizes. They opened in July and on the 22nd of that month, Roberts appeared in the dock at Birmingham before Mr Justice Gorman. The case for the prosecution was put by Mr Richard O'Sullivan, while Roberts was defended by Mr R.K. Brown and Mr A.P. Marshall. Despite his earlier statements, Roberts pleaded not guilty to murder. He admitted that he was responsible for his wife's death but now said that he never intended to kill her.

There were few witnesses to call. Carmen Brown, Roberts' daughter, testified that her father resented the close relationship she had enjoyed with her mother. This was made even more acute when Carmen's uncle, who was Doris' brother, moved in with her. Roberts deeply objected to the closeness the family had and especially resented his brother-in-law sleeping in the same room.

Dr James Mathewson Webster had made a post-mortem examination of the body and he stated that there were severe injuries to the head. The skull had suffered gross fractures due to multiple blows but the attack must have been sudden, for there were no defence wounds on Doris' hands.

Roberts went into the box to explain his actions on the morning of May 31st. He stated that the previous year, he had been accused of stealing some money. He was searched and his fingerprints were taken but he was innocent and no charges were ever preferred against him. The matter preyed on his mind, though, especially when his wife kept referring to it and saying that she thought he was guilty after all.

After having been unemployed for some time, Roberts was about to start a new job and had put some money on the table for his weekly expenses. After Doris had picked up the money, she put it into her own purse and dropped this down her blouse. Once Doris' body had been found by the police, the purse was found, just where Roberts said she had placed it.

Roberts was asked what was in his mind when he picked up that first hammer and he replied that he had not intended to kill her. He just wanted his money back, so that he could go to work and he did not realise what he had done until he saw his wife lying on the floor. Roberts claimed that he had picked up the hammer because he thought Doris was neglecting her duties to him, adding that 'the feeling just came over me to hit her'. He knew he had killed her but he had done so in a moment of passion and was not responsible for his actions. Once again, though, Roberts seemed more concerned for his property and added that he wanted none of it to be given to his children. Instead, he wanted everything he had to go to an institution for old people.

Having been found guilty and sentenced to death, Roberts thanked the judge before being taken down to the cells. He did not appeal against that sentence and no reprieve was forthcoming. On the morning of Tuesday, August 2nd, 1955, Corbett Montague Roberts was hanged at Birmingham by Stephen Wade and Harry Allen.

British justice had certainly moved swiftly on this occasion for it was just nine weeks to the day since Roberts had killed his wife.

CHAPTER TWENTY-FIVE

DAYLIGHT ROBBERY

ALTHOUGH David Alan Keasey was only 21 years old, he was already quite a successful businessman and ran his own gent's outfitters shop at 21 Wolverhampton Street, Dudley.

At a few minutes before 5.30pm on Friday, May 17th, 1957, a young man walked into the shop, to all intents and purposes he was just another customer. At the same time, a schoolboy, 15-year-old David Hiscox, happened to be standing outside and just a couple of minutes after the man had entered the shop, David heard a loud bang which was immediately followed by a scream. Within seconds, the door to the shop was thrown open and the young man dashed out into the street and ran off towards High Street shouting, "There's a man in there had a fit."

David Hiscox returned to his home at 19 Russell Street. Not long afterwards, Doreen Bell, who was David Keasey's fiancée, went into the shop to find two men leaning over David, who lay on the floor behind his counter. Neither man had any idea what had happened but an ambulance was summoned and David Keasey was rushed to hospital. There he was found to be dead, the cause being a bullet wound in his back.

The police, having spoken to David Hiscox, were able to release a general description of the man seen running from the shop, after the loud bang. The man they were seeking was: 'About 30 years old; 5ft 10ins tall; hatless and wearing a raglan type raincoat.' The same man had also stopped a woman further along the street and asked her to fetch a doctor to the shop where a man had 'had a fit' and she stated that he spoke with a Black Country accent, so was probably a local man.

A police search of the shop in Wolverhampton Street had revealed money in the till and in David Keasey's pockets, so robbery did not appear to be the motive for the crime although, of course, it might later be shown that an attempt at robbery had been made, once the killer had been captured. Scotland Yard were called in and that same night, Detective Superintendent G.A. Miller and Detective Sergeant Sydney Gentle travelled to Birmingham from London.

It looked as though the gunman might have struck again when a man named George Richard Drew, who lived at Hilary Crescent on the Bramford Estate at Coseley, rushed into his local police station on May 21st. He reported that he had been on his way to work when he was held up by a powerfully-built man wearing an old belted raincoat and with a black trilby hat pulled down over his eyes. The man had pulled out a gun and forced Drew to empty his pockets. Drew was unable to give a description of his assailant, though, because not only did his hat cover the top half of his face, but he also had a scarf wrapped around the bottom part of his face.

By May 22nd, Superintendent Miller reported that most of the customers who had been into Keasey's shop on May 17th, had come forward. The police were now questioning bus crews in case the killer had made good his escape on public transport. On the same day, David Keasey was buried, the service taking place at Tividale Methodist Church.

June 11th was a significant date for the family of the dead man for that was the day on which he should have been married to Doreen Bell. Superintendent Miller used the date to appeal for information about anyone who had changed their habits or routine since May 17th.

The case was finally broken towards the end of June when a 17-year-old youth, John Albert Aston, who lived in Albion Road, Smethwick, told the police of a conversation he had recently had with a friend. John Aston said that in late May or early June, he had been digging over his front garden when this friend came to the front gate and they fell into conversation. It was during what was otherwise an ordinary discussion that the friend admitted that it had been him who had 'shot the fellow at Dudley.' Having heard this, the police, led by Superintendent Miller, paid a visit to Lones Road, Smethwick, the house where 24-year-old Dennis Howard lived.

Dennis Howard certainly had a fascination for guns, for the police found an arsenal of weapons there, including two Smith and Wesson revolvers, but it was when they discovered a Mauser automatic pistol that Howard remarked, "That's the one I shot Keasey with at Dudley. Mind you, we had a fight and in the struggle I shot him. I asked him for the money out of the till. I had the gun out. He grabbed me by the arm and I pulled the trigger. I carried the gun to make me brave." Howard was taken into custody and charged with murder.

On June 24th, Howard made a four-minute appearance before the magistrates, when a seven-day remand was requested and granted. After that hearing, Howard was given permission to see two of his brothers who had been present in court. The second appearance took place on July 1st when Mr N. Bayley, for the defence, made no objection to a further remand, until July 9th.

It was on July 9th that the evidence was heard, the prosecution case being put by Mr David Prys Jones. John Aston told the court of an earlier visit to Dudley with Howard and another companion. Howard had given both Aston and his friend a gun, both Smith and Wessons but there was something wrong with the one Aston had, for the hammer would not click. A few days after this incident, Aston's parents had found the gun and having discovered where it came from, insisted that it be given back to Howard.

In addition to this testimony, there was other evidence against Howard. The cartridge case which had been found behind the shop counter, close to David Keasey's body, was shown to have been fired from the Mauser automatic and a thumbprint found at the scene matched Howard's prints, which were taken after his arrest. Finally, Howard's own statement was referred to. In this he had admitted that he had gone in to the shop and asked Keasey for a blue pullover. Keasey went to the back of the premises to fetch it and when he returned, Howard pulled out the gun and demanded the money out of the till. Rather than submit to being robbed, Keasey had closed with Howard and a struggle had followed in which the two protagonists' arms were entangled. Howard had his hands behind Keasey's back when he pulled the trigger and Keasey fell to the floor. Howard had run out of the shop shouting that there was a man inside who needed help.

All this was more than enough to send Howard for trial and that opened at Worcester on October 17th before Mr Justice Hinchcliffe. The trial lasted for two days, during which the Crown case was put by Mr G.G. Baker and Mr Patrick Medd, while Howard was defended by Mr R.G. Micklethwait and Mr Stephen Brown.

By the time this case came to court, the 1957 Homicide Act had been passed, meaning that there were only five circumstances under which the death penalty could be applied after a guilty verdict in a murder trial. The last execution in 1955 had been that of Alec Wilkinson on August 12th. There had been no hangings at all in 1956, while these amendments were being discussed, and since the Act had been passed, only one man, John Wilson Vickers, had been executed in 1957. Howard, though, was now facing that same penalty since one of the circumstances where hanging could be applied was murder involving the use of a firearm, and where death occurred during the commission of a robbery. Dennis Howard was on trial for his life.

On the second day of his trial, Howard stepped into the witness box to give his own version of the events inside the shop at Wolverhampton Street on May 17th, 1957. At one stage, Mr Baker for the prosecution asked Howard, "Have you noticed that you have never expressed any regret for this?" Howard did not reply.

Turning to the day of the shooting, Howard said that he had decided to commit the crime while he was in Dudley, but he had never intended to shoot anyone. Indeed, he had only taken the gun out with him to test it as it was not working properly, had not even intended using it in the robbery, and did not hold a licence for any of his weapons. Later still in his evidence, though, Howard admitted cocking the gun before going into the shop, for extra morale, and said that he had his finger on the trigger to 'look more businesslike and effective.' Howard said that the shooting was accidental but under cross examination, had to admit that he had never mentioned this to the police at the time of his arrest.

In his summing up, Mr Justice Hinchcliffe, realising that the idea of the death penalty might prey on their minds, told the jury, "It would be utterly wrong of you to return a verdict of manslaughter just because you don't like the sound of murder. Justice could not be done in this country if juries were looking over their shoulders, wondering what the result of their verdict might be." The jury took those words to heart and duly found

Howard guilty of capital murder, whereupon Mr Justice Hinch-cliffe sentenced him to death.

On October 22nd, it was announced that the execution had been fixed for November 6th, but this was postponed when notice of appeal was entered. That appeal was heard on November 18th before the Lord Chief Justice, Lord Goddard, and Justices Devlin and Pearson, although Howard had elected not to be present in court during the deliberations.

For the defence, Mr Micklethwait said that at the trial he had pressed for a verdict of manslaughter and he now hoped that the appeal court would now substitute this verdict. In the early part of the trial, while the jury had been absent, the judge had ruled that the prosecution were not allowed to bring up the fact that there was evidence that Howard had broken into other premises in Birmingham, as this might prejudice the jury. At one stage, however, Howard had been asked, "When you were out with Aston and the other man, what did you do?" Although the judge ruled that Howard need not answer, the question itself was bound to give the jury the impression that Howard had been concerned in a previous incident in which a firearm was carried. In the event, the judges ruled that this was largely irrelevant since Howard had admitted that he had cocked the pistol before he went into the shop. If that was the case, how could it possibly make it any worse if the jury suspected that he might have used a gun before? Since the pistol was cocked, it was clear that Howard meant to use it and the killing was therefore planned. The appeal was dismissed.

Howard's only hope now was for the Home Secretary to recommend a reprieve. On December 2nd, it was announced that no such recommendation was to be made and the death sentence would be carried out.

At 9.30am on Wednesday, December 4th, 1957, Dennis Howard was hanged at Birmingham by Harry Allen and Royston

Rickard. Only a few pressmen and police officers were stationed outside the prison at the time, but a typist who worked at Winson Green and a baker's boy waiting to make a delivery, had to stand across the road until they were allowed to enter the prison. It was the last execution in 1957 and only the second since the passing of the Homicide Act.

CHAPTER TWENTY-SIX

ALIBIS

AT APPROXIMATELY 6.40pm on Saturday, 2nd June, 1962, Margaret Jean Bradley, a nursery nurse, was standing at a bus stop outside a newsagent's at 176 Lea Bank Road, Edgbaston, when she heard a sound which she thought might be a car back-firing. Soon afterwards, Margaret saw a man leaving the shop and although she could not see his face clearly, she later described him as being either a dirty white man, or a pale-skinned coloured man. At about the same time as this incident was taking place, Louisa Bates, the proprietor of the shop, entered from the back of the premises and found her son, 47-year-old Thomas Arthur Bates, lying on the floor among upturned sweet bottles and scattered newspapers. Thomas had been shot and was already dead.

By the Monday, the police, after speaking to Margaret Bradley, issued a general description of the man she had seen. He was described as being: 'Aged between 30 and 40, 5ft 8ins tall, of slim build with prominent cheek-bones and eyes described as long narrow slits. He was wearing an old brown trilby hat with a dark band – medium brown three-quarter length overcoat with patch pockets and grey trousers.'

The officer in charge of the case, Detective Chief Superintendent Gerald Baumber, said that he was particularly interested in tracing two boys and a girl, all aged about 11, who had been seen playing close to the newsagent's at the time Thomas Bates had been shot. The next day, Chief Superintendent Baumber said that his officers were also interested in talking to a coloured man with an unblemished skin who had been wearing a Robin Hood-style hat which had a feather in it, and winkle-picker shoes. He, too, had been seen in the area at the time of the shooting and might have seen the killer running from the scene.

On June 6th, the police swooped on a number of addresses in Birmingham and many coloured men were taken to Ladywood police station to be interviewed and eliminated from the inquiry. One of those men was 19-year-old Oswald Augustus Grey, a man who had been unemployed for the past year and who lived at 47 Cannon Hill Road, Edgbaston. The police received information that Grey had once had a gun in his possession, and it was then that officers began to interview him about the murder of Thomas Bates. After much questioning, Grey, who changed his story repeatedly, first saying he had never had a gun, then saying he had one but had now thrown it into the canal, and finally admitting that he did have a gun and it was still in his possession. He was charged with stealing this weapon, which belonged to Mr Hamilton Bacchus of 60 Varna Road, Balsall Heath. It was on that charge that Grey first appeared before the stipendiary magistrate, Mr J.F. Milward, on June 7th, when he was remanded to the following day.

The gun which Grey was accused of stealing had been found hidden beneath a wardrobe at his home in Cannon Hill Road and tests soon showed that this was the weapon which had been used to shoot Thomas Bates. That evidence, plus a positive identification at an identity parade, led to Grey being charged with murder when he made his second appearance before the magistrate. The prisoner was remanded again, this time until June 15th.

By June 15th, Grey was represented by Mr F.G. Owen who made no objection to a further remand but added, "This man absolutely denies he is the man who shot the newsagent." On June 22nd, yet another remand followed and it was not until June 29th that Grey was sent for trial on what would be a capital charge.

The trial of Oswald Grey opened at Birmingham on October 10th, 1962, before Mr Justice Paull, and the proceedings lasted for three days. Grey was defended by Mr A.E. James, who was assisted by Mr John Owen, while the case for the Crown was led by Mr Graham Swanwick, assisted by Mr James Ross.

One of the major problems for the prosecution was that Margaret Bradley, and indeed other witnesses who had since come forward, all denied that Oswald Grey was the man they had seen coming out of the newsagent's shop after Thomas Bates had been shot. The description given by Margaret Bradley was closer to a Mr Cleghorn who had apparently gone into the shop just after the shooting, seen Bates on the floor and run to telephone for the police from a call box nearby. Margaret, however, swore that not only was Grey not the man she had seen, but neither was Mr Cleghorn, implying that the man she had observed was indeed the assailant but that this man was simply not Grey.

Anna Maria Scott, who lived in Bishop's Avenue, Ladywood, had also seen a coloured man close to the shop at about the time of the shooting but she also testified that this man was definitely not Grey. The same was said by Annette Evans, who had been in the newsagent's at 6.20pm, some 20 minutes before the shooting. At the time, there had been a coloured man there and when Annette left, he remained inside the shop and Annette noticed that he seemed particularly interested that she be served before him. The man she had seen was taller than Grey at 5ft 10ins, was broader and had straight hair. Grey was certainly not the man.

Marion Beatrice Woolley lived at 139 Great Colmore Street and she, too, had been close to the newsagent's shop on June 2nd. She had seen a coloured man, standing near the shop, looking around furtively as if to see if the coast was clear. The man took a handkerchief from his pocket and fastened it behind his head before walking directly towards the shop. Approaching the premises, the man pulled the handkerchief down over his face. Marion described this man as being 35 to 40 years old with hollow cheeks. This description was confirmed by Carole Woolley, Marion's daughter, who was with her mother at the time. Both women said that this man was not Oswald Grey.

The fact remained that the strongest piece of evidence against Grey was the fact that the murder weapon had been found in his rooms. Grey tried to explain that although this may well have been the murder weapon, it had not been in his possession at the time the crime was committed. The gun in question was a 7.65mm Walther automatic, and he claimed that he had given it to a man nicknamed Mover. The name of this 'Mover' was in fact Harris Karnfi, and Grey insisted that he had met him in a cafe in Mary Street, Balsall Heath, on the morning of June 2nd. That night, at a party in Burbury Street, Karnfi returned the weapon to Grey, who hid it underneath his wardrobe. At the crucial time, therefore, the gun used to kill Thomas Bates could not have been used by Grey.

Unfortunately for Grey, Karnfi denied this story completely and produced two witnesses, Dolores Kennedy and her sister Barbara, who testified that he had been in their company from 11.00am on June 2nd, until 10.00pm. He could not, therefore, have been in Lea Bank Road at the time of the shooting. Further, when Grey also said that he had been in a pub with his father, Felix Grey, and a friend, Phyllis Shields, when Bates was shot, they confirmed that they had spent some time with Oswald that day, but had no idea at exactly what time beyond saying that it was early evening.' Worse was to come when the owners of the cafe in Mary Street, Cephas Smith and Effie Dora Rose, testified that Grey, a man they knew well, had not been in their establishment on the day in question and so could not have met Harris Karnfi there and handed over the gun.

Grey had admitted changing his story a number of times but claimed that was due in part to the fact that he was frightened of the police. During their questioning of him, Grey claimed that certain officers had used 'third-degree methods' on him, including physical violence. The prosecution then called Superintendent Baumber, Chief Inspector J. Benbow, Detective Inspector H. Robin and Detective Constable Colin Walker, all of whom had been involved in the interrogation of Grey. All four officers denied that there was any truth in Grey's allegations.

Once Grey's alibi had collapsed and witnesses testified that he was lying about Karnfi, the jury could find no way to explain away Grey's possession of the murder weapon and so, after 50 minutes' deliberation, they found him guilty as charged and he was sentenced to death.

The execution date was set for October 30th but when, on October 19th, Grey's defence team announced that he was to appeal, this was postponed. The appeal was heard on October 29th, before Lord Parker, the Lord Chief Justice, and Justices Gorman and Salmon. The grounds of the appeal were that Grey was simply not guilty and that the trial verdict had been unreasonable and could not be supported by the evidence.

Giving the court's judgement, the Lord Chief Justice said that by his own admission, Grey had stolen the murder weapon. The crime had taken place between 6.30pm and 6.45pm and the evidence indicated that the pistol was in Grey's possession at that crucial time. Grey had claimed that in fact the pistol was with

'Mover' at this time, but although this man was of bad character, he had given evidence for the prosecution and himself had an alibi for the day of the shooting. Finally, Grey had lied to the police about his possession of the gun and, in all, had told five different stories. There was no way that the conviction could be overturned and the appeal was consequently dismissed.

On November 6th, a final appeal was made to the Home Secretary in an attempt to obtain a reprieve for the condemned man. When, on November 18th, it was announced that this had also failed, Grey knew that his last hope had gone and the sentence would be carried out.

On the morning of Tuesday, November 20th, 1962, Oswald Augustus Grey, who had by now turned 20, was hanged at Birmingham by Harry Allen and Samuel Plant. At the time, there was a demonstration outside the prison when four university students stood in silence carrying anti-capital punishment slogans. It was the last-ever execution at Winson Green and only five more men would face the same penalty in any other prison.

APPENDIX

To aid the student of true crime, I include a list of all the executions which have taken place at Birmingham this century. Many of the stories behind these names are, of course, included in the main body of this book:

John Joyce, 20th August, 1901
Charles Samuel Dyer, 5th April, 1904
Samuel Holden, 16th August, 1904
Frank Greening, 13th August, 1913
William Allen Butler, 16th August, 1916
Louis Van de Kerkhove, 9th April, 1918
Henry Thomas Gaskin, 8th August, 1919
Samuel Westwood, 30th December, 1920
Edward O'Connor, 22nd December, 1921
Elijah Pountney, 11th August, 1922
William Rider, 19th December, 1922
John Fisher, 5th January, 1926
George Sharples, 13th April, 1926
James Joseph Power, 31st January, 1928
Victor Edward Betts, 3rd January, 1931
Jeremiah Hanbury, 2nd February, 1933
Stanley Eric Hobday, 28th December, 1933
Dorothea Nancy Waddingham, 16th April, 1936
James Richards and Peter Barnes, 7th February, 1940
Eli Richards, 19th September, 1941
Arthur Peach, 30th January, 1942
Harold Oswald Merry, 10th September, 1942
William Quayle, 3rd August, 1943
James Farrell, 29th March, 1949
Piotr Maksimowski, 29th March, 1950

William Arthur Watkins, 3rd April, 1951

Horace Carter, 1st January, 1952

Leslie Green, 23rd December, 1952

Frederick Arthur Cross, 26th July, 1955

Corbett Montague Roberts, 2nd August, 1955

Ernest Charles Harding, 9th August, 1955

Dennis Howard, 4th December, 1957

Matthew Kavanagh, 12th August, 1958

Oswald Augustus Grey, 20th November, 1962

In addition, the following executions took place
at Warwick prison:

George Place, 30th December, 1902

John Davis, 1st January, 1907

Edwin James Moore, 2nd April, 1907

Harry Taylor Parker, 15th December, 1908

The following men were hanged at Stafford jail:

James Arthur Shufflebotham, 2nd April, 1901

William Lane, 12th August, 1902

Henry Jones, 29th March, 1904

Frederick William Edge, 27th December, 1905

Joseph Jones, 26th March, 1907

Joseph Edwin Jones, 14th April, 1909

George Loake, 28th December, 1911

Josiah Davies, 10th March, 1914

Finally, the following executions took place at Worcester:

Samuel Middleton, 15th July, 1902

William Yarnold, 5th December, 1905

Thomas Fletcher, 9th July, 1913

Djang Djing Sung, 3rd December, 1919

BIBLIOGRAPHY

Newspapers:
Birmingham Daily Mail
Birmingham Daily Post
Birmingham Evening Mail and Despatch
Birmingham Mail
Birmingham Post
Birmingham Post and Birmingham Gazette
Birmingham Weekly Mercury
Coventry Evening Telegraph
Evening Sentinel
Midland Counties Express
Midland Counties and Wolverhampton Chronicle
Midland Daily Telegraph
Rugby Advertiser
Staffordshire Sentinel
Sunday Mercury
Sunday Mercury and News
Weekly Mercury
Wolverhampton Chronicle and Midland Counties Express

Assizes Documents:
ASSI 13-31 Joyce
ASSI 13-34 Dyer and Holden
ASSI 13-36 Davis
ASSI 13-43 Greening
ASSI 13-46 Butler
ASSI 13-48 Kerkhove
ASSI 6-54/9 Gaskin
ASSI 6-54/8 Sung
ASSI 6-55/6 Westwood
ASSI 6-57/1 Pountney
ASSI 13-55 Fisher
ASSI 13-57 Power
ASSI 13-60 Betts
ASSI 13-62 Hanbury
ASSI 6-68/3 Hobday
ASSI 13-71 Richards
ASSI 6-72/8 Peach
ASSI 13-72 Merry
ASSI 13-73 Quayle

INDEX